Watchman at the Gates

American Warriors

Throughout the nation's history, numerous men and women of all ranks and branches of the US military have served their country with honor and distinction. During times of war and peace, there are individuals whose exemplary achievements embody the highest standards of the US armed forces. The aim of the American Warriors series is to examine the unique historical contributions of these individuals, whose legacies serve as enduring examples for soldiers and citizens alike. The series will promote a deeper and more comprehensive understanding of the US armed forces.

Series editor: Joseph Craig

An AUSA Book

WATCHMAN
AT THE GATES

A Soldier's Journey
from Berlin to Bosnia

General George Joulwan
with David Chanoff

Foreword by Tom Brokaw

UNIVERSITY PRESS OF KENTUCKY

Published by The University Press of Kentucky,
scholarly publisher for the Commonwealth,
serving Bellarmine University, Berea College, Centre
College of Kentucky, Eastern Kentucky University,
The Filson Historical Society, Georgetown College,
Kentucky Historical Society, Kentucky State University,
Morehead State University, Murray State University,
Northern Kentucky University, Spalding University,
Transylvania University, University of Kentucky, University
of Louisville, and Western Kentucky University.
All rights reserved.

Editorial and Sales Offices: The University Press of Kentucky
663 South Limestone Street, Lexington, Kentucky 40508-4008
www.kentuckypress.com

Photographs are from the author's collection.

Library of Congress Cataloging-in-Publication Data

Names: Joulwan, George A. (George Alfred), 1939– author. I Chanoff, David,
    author. I Brokaw, Tom, writer of introduction.
Title: Watchman at the gates : a soldier's journey from Berlin to Bosnia /
    General George Joulwan with David Chanoff ; foreword by Tom Brokaw.
Other titles: Soldier's journey from Berlin to Bosnia
Description: Lexington, Kentucky : The University Press of Kentucky, [2021]
    I Series: American warriors series I Includes index.
Identifiers: LCCN 2020053332 I ISBN 9780813180847 (hardcover) I ISBN
    9780813180854 (pdf) I ISBN 9780813180861 (epub)
Subjects: LCSH: Joulwan, George A. (George Alfred), 1939– I
    Generals—United States–Biography. I United States.
    Army—Officers—Biography. I North Atlantic Treaty
    Organization—Biography. I Yugoslav War, 1991–1995—Bosnia and
    Herzegovina—Personal narratives, American. I Vietnam War,
    1961–1975—Influence. I United States—History, Military—20th
    century—Anecdotes. I Cold War—Biography.
Classification: LCC E840.5.J68 A3 2021 I DDC 355.0092 [B]—dc23

This book is printed on acid-free paper meeting
the requirements of the American National Standard
for Permanence in Paper for Printed Library Materials.

Manufactured in the United States of America.

Member of the Association
of University Presses

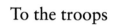

To the troops

Contents

Illustrations follow page 124

Foreword

When we do an inventory of America's manifold strengths, the soundtrack is the national anthem with a squadron of fighter jets at warp speed roaring above a parade of uniformed men and women in close formation, reminding us that when this moment is over, they're back to their duty of securing our safekeeping while the game, the race, the patriotic event goes on.

Who are those who put on the uniforms and step into harm's way? By their commitment to military service, we know they are risk takers. They live by a demanding code of conduct. They're simultaneously warriors and statesmen, innovators and by-the-book students of long-established conduct.

Among these exceptional individuals, a few stand out.

One is my friend George Joulwan, a classic American story. The grandson of Lebanese immigrants, George heard the call of duty as an outstanding football lineman who passed up the bacchanal weekends of civilian gridiron temples and chose West Point, the storied army academy, instead.

He was catapulted into Vietnam at the most dangerous time in that brutal war, learning the lessons of unconventional wars the hard way.

By chance, he became close to a more senior officer, who in turn was recruited by the White House to manage the closing days of his commander in chief, President Richard Nixon. George was White House deputy chief of staff then, which gave him a front-row seat for the last acts of the Watergate drama.

It was then that as NBC's White House correspondent I came to know George and appreciate his mischievous sense of humor framed by a buttoned-up military code of loyalty.

From that unlikely launching pad, George became one of America's most accomplished senior military commanders during the tumultuous days of Central American and European upheaval, the collapse of the Soviet Union, and the rise of murderous tribes in the Middle East. He was on the front lines of the Cold War stand-off in Germany, when outgunned US and North Atlantic Treaty Organization (NATO) forces faced the massed Soviet tank armies. As a newly minted West Point lieutenant, he was there when the Berlin Wall went up; twenty-eight years later he was US forces commander when the Iron Curtain collapsed and the wall came down. No one has told the story of the strategy and tactics of that potentially catastrophic confrontation better. In the culminating command of his career, George led a sixty-thousand-strong NATO army into the Balkan killing fields, putting a stop to the genocidal massacres that were the worst ethnic killings in Europe since World War II.

As a warfighter and a strategist, George was present at most of the crucial events of the last part of the twentieth century, which still resonate strongly through America's military and political challenges today. *Watchman at the Gates* should be required reading for aspiring military commanders, young political scientists, and candidates for public office— indeed, for anyone who either needs or simply wants to know what it means to lead the men and women who put their lives on the line to keep us safe.

I just wish George had been a little more forthcoming with me during the final days of Watergate!

Tom Brokaw
March 2020

Introduction

My story is a soldier's story. In many ways it's a story every soldier can relate to because many of the events in my life were shared by other soldiers of my generation. I spent two tours in combat—in my case that meant in Vietnam—mostly in relatively small but deadly fights with Vietcong and North Vietnamese regulars but also in a couple of big battles. I was promoted from rank to rank. I trained hard, I fought, I commanded, first smaller units, then larger ones. I studied and taught at the US Army's war colleges, and I strove always not just to follow but also to understand the profession I had chosen—its customs, its values, its relationship to the civilian and political worlds it was part of but also apart from. I never considered myself anything other than a soldier, and I never aspired to be anything else. I thought that defending our country and the democratic values it stands for was as high a calling as one could wish for.

I learned how to serve that calling in places like Bosnia, El Salvador, the Congo, and the jungles and rice paddies of Vietnam. My first deployment fresh out of West Point was opposite Germany's Fulda Gap, where our outnumbered and outgunned forces faced the Soviet Union's massed tank armies. I was stationed opposite Fulda again as a company, brigade, and divisional commander and then finally as a corps commander, still confronting the same strategic problem.

I was in West Germany while the Berlin Wall was going up, when American and Soviet tanks faced each other across the barbed wire and President Kennedy gave his "Ich bin ein Berliner" speech. The hundreds of little flower and cross memorials marking where East Berliners had been shot down trying to escape to freedom made a lifelong impression on me. I was in Germany again when the Iron Curtain lifted and the Wall came down, when tens of thousands of East Germans walked and drove in their little Trabants across the border with tears of joy in their eyes and were met by equally joyful crowds of West German friends and relatives.

In Germany and elsewhere, I learned the necessity of alliances. I put that lesson to use fighting the drug cartels in Latin America and then in the Balkan War. As the North Atlantic Treaty Organization's (NATO) military chief, I led a sixty-thousand-soldier army into Bosnia that implemented

1

the Dayton Accords and put an end to the massacres and ethnic cleansing going on there.

NATO forces in Bosnia came from thirty-three countries, including a brigade from Russia. I saw the partnership we forged there as a stepping stone to a wider, ongoing strategic cooperation between the United States and Russia. Our collaboration in Bosnia led to the NATO-Russia Founding Act of 1997, which formally ended the Cold War, but American and Russian national interests coincided or ran parallel in many other areas as well. We had mutual interests then; we still have them today, even as we fall further into a period of renewed conflict. I knew that neither the Russians nor ourselves could simply put away many decades' worth of hostility and distrust, but I thought that cooperation in endeavors of mutual interest could become a pathway toward more trust and a way out of the old antagonism. I pursued that strategy vigorously until my retirement as supreme allied commander.

As commander in chief (CINC) in Latin America and Europe and as commander of NATO's forces, one of my primary jobs was to advise the political leadership—the president and secretary of defense, on one hand, the NATO secretary-general and council on the other. As often as possible, I tried to anticipate the needs of these decision makers and give proactive advice so that the feasibility and risks of potential engagements would be clear. I emphasized always the fundamental requirements for successful military action—clarity of mission, unity of command, robust rules of engagement, and timely direction from the political leadership. These were lessons I had learned from the critical events I had witnessed and been part of in Germany, Latin America, Vietnam, and the Watergate White House, where I had been Alexander Haig's deputy when he was Nixon's chief of staff.

Another truth I absorbed from my time as a newly minted platoon leader to my final appointment in Europe was that allies and coalitions are required to deal successfully with large, complex challenges. The worldwide challenges we faced during the long Cold War were too great for us to overcome by ourselves. The challenges we face today are equally vast and a great deal more complex. We stand in need of partners whose fundamental values we share as well as others with whom we have strategic interests in common.

Allies, coalitions, partnerships are the key to furthering our national interests. But to survive as who we are and who we have always been, we need above all to keep to our moral purpose as a nation. That was my takeaway from Bosnia and from the other critical arenas of my life as a soldier. Looking back, it is the theme of the story this book tells.

1

Learning Values

Every New Year's Eve when I was growing up, our entire clan, maybe twelve or fifteen families, plus friends and neighbors would crowd into the big living room in my grandfather Michael's house on Minersville Street just before midnight.

Grandpa Michael and Grandma Mantura Joulwan—Giddu and Sittu to us—lived in what we called the Big House. They were at the center of the Lebanese families who came to Pottsville, Pennsylvania, from their Maronite mountain village of Toula toward the end of the nineteenth century. Pottsville was nestled among the high hills of central Pennsylvania, Broad Mountain, Mt. Hope, Mt. Carbon, and others, which reminded Michael of the mountains of his home, so that's where he decided to settle down.

Grandpa Michael was the first Lebanese to arrive in Pottsville as a penniless twenty-three-year-old who spoke no English and had no employable skills. But Pottsville was in the anthracite-coal-mining region, and wherever you went in that region, there were communities—"patches" in the local speech—of immigrants drawn to the coal fields: Germans, Irish, Lithuanians, Ruthenians, Slovaks, Poles, Hungarians, Ukrainians, and others, many of whom spoke no English, so not speaking the language was no impediment to Michael as he tramped from place to place with a peddler's pack on his back full of religious articles and notions.

Michael eventually made enough money to open a small shop; then he went back to the old country to find a wife. In Toula, he found Mantura Daher. She apparently liked him, but she had no intention of going to live in "the Wild, Wild West," which is what the people in Toula called the United States. The family lore didn't say how he persuaded her, but somehow he did, and in 1894 she came to Pottsville with him, went to work next to him, and started having children, all of whose names they took straight out of the Bible: John, Joseph, Paul, Solomon, Sarah, and Alice, my mother, whose name wasn't biblical, though no one from my generation knows how that happened.

Michael Joulwan was an enterprising man, and some years after he brought his bride back from the old country, he went into the real estate

3

business. He became a prominent member of the church—St. Patrick's Roman Catholic on Mahantongo Street, abutting the Yuengling Brewery, which some thought (and some still think) ironic. The Lebanese Christian community in Pottsville was too small to have its own church, but the Maronites were in communion with Rome, and St. Patrick's welcomed them, so that was where they worshipped. As our family's patriarch, Michael played an important role as counselor and adviser on everything from business and financial matters to spiritual concerns. He and Mantura were also a connection to the foods, the music, the language of the old country, a link that was fraying badly among the assimilated kids of my generation. But every New Year's Eve we all gathered at Grandpa Michael's house, no matter what other plans we might have.

With the entire clan crowded around, at the stroke of midnight Michael would stand up, and everyone in the room would take a knee as he brought in the new year with a prayer, blessing all of us, husbands, wives, children, grandchildren, girlfriends, friends, and neighbors. My last two years in high school I brought my girlfriend at the time. "I love it," she said. "This is the true way the new year should come in."

You could never tell who might be there. Grandpa Michael didn't care whether you were white, black, pink, blue, Jewish, Arabic, Protestant. You were welcome in his house. There was a black church and cemetery across the street, and his black neighbors were as welcome as everybody else. "Everyone is welcome here," he told me on more than one occasion; he wanted to make absolutely sure that I and everyone else in the family got the message.

I always thought he brought that attitude over with him from the old country. From what I understood then, Lebanon was a rough place, with Sunni and Shi'a Muslims, Druze, Christians, and Jews living close by each other in the mountains and down on the coastal plains. Maybe not too different from the many ethnic and religious communities that populated Pottsville and its surrounding towns and hamlets. Michael was so deeply grateful for the opportunity America had given him to build a new life that it was an article of faith with him that everyone else who came here should have the same chance. He and Mantura lived that belief.

Their door was always open, and the kitchen seemed to run all day every day, producing the wonderful aromas of Lebanese foods. People would stop by for lunch or dinner—not just family but also neighbors and just passersby. Their dinner table always seemed to be crowded. If someone looked as if he were on hard times, he was likely to get pulled in off the street.

Like many children and grandchildren of immigrants, I regret that I didn't spend much time talking with my grandparents about their past lives in the places they came from. I was more interested in sports and girls than I was in how they had lived back then. But later in my life I learned a great deal more. As supreme allied commander of NATO forces, I was the American general responsible for the Middle East as well as for Europe and Africa. I got to know Lebanon well then, and I got some idea of why my grandfather Michael may have decided to leave his village.

Although Lebanon's various communities experienced periods of tolerance and relative peace, their history was also marked by violence. The Maronites were a Christian minority among Muslims, so times for them were often rough. Sporadic fighting had occurred through the early nineteenth century, culminating in the so-called Mt. Lebanon War in 1860, when the Druze, in conjunction with the ruling Turks, massacred many thousands of Maronites and destroyed hundreds of villages. The region had been part of the Ottoman Empire since the sixteenth century, but with Ottoman power breaking down in the late nineteenth century, sectarian antagonisms and bloodshed were a constant. To what extent Grandpa Michael might have been involved in or subjected to any of that, I didn't know, but given the history it wasn't hard to see why in his early twenties he decided to leave and try his luck in "the Wild, Wild West." It was also easy to surmise why tolerance and acceptance of others were so high on his scale of values. He had seen what the opposite led to.

Not that Schuylkill County and its capital, Pottsville, were oases of tranquility. Pottsville and its surroundings had been the hotbed of the Molly Maguires, an underground secret society whose violent origins were back in Ireland but that had arrived in Schuylkill County with the Irish immigration of the 1840s and 1850s.

The miners in the anthracite region, many of them Irish, were often involved in strikes and riots aimed against the predatory practices of the mine owners and bosses. Miners who were members of the society figured significantly in the violent confrontations and occasional murders of foremen and bosses. During the Civil War, the "Mollies" took leading parts in the antidraft riots and uprisings that centered on Pottsville and the surrounding coal towns.

When the war was finally over, labor militancy merged into a sort of class warfare, again with Mollies in leading roles. In the mid-1870s, a spate of murders led to the arrest of Molly Maguire leaders, and on June 21, 1877, ten of them went to the gallows at the same time. Four were hanged in Mauch Chunk (later renamed Jim Thorpe for the great Native

American athlete) and six in Pottsville. It was the so-called Day of the Rope, the largest mass hanging in Pennsylvania history.

So Pottsville before Grandpa Michael's arrival wasn't peaceful. It wasn't peaceful afterward either. Ongoing tensions between mine operators and miners had led to the creation of the United Mine Workers Union. In 1897, nine years after Michael settled in Pottsville, the sheriff of Luzerne County, with more than a hundred deputies at his back, met a strikers' march in Lattimer, thirty or so miles from Pottsville. He ordered the marchers to disperse, and when they didn't, the deputies fired into the crowd, killing nineteen and wounding many more. The infamous Lattimer Massacre led to a great upsurge in union membership and gave the union a national platform.

Coal mine confrontations continued long after this, but when I was growing up, the Civil War riots and the Molly Maguires and their Pinkerton enemies were just part of the distant past that everyone—at least my contemporaries—sort of knew about but weren't very concerned with, if at all. Violence in my youth had been considerably domesticated, if that's the right way of putting it, by being transferred to football field confrontations. Sports were big in Pottsville, and football was by far the biggest.

Pennsylvania was renowned then for the toughness of its high school football teams, especially in the coal-mining and steel-making regions. A slew of college and National Football League stars came out of these places, among them Mike Ditka, Chuck Bednarik, Lenny Moore, Joe Montana, Jack Hamm, and Johnny Unitas. Penn State is known as Linebacker U, but well before that nickname took hold, Pottsville had its own NFL team, which won the NFL championship in 1925—not a widely known fact outside of Schuylkill County, but true and still an object of both pride and bitterness. That team was the Pottsville Maroons.

The Maroons of 1925 were coal miners, firemen, former college players, and three pro players the team poached from the Canton Bulldogs. The Maroons had earlier played in the Anthracite League, which included teams from other eastern Pennsylvania coal towns, but in 1925 they joined the five-year-old National Football League. In their first seven games that season, they outscored their opponents 179 to 6. They ended the season with a 21–7 win over the Chicago Cardinals, which gave them the NFL championship. The title was stripped from them, though, when they played an after-season exhibition game against all-stars from Notre Dame, the dominant college team at a time when college football was considered far superior to the ragtag professional teams then playing. The Maroons won that game 9–7, but the league's commissioner suspended them for playing the game in Philadelphia, supposedly violating the territorial rights of Philadelphia's NFL team, the Frankford Yellowjackets (forerunners of the Philadelphia Eagles). Bitterness over that treatment and efforts to reinstate the Pottsville title went on for many decades.

The Maroons' Tony Latone was arguably the top running back of the era. His bronzed football boot sits on display in the Schuylkill County Historical Society. Red Grange, whose electric play drew giant crowds, took part in a barnstorming game against the Maroons in 1927 for a fee of $500. On the first play, he was knocked cold. When he cleared his head and got back into the game, he was knocked out again. According to one supposedly accurate account, Grange got up the second time, said, "To hell with the $500. It ain't worth it," and walked off the field.

In a book about the team, *The Breaker Boys,* author David Fleming recounts that the Maroons once humiliated coal-region rival Coaldale so badly that Coaldale fans shot up the Maroons' train as they were leaving town. That sounds extreme, but not too long before my time playing football for Pottsville High School, our Minersville rivals used to bring a coffin with them to away games, suggesting to their opponents what was going to happen to them once the game started. It's possible that visual might have had its antecedent in the "coffin notices" the Molly Maguires used to send as warnings to enemies they were planning to murder.

I grew up playing football, basketball, and baseball, always competing hard against my twin brother, Jimmy. In football, I was a center, he was the quarterback; in baseball, he was the pitcher, I was the catcher; in basketball, he played guard, I was a forward. Being a twin meant we always had a buddy to throw a ball with or shoot baskets with or fight with; it made for a close bond between us. Jimmy and I were more competitive against each other than we were against rival teams.

Since we lived on East Norwegian Street, on the poor side of town, our pickup games drew kids of every kind, whose families came from places you could hardly pronounce. But it didn't matter where you came from. It didn't matter if you were black or white or whatever kind of strange nationality. If you could play ball, you were on the team. That was the entry fee for coming in. You didn't judge kids by where they came from, only by whether they could help you win those dead-serious, all-day games on the sandlots and outdoor macadam courts.

When Jimmy and I got through junior high school, we split up; I went to the public school, Pottsville High, and he decided to go to Nativity Catholic, where he became a star everything. My school, Pottsville, played in the East Penn League, one of the roughest conferences in Pennsylvania, including Allentown, Bethlehem, Easton, and Hazelton—all bigger towns than Pottsville, which meant we were usually playing teams with bigger guys and bigger benches. You had to figure out how to beat teams like that; it was always a struggle of little guy against big guy, small town against big town. I liked that. Matchups like that appealed to my competitive nature; they also made me think. I couldn't just run over guys who were bigger and stronger. I had to be agile and quick, and I had somehow to out-think them. (That wasn't bad practice for my future of facing off against the massively superior Soviet forces on the East-West German border.) It was very rewarding to me when I made all-state as center. I was competing against some of the top high school athletes in the country. I also managed to make all-state honorable mention in basketball as a forward. I was only five-foot-eleven, but I was good under the boards. I knew how to use my strength, and I had sharp elbows.

Being all-state football in Pennsylvania meant that I was courted by a number of big-name college teams. Penn State's Joe Paterno had dinner with us; he was Rip Engle's assistant coach at the time. Other coaches came to recruit me, from Pitt and Syracuse and Miami and other schools. Some talked with me in my home; others took me for rides in their cars, letting me know that if I signed up, their school would give me a car like the one I was riding in.

Since I was playing basketball, too, it was hard for me to visit many schools, but one I went to see was Miami. I liked the weather there; central Pennsylvania in the winter was no joke. The assistant showing me around said, "NCAA rules permit us to give you an allowance for laundry. We'll do that, but you just drop your stuff off here and stop by to pick it up the next day." We looked in at the cafeteria.

"We can pay you so much for meals, so we'll do that; plus, we'll give you a book of tickets, so you can just go in and eat." That evening we passed by the lighted gym. "Off season we can give you a job."

"Really?" I said. "What kind of job?"

"Well, your job would be to check that the janitors have turned the gym lights off at night."

"That would be my job? I could do that from here."

"Right," he said.

The football players lived in nice, two-person apartments—two bedrooms with a shared kitchen and living room, directly across the street from the girls' dorms. So that was interesting. The whole thing was tempting until I went out to see the spring football practice. The team was training, and a number of big muscular guys were carrying towels and water out to the field—football scholarship guys who didn't make the team.

"That's not what I had in mind," I said. "I wouldn't want to be doing that."

When I got back home, I received a letter from the coach. "I understand and appreciate what you said. We're offering you a five-year scholarship with a guarantee of no work of that sort. The scholarship is good for five years even if you get hurt the first day of practice and are unable to play for the rest of your time as an undergraduate." I was very tempted.

I was also recruited by the navy and army academies, although the US Naval Academy wanted me to go to prep school for a year. Penn State's Pottsville campus Reserve Officers' Training Corps (ROTC) was run by a Major Nicholson, who suggested to Colonel Red Blaik, the famous army coach, that he might invite me to visit, which he did. I was seventeen years old when I went up to West Point. My playing weight was around 180 pounds, on the small side for our high school league, very small for Division One college football, even back in 1957. Many of the recruiters had told me, "You'll have to beef up." But Coach Blaik said, "You could play here now." He showed me pictures of army's unbeaten 1945, 1946, and 1947 teams that featured Doc Blanchard and Glenn Davis, both Heisman Trophy winners.

"Those teams' average age was eighteen," Blaik said.

Then he introduced me to his starting center, Jim Kernan, who was about my size.

"But I want to be clear," Blaik said. "If you come here, your first mission is to graduate and become an officer in the United States Army. Football comes after that." All told, I received recruiting offers from fifty-plus schools, which was more than a little overwhelming. But Blaik was the only one who said anything like that, which impressed me.

I had never thought about a military career. My father had lied about his age to get into the navy during World War I, but that was mainly to see places other than Pottsville. He never considered making a career of it, and he never encouraged either my brother, Jimmy, or me in that direction. My mother and my four older sisters talked to me as I was getting near graduation. "George, you should really think about what you want to do with the rest of your life." But they weren't thinking about the military any more than my father was.

I did think about my future, at least to some extent. Football was a big part of my life, but I never saw professional football as a possibility. Coaching definitely was, though. I admired my coaches; they were the best people I knew. I was co-captain of our football team and captain of our basketball team, so I had at least some experience in motivating my teammates. I saw the challenge of it, which appealed to me. Coaching was something I thought I'd enjoy.

Although I wasn't thinking about going into the army, Pottsville was a place with a long attachment to America's military. In Pottsville, patriotism was a strong value.

I was born in 1939, at the end of the Great Depression. When I was young, the country was in the throes of World War II. Rationing was in effect for food, clothing, and all kinds of commodities. I was too young to understand the hardships people were enduring, but there was a feeling among everyone that they needed to sacrifice in order to help the war effort. I heard enough talk about that as I grew older, so it made an impression on me. In 1945, the troops were welcomed home, including my cousin Paul, who had fought against the Germans, had been taken prisoner, and had escaped from a prisoner-of-war camp. To this day I remember the returning soldiers marching down Main Street to Garfield Square, with its statues and Civil War cannons. I remember the parade, the fire trucks, the crowds. I remember everyone singing.

In Pottsville, Memorial Days were big events. Each Memorial Day a parade wended its way to Garfield Square, where speeches were given and patriotic songs sung. All the town's schoolchildren took part. Girl and Boy Scouts marched in uniform, the school bands played, including the high school girls' bagpipe band. Little League teams marched, as did the Penn State Center Drum and Bugle Corps, the city council, the school board, students from Pottsville High and Nativity Catholic, National Guard units. Everyone was caught up in the civic pride, inseparable from military traditions and history going back to the American Revolution.

One of George Washington's drummer boys at Valley Forge was from Orwigsburg, right next to Pottsville, and the county had raised several companies of militia, the first of which joined Washington on the heights outside of Boston in 1775. Garfield Square was a Civil War memorial site, and Pottsville played a memorable role at the very beginning of the fighting then. When Fort Sumter came under fire in April 1861, Abraham Lincoln called for volunteers to defend Washington, DC. Pottsville sent the National Light Infantry and the Washington Artillerists, two local volunteer companies. Other companies came from neighboring counties. Marching through Baltimore, the Pennsylvania First Defenders (as they came to be called) were attacked by a mob of Confederate sympathizers, and many of them were injured. The most seriously hurt was Nicholas Biddle, an African American member of the Artillerists. Some believe he was the war's first Northern casualty. Eight Civil War Medal of Honor winners came from Pottsville and its surroundings, and many more earned that honor in other wars. A long list of generals and admirals hailed from the Pottsville area.

So even though the Joulwans weren't a military family, I grew up in a place that was proud of its military heritage. I wasn't thinking about West Point before I met Coach Blaik, but what he talked about appealed to me. It set him apart from the other coaches and recruiters I had met. I may not have been thinking about going into the army, but I was open to it.

The times also had something to do with how I was thinking. I graduated in 1957, in the middle of the Cold War. Sputnik went up in the fall of my senior year. The threat of thermonuclear war with the Soviet Union was in the air, the feeling that America was being challenged. I felt instinctively that the military would appeal to my competitive instincts both as a football player—I could play for Coach Blaik—and as the leader of a platoon instead of a football or basketball team. I had a feeling that the military could be a profession that would allow me to channel a lot of who I was. So when it turned out that I could get an appointment to West Point from our congressman, I decided to go.

When the time arrived, my father drove me to West Point, along with another incoming cadet, Mike Brady from Indiana, a high school quarterback who also planned to play football. We had been in touch and decided that he would come to Pennsylvania first, and we would go up together. When we got to West Point, I said, "Go check in to your room. Let's plan to meet at 5:00 in the cafeteria and have a milkshake." Needless to say, I didn't get to meet Mike at 5:00 for a milkshake.

The next time I saw him was two weeks later when I noticed him double-timing at attention around the barracks area. I'm sure his experience when he checked in to what was called "Beast Barracks" was the same as mine, which was simply one of shock. I had been wined and dined at Syracuse University, where Jim Brown had just graduated the previous year, leading the team to the East Coast championship and the Cotton Bowl. I had visited the University of Miami, which was ranked sixth in the nation, where the football players lived in nice apartments across from the girls' dorm and enjoyed perks fit for a king. I had been driven around in convertibles. Then I got to West Point, said good-bye to my dad, and next thing I knew my face was up against a gray wall with a senior cadet behind me barking, "Stand at attention! Drop that bag! Pick up that bag! Drop that bag! Get your neck in!"

I thought, "What the hell? What did I get myself into here?"

Up until my first year, the Corps of Cadets had always been organized by size, so that the biggest cadets, including most of the athletes, were in Companies A-1, B-1, and so on, while the smaller cadets were in A-2, B-2, and so on. In my plebe year, the academy changed that formation, and I ended up by chance in a company that had mostly smaller and shorter cadets. I was tall and big for that company; plus, I was the only one who played football. I stood out, which meant I was a great target for hazing. My plebe friends from the football and basketball teams were reluctant to visit me; they would have been courting the same harassment.

The atmosphere for plebes was one of constant chaos and pressure, but that first day, with my face up against the wall, I felt something click. Right after the shock faded, my first thought was, "These bastards aren't going to get the best of me." That idea settled in quickly, which saw me through Beast Barracks and into the regular Cadet Corps once that initial summer break-in was over. The harassment was arbitrary and a pain in the neck, but I didn't find it overwhelming.

"How many lights in Cullum Hall, mister?"

"Three hundred and forty lights, sir."

"How is the Cow, mister?"

"Sir, she walks, she talks, she's full of chalk . . ."

"Mister, what do plebes rank?"

"Sir, the superintendent's cat, the commandant's dog, . . . and all the admirals in the whole damned navy."

"Mister, what is Schofield's definition of discipline?"

"Sir, the discipline that makes the soldiers of a free country reliable in battle is not to be gained by harsh or tyrannical treatment."

You had to have a sense of humor.

Many of my fellow plebes did have a hard time with the pressure. It was confusing, abrasive, and could easily make an eighteen-year-old kid angry and fed up. But I found that I was able to buck people up. I tried to encourage other cadets who were having problems. I could get them to laugh about the hazing and help them see that they could stick it out instead of quitting. I found I was comfortable in that role. It was an important thing to discover about myself.

I didn't mind the discipline; my inclination was to take any threat or tough treatment as a challenge. I enjoyed the physical challenges, too—the 5:00 a.m. runs, the combat training, the forced marches. I was up for all that. I also found myself figuring out how to beat the system. At first,

"Beasties" had no privileges at all; then slowly we were given something here, something there.

"You four get a quarter each. You can buy anything you want with it."

There wasn't much each of us could buy with a quarter, but if the four of us put our quarters together, we could get a pint of ice cream and share it. So instead of the pittance they gave us being a downer, it became an upper. We weren't really beating the system; we were working it. That might have been trivial, but it felt like a big victory. At every turn, big and small, you needed to figure out how to work as a team. That was really how you survived, with the support of your buddies. You couldn't do it alone.

As a Beastie, when you ate, you had to stare at the top rim of your plate and were allowed to chew your food only three times before you swallowed it. That rule was relaxed when you finished summer training and joined a regular company. But even then you had to eat "braced," sitting rigidly with your neck cranked back.

As a football player, I got out of that requirement. Football players didn't have to eat braced, and they fed us better, steaks and lots of carbohydrates. Also, most of the waiters were from eastern Pennsylvania, Shamokin, Hazelton, and other places near Pottsville, so they used to slip me extras under my chair.

After football season, though, it was back to eating braced. But in June Week that year an opportunity came along to get out of it—"fallout" in West Point terms. We plebes could get fallout from eating braced all week if we could successfully carry out a covert operation of our own invention. That was the challenge from our company's upperclassmen.

In our training that year, we had learned the elements of a "five-paragraph field order," a standard method of planning a military operation that defined the situation, the mission, the execution, the logistics, and the command/communication. If we could execute a covert five-paragraph operation, we would enjoy the freedom to eat like normal human beings for an entire week.

The operation the six of us conceived had to do with George Washington's horse. At Trophy Point overlooking the Hudson River was an equestrian statue of the first president mounted high on a monumental granite pedestal. June Week was when all the cadets' families came up to visit, and Trophy Point was an especially picturesque setting that always attracted a lot of visitors. Given those facts, it seemed to us it would be a great thing to paint the prominent testicles of Washington's horse a bright red—in retrospect an adolescent stunt, but then we actually were adolescents, even if we were in training to be soldiers. And to carry out this stunt we would need to utilize our five-paragraph-order field training, so it was going to be military all the way. First, we analyzed the situation and defined the mission; then we planned the execution. The six of us would make our way clandestinely in the dark of night three or four hundred yards across the parade field to Trophy Point. At the statue, mounted on its high pedestal, three of us would link arms, two would climb on our shoulders, and our painter would clamber up on theirs with a can of paint and paintbrush and do the job. We knew that if we were caught, we'd be dead ducks.

At 0100 (1:00 a.m.), the six of us left our dorm and went out into the pitch-black night dressed in black pants and black parkas. We took with us a can of red paint and a paintbrush, which we had a cab driver buy for us in town so that nothing could be traced back to us without a full-scale police investigation (this part of the plan came under "logistics"). As we hustled across the field, we saw car lights coming along the adjacent road, so we hit the ground. Then we saw another set of lights coming. It was 1:00 a.m. "Where the hell is all this traffic coming from?" I whispered as we crawled toward our target.

When we got to the statue, the three biggest of us stood together while the next two clambered up onto our shoulders; then my roommate, Pat, who had been a wrestler in high school, climbed to the top and painted the horse's balls a shining crimson. Then we got out as fast as we could and made it back to barracks, except that in the excitement Pat left the paint can and brush up on the pedestal under the horse.

The next morning our company assembled for a march out exactly to Trophy Point, which we had no idea was going to happen. We came out of the barracks, made a turn, and headed straight for the horse. In the distance, we could make out two red spots on the horse's underside. As we got closer, the red spots grew larger and larger until the entire company had a crystal-clear view of the desecration, the six of us perpetrators trying hard to choke back our snickering.

This was going to be great. I was already savoring the fallout. But we hadn't quite thought through all the potential consequences. Some of West Point's officers—the captains and majors and colonels—lived with their families on campus. Others invited their families up for June Week, and as word about the horse spread through the chain of command, we heard that the officers weren't amused and that they were intent on finding the people who committed the defilement.

We were afraid the hammer was going to fall—we knew they were looking hard for the perpetrators. I started to feel guilty about all of us getting into trouble, so I decided to take the heat. Our cadet company commander was Tom Sands, a great guy, a graduating first classman while I was a plebe. In June Week, seniors, or "Firsties," were allowed to purchase cars (assuming they had the money) and bring them to campus, so he had his there, and I was helping him wash it.

Halfway through the wash job, I said, "Sorry, sir, I've got something I've got to tell you. You know the statue of Washington's horse, the red balls? I'm one of the ones responsible for it." I was trying to tell him this in a way that would make him proud of our exploit—"We went out there in the dead of night, planned our mission, executed it," and so on—but I didn't know if that was going to work.

"But I want to tell you that if anything bad comes of it, I will take the heat for it. I don't want you or any of the company to suffer . . ."

In the middle of this confession, Tom looked up and laughed. "I thought that was great," he said. I squirted his car some more, then got out of there as fast as I could. The incident didn't die, though. The administration never did find the guilty parties, and my classmates were still talking about it at our fiftieth reunion. We'll probably be talking about it at our sixtieth. You had to have a sense of humor.

The relaxed eating standards I got for playing sports and for a couple of other accomplishments were the only break I got, though. There was a "Blue Book" of rules and regulations that every cadet had to know by heart, including exactly how to dress, how to fold his clothes, and how to arrange his medicine chest—"toothbrush to the right, bristles up." Many of those rules seemed superficial and unnecessary, but the large number that you disciplined yourself to learn and follow had a cumulative effect. You found yourself paying attention to detail the way you had never done before. Even the apparently nonsensical memory challenges—"How is the Cow?" "How many this or thats are in some hall?"—had a purpose: Keep things in mind. Remember them. Even trivial details can be significant. I didn't realize it at the time, but West Point was trying to instill these mental habits in the army's future officers.

Playing football for Red Blaik was another lesson in discipline and attention to detail. I was on the plebe team my first year, made the varsity traveling squad my second, and lettered my third and fourth years. I watched closely how Blaik motivated the team and how he kept a gimlet eye on absolutely everything that happened on the practice field. He had a platform that was twenty or so feet up. He could see everything and everybody from up there, and every player and assistant coach knew he was watching. His eyes were everywhere, and if you screwed up, you'd hear his whistle blow. He'd tell us beforehand exactly how the practice or scrimmage was going to go, and that was exactly how it went, down to the minute. Blaik analyzed every play in every game using film; he was one of the first coaches to do that. Over the years, twenty of his assistant coaches went on to become head coaches, including in the NFL. The Green Bay Packers' Vince Lombardi, maybe the greatest football coach of all time, was one of his assistants. Lombardi wrote that under Blaik he learned what attention to detail meant and how important it was.

Blaik left West Point in 1958, after the team went undefeated and finished third in the nation. The team that year boasted three All-Americans. In my junior and senior years, I played under his successor, Dale Hall, who had played under Blaik on army's teams with Doc Blanchard and Glenn Davis. We played against great teams in 1959 and 1960—Pittsburgh with Mike Ditka, Syracuse with Ernie Davis. My senior year we beat Syracuse 9–6 and tied Pitt 7–7. Unfortunately, we lost to navy and its great running back and Heisman Trophy winner Joe Bellino, but we played them even up; the final score was 17 to 12.

In my senior year, I played two ways, center on offense, nose guard on defense. I also played on our special teams. At the end of that year, I won the team's offense and defense awards—the most blocks, the most tackles, according to statistics kept by the coaches. Of course, you don't think about those kinds of things as you're playing, so the awards came as a surprise to me. I was given a caricature of me drawn by someone from the *New York Times* that I still have up on my study wall, a happy memento of my last season playing football. I loved football at West Point. It was a continuation of everything I found rewarding about it from the time I was in high school. In a way, it was also a break from the relentless rigor of West Point academics and military training. But Coach Blaik had told me when I first visited that becoming an officer would be my first job, football would be secondary, and so by the end of my plebe year I recognized that the military learning and conditioning had stuck.

In that first year, my mentality went through an evolution. By the end of it, I was attentive to detail in a way I had never been. I was conditioned not only to attend to details but to remember them. My whole mental orientation had become disciplined in a way I couldn't have imagined as a high school student. By the time I finished my plebe year, I was no longer a civilian.

Another aspect of plebe life that began to take root was the value system I was exposed to at every turn. West Point reinforced the values I had absorbed from my family and from growing up in Pottsville—the patriotism, the work ethic, the inclusiveness. But unlike in normal, everyday life, in academy life there was a continual emphasis on ethical conduct, honesty, and the taking of responsibility for your actions. As a cadet at West Point, you were instilled with the need for moral courage, the obligation to choose the harder right rather than the easier wrong. That was a unique culture for a university. The atmosphere, the discipline, and the camaraderie had a profound impact on me. The traditions of duty, honor, country weren't just some motto, as they might have seemed when I first heard them articulated. By the end of my first year, I knew they were important. They were the institution's core beliefs, and they were becoming my own as well.

2

Germany

The Wall

The first time I was in Berlin, the wall hadn't been built yet. It was the summer of 1960, the end of my third year at West Point. That summer I was sent to Germany as part of the army's program to give cadets experience of what it was like to lead a platoon. Even then, before the wall, the city was a flashpoint. In 1948, Stalin's decision to starve West Berlin to death had precipitated the Berlin Airlift and might easily have touched off World War III. Now Nikita Khrushchev was calling West Berlin a "cancer," "a bone in my throat." In 1958, he had given President Dwight D. Eisenhower an ultimatum, demanding that the United States evacuate its forces from the city. Eisenhower had disregarded him. Khrushchev repeated the threat in his first meeting with President John F. Kennedy. No one I knew was aware how close we were to war. It wasn't until years later that we learned Khrushchev was deciding if it was worth chancing a world war to take West Berlin by force.

But with all the tension, Berlin still seemed like at least a seminormal place. The border between East and West was open. Trams and subways ran between the city's two parts, and traffic moved from one sector to the other. East Berliners traveled to and from jobs in the western part; friends and families visited across the demarcation line. In my brief time in the city, I went to a nightclub with phones on the tables; people called and invited each other to dance. There was a friendly spirit in the air. Berliners seemed like a fun-loving people, despite the anxiety they had to live with.

I graduated in 1961 and was posted to Germany in 1962. As a newly minted second lieutenant, I was assigned to the Thirtieth Regiment of the Third Infantry Division, the so-called Rock of the Marne Division, which was face to face with the massed Soviet tank armies on Germany's East–West border. When I saw Berlin again, it was a changed place.

In the summer of 1961, the Berlin Wall went up overnight. Berliners woke up on the morning of August 13 to find East German workers tearing up streets, stringing barbed wire, and emplacing concrete elements

18

and cinderblocks along the boundary between the city's two sections. The whole city was taken by surprise. West Berliners were stunned. East Berliners panicked. Many tried to race across the barbed-wire barriers as they were going up. The wall separated families and suddenly threw people out of work. When I got there, East German workers were reinforcing the wall with concrete, raising the barbed wire, adding emplacements and bunkers for troops, a moat to keep cars from ramming through the wall, watchtowers, floodlights, a "death strip" with trained machine guns and vicious patrol dogs. East Berliners were being shot down as they tried to escape. I didn't see any of the fun-loving spirit I had seen before. West Berliners seemed somber and anxious about their future.

The East German regime called the wall an "antifascist barrier" meant to keep spies and other "bad elements" from entering the Soviet Zone. But in fact it wasn't built to keep enemies out; it was built to keep East Berliners in. Before the wall went up and the border was sealed, more than three and a half million East Germans had escaped to the West, more than one-fifth of East Germany's entire population. Many doctors, engineers, scientists, and teachers were among the millions getting out. East Germany was hemorrhaging people, especially its professional class.

The wall stopped that. Along the West Berlin side, I saw the crosses and flower memorials that marked where East Berliners had been killed trying to flee, crashing cars and trucks into the barriers in attempts to break through, climbing over or tunneling under it. I had been following incidents in the news while still in the United States, but seeing them in person was shocking. People trying to come through were getting caught on the barbed wire. Where apartment buildings abutted the wall, people leaped out of second-story windows trying to escape to freedom. "What's going on here is barbaric," I thought. "It's not human. A government that would do this to its own people, what else might it do?"

From there, I began thinking about why we were in Germany. Not that I had questioned it before, but now I had a very clear understanding of the reason. Soldiers need to know why they're doing what they're doing, what they're putting their lives on the line for. As I reported to my regiment in Schweinfurt, I had no doubts about why I was there.

Graduating from West Point, I had chosen to go into the infantry instead of one of the army's other branches. My first German experience as a cadet platoon leader had settled my mind on that. My company commander then was a crusty old Korean War veteran. "You're going to be platoon leader," he told me. "We're going on a field exercise. You're in charge!" So, with my cadet-rank insignia of three bars on my collar, I went down to the platoon and took charge.

A day or two later there was some infraction by one of the platoon members. I got a rude awakening when the company commander called me in and chewed me out. "You're responsible for everything this platoon does," he said, not gently. "I put you in charge, so get in charge!" With a lot of help from the platoon sergeant, for the next thirty days I had an in-depth learning experience about what it meant to be a leader. The challenge was to get forty men to willingly do what I wanted them to do. This was similar in a way to getting a football team to work together. Getting a handle on how to do that appealed to me, which was why I chose the infantry. I had no idea I would be doing essentially the same thing, just on a larger and larger scale, for the next thirty-six years of my life.

Now, in 1962, two years after my cadet leadership experience, I was reporting to the Third Infantry Division in Schweinfurt as a commissioned second lieutenant. The Third Infantry was a storied division. In World War I, it had held against a massive German assault in the crucial Second Battle of the Marne. In World War II, it had performed heroically in North Africa, Sicily, Italy, and France. Audie Murphy, the Medal of Honor winner who was the most decorated soldier of the war, was a Third Division veteran. Now the Third was right at the center of the Allied defense against a potential Soviet assault on West Europe, opposite the Fulda and Meiningen Gaps through the Thuringian range of hills and mountains, which was the most likely attack route (along with the North German plain) for the Soviet tank armies.

With seven or eight other new lieutenants, I stood in the office of Colonel William DePuy, commander of the Third Division's First Battle Group. We were arranged there in a line, and I had gotten myself onto the right end, thinking that Colonel DePuy would start there. But instead he started from the left, which meant I went last. As he asked each new lieutenant what he thought about why he was there and what he wanted to do, I was getting more and more nervous. I knew there was only one platoon leader slot open, and I was sure someone else was going to ask for it. But for some reason none of the others did, and when DePuy came to me, I said, "Sir, I came to command a platoon. Give me a platoon. That's what I want to do."

After everybody left, DePuy called me back in. "You've got the second platoon, Delta Company," he said. "Report to the company. We're moving out tomorrow at 0530. Get your people ready!"

The next morning we moved out across the German countryside, which did a lot of damage to the terrain, but as I quickly learned, DePuy was all about fast movement, maneuver, and the most realistic training possible. If a Soviet attack did come, the Third Division would be in the direct path of a Russian and Warsaw Pact juggernaut. Preparation for that assault required mobility and an intimate knowledge of the terrain, which meant the kind of hard field exercises into which I was now plunged.

We moved out in new M-113 armored personnel carriers, and at the end of the day we were digging in our first defensive line when a helicopter put down next to us and out stepped Colonel DePuy, immaculate in pressed fatigues. I reported to him, and he said, "I want to walk your line"—that is, he wanted to inspect how we were dug in, to check that everything was done right. I had just arrived the day before. I didn't even have my legs under me yet. He obviously hadn't chosen my platoon by accident.

We moved down the line, DePuy asking the soldiers dug into their foxholes, "Who's on your right? Who's on your left? What's your mission? Their fire interlocks with yours. Do you know who they are? Do you trust them?" When we came to the machine-gun position, he got down on his stomach in the mud behind the gun. He looked up at me. "The machine guns protect not just their own platoon but the flanks of the adjoining platoons. We need to tie everything in." He turned to the assistant gunner. "Let me see your range card." The gunner gave him the card—it showed eight hundred meters of grazing fire: eight hundred meters where the machine gun's flat trajectory fire could rake an enemy advance. "Walk out there," DePuy told the gunner. The gunner walked out. He hadn't gone more than fifty yards before he walked down a depression and disappeared from sight. Apparently we did not have eight hundred meters of grazing fire. DePuy looked at me. "Whose responsibility is it to check this out?"

"Mine, sir."

"That's right. This is the most important weapon system in the platoon. This is something you check. Get your platoon sergeants squared away. I need you to understand what my priorities are."

Twenty-four hours in command, and I had already screwed up. That night we moved out again. By daylight we were dug in to our second defensive line. *Whop, whop, whop,* in came DePuy's helicopter. "Let's walk out five hundred meters," he said. We walked out. We looked back at my platoon, dug in on a hillside. "You're a Soviet commander," he said. "You're going to attack this hill. What would you do?"

"Sir, the first thing I'd do would be to call in artillery."

"Right, that's the first thing a Soviet commander would do. Where would your aim point be?"

I looked at the hill. "Right at the top of the hill, see that big tree? That's where I'd aim."

"Good. If a Soviet regiment attacks, you've got to expect massive heavy artillery. That's how they do it."

Back in our positions, DePuy said, "Let's walk the line." We walked the line, the same as the day before. "Who's on your right? Who's on your left? What's your mission?" We came to the machine gun. "Let me see your range card."

"The machine gun position is good," he said. "The range card is good. The protective line is good."

I breathed a sigh of relief. Then he said, "Look up."

I looked up. I had put the machine gun directly under the tree I had just told him a Soviet commander would use to register his fire.

Colonel William DePuy had come out of World War II with a reputation as a fighter. He had started the war as a new lieutenant and had received a field promotion to major during the Normandy campaign. He had fought on Utah Beach and right up through the Battle of the Bulge and beyond, finishing the war as a lieutenant colonel. He was short in stature and slight, but he had a commanding presence. He was, as I quickly found out, a superb trainer.

DePuy had studied for a time at England's Imperial War College, which had influenced him to a degree. He had a gift for marrying strategy and tactics. He understood the movement of armored units, of infantry units, of the need to have cross-reinforcement of armor, infantry, and air force, all working together. And he took his idea of how to fight all the way down to the platoon and squad level. If we did have to fight the Soviets, how should we build our defense? What was the best way of maneuvering so we could conduct an active defense rather than just sitting there waiting to be crushed by the massed Soviet and Warsaw Pact armies?

I started learning his lessons from that first day as a platoon leader: how you pay the closest attention to every detail, how you dig in, how you move, how you train your troops so they can accomplish the hard, strenuous tasks you are demanding of them. That's what he was about; I bought in to all of it.

In addition to his strategic and tactical creativity, DePuy had an unusual ability to talk not just to higher-level commanders but to green second lieutenants like myself and to sergeants and privates as well. He had an easy way of communicating with common soldiers. He sat down and spoke with them, always teaching, always explaining, and they understood that in all of his grueling training he was really looking out for their welfare. The better they knew how to do what he demanded of them, the better their chances of coming out of battle alive.

I had been in Schweinfurt for only six months when DePuy left for another assignment, but in that time he put me through his teaching process. He took me along with him in his thinking, which got embedded in my own approach as I rose in rank. How do you maneuver? How do you mount an overwatch and leapfrog, where one element protects another as the second moves forward? How do you fix an enemy coming at you while bringing your other assets to bear on his attacking forces and eroding or destroying his reinforcements?

DePuy was developing his ideas about active defense in response to the great strategic problem posed by the overwhelming superiority of Soviet and Warsaw Pact armies facing us in Germany. This wasn't some theoretical military-political game playing. The potential for real military conflict was a constant during all the hard Cold War years, a threat that peaked frighteningly on more than one occasion.

The Berlin Airlift in 1948, which countered the Soviet attempt to starve West Berlin to death, was one instance everyone knew about. Had the Soviets shot down one American plane, it would have led to a general conflagration. A lesser-known near-war occasion took place in 1961, exactly a week after the wall started to go up. As the initial concrete barriers were being set and the barbed-wire fences thickened and extended, President Kennedy sent Vice President Lyndon Johnson and former West Berlin military governor General Lucius Clay to demonstrate America's commitment to the city. At the same time, an American armored column crossed the border from West Germany into East Germany and headed up the autobahn to reinforce the Allies' Berlin garrison. West Berlin was an Allied enclave in the heart of East Germany, a hundred miles from the border through hostile, unpredictable territory.

The column, with its APCs and tanks, moved through East Germany on high alert for any effort to stop them. The tension was almost unbearable. When the first elements rumbled into West Berlin, people swarmed around them joyously, planting flowers in the tanks' gun barrels. Everyone knew what might so easily have happened and what still might happen as Allied and Soviet forces faced off along the two sides of the city.

It was against this background that DePuy began conceptualizing a new strategy aimed not just at delaying a Soviet assault until reinforcements could arrive from the United States but at defeating it with the forces on hand. The Soviet war plan was to attack with echelon after echelon, create a penetration with overwhelming numbers, then exploit the penetration and reach and cross the Rhine River within twenty-four hours, essentially eliminating West Germany's ability to survive as an independent state. If the Soviets were able to keep to that time table, there would be no chance for new American forces to arrive before West Germany was swallowed.

As commander of the battle group directly opposite the Fulda and Meiningen Gaps, DePuy was focused on this problem early on. He believed that an active, fast-moving defense conducted by mobile elements could halt an initial Soviet thrust, but the key to success would be to badly damage the second and third Soviet echelons that were coming behind. We might take out the first fifty tanks, but five hundred were coming behind them. If we couldn't simultaneously attack deep to disrupt, delay, and attrit the following echelons, we were going to end up in deep trouble. All of our exercises and training were predicated on the fact that we were the element charged with stopping a Soviet onslaught.

DePuy moved on from Germany to Vietnam, where I met him again when I was assigned there as a company commander in 1966. At that point, he was my division commander, and unlike most of his peers he was always looking at the battlefield in terms of maneuver. That's what he had done with his battle group in Germany, and that's what he did with his battalions and brigades in Vietnam. Speed and deception were his stock in trade. Shocking the enemy with rapid movement and firepower. Fixing the enemy on a defensive line organized around his innovative firing positions, then hitting their oncoming forces with all the power of his combined arms. These were central elements of DePuy's warfighting strategy. He brought them with him to Vietnam, and they became key to the AirLand Battle doctrine he helped develop as head of the US Army's Training and Doctrine Command later in his career. It's no exaggeration to say that he was the chief architect who rebuilt the American army that came out of Southeast Asia so depleted and demoralized.

DePuy's strategic thinking was an important part of the background I brought with me when I fought under him in Vietnam and many years later when I became a division and corps commander, facing essentially the same problems he faced when I was one of his platoon lieutenants in my very first deployment.

DePuy's training and warfighting methods weren't the only lessons I learned early on in Germany. The German language had been one of my concentrations at West Point, and since I spoke it to some degree, I heard, "Lieutenant, you are now the liaison officer to the German Second Corps. We're exercising with them, so get up to their command center in Heppenheim and report to the corps commander."

The German Second Corps commander was a three-star general, so it didn't occur to me that I would be having any contact with him after I introduced myself. I expected them to embed me with one of their units in this war game and put me together with one of their communications officers. Since I was going to be in the field with them, I took my sleeping bag, my toothbrush, and a change of socks and headed up to Heppenheim.

When I reported to the corps commander, though, he told one of his officers, "The lieutenant's going to be staying here. Show him his quarters," which turned out to be a nice old-style German hotel room, with its own bathroom. It's not easy to describe the kind of luxury that seems when you're expecting to sleep on the ground and use a slit trench with the rest of the men.

But instead of bivouacking in the field, I was stationed in the command headquarters, monitoring the maneuvers with senior members of the German Staff and communicating back and forth with the exercise controllers from the American Seventh Army in Heidelberg. Most of the German officers were veterans of World War II. Every morning the chief of staff would call the officers to attention and brief the corps commander—the most professional briefing I had ever heard. Then later in the day the members of the staff would sit around, have a beer together, and discuss the situation. I was listening to these high-level tactical, intelligence, and logistics officers discussing military operations in a way I had never heard before. At twenty-three years old, I was a little dazzled to be there with such people. I found out early on how much there was to learn from allies and partners.

As the exercise developed, I got a call from Seventh Army control. "Tell Second Corps there's an airborne drop in their rear, and they need to react to it." This exercise was, as most of them were, a game against a hypothetical Soviet attack through the Fulda Gap. The German Second Corps was playing the Allied reserve element. We knew that a Soviet frontal assault would likely be accompanied by an airborne drop behind our lines, and here it was. The reserve needed to respond.

The German chief of staff was a giant, six-foot-seven-inch paratroop officer and Alpine specialist. I told him in German what was happening. "Control wants to know," I said, "what is your reaction?" "Komm mit mir," he said. We went to the maps. "Here we are," pointing. "Here's where you say the airdrop is. Now, we're going to go back to your control headquarters in Heidelberg because I need to tell them in person that I'm doing nothing. I'm going to watch it. I'm not going to do anything except watch."

We drove the twenty miles or so to Heidelberg, where I introduced the German chief to the control officers, almost all of them Americans. I asked him, "General, what is your reaction to the airdrop going to be?"

"Let me explain," he said.

He went to the map spread on a table. He was so tall he had to get down on his knees to show what the Second Corps reserve was going to do. The American officers clustered around him.

"Here is the front line," he said. "Here's where you say the enemy airdrop is. Here is my position." I was doing my best to translate. I spoke German, but I wasn't used to the military lingo. It was hard to keep up.

"I am going to do nothing except observe," he said. "The Soviet marry-up force will take I don't know how long to get there, if they get there at all. And if they don't marry up, all these people are going to do is just sit there. They're not capable of much else. If they try, they know they'll get torn to shreds. So we're not going to attack them because a much bigger threat might develop somewhere else. So my judgment is that we're just going to observe."

As he was saying this, the American controllers were pulling their hair out. "You've got to react," they insisted. "We can't have these people behind our lines!"

"Nein," said the German. "I'm the reserve for the entire front. If we commit the reserve, that opens us up to anything else that happens. You give me something that makes me move, and I'll do it, but this airdrop doesn't make me move. I'm going to hold the reserve where it is and watch what they [the Soviets] do."

This went directly counter to American instincts. The natural American reaction is if you see a problem, you react to it. You take care of it if you can. That was certainly how I thought. On a football field or basketball court, if you see a play developing, you react, you try to break it up. But as I was watching this encounter between the German chief of staff and the American officers, I was thinking, "Wait, the Germans are saying, you have to think of the next step and the step after that. You can't just react; you have to think it through. You have to consider that if you commit the reserve, which I would have done, then you're vulnerable elsewhere. So you need to assess: How much of a threat is this airborne drop to your rear? If it becomes serious, if they're preventing you from getting supplies up, if they're hitting your rear, that's one thing. But none of that was happening. So he is watching it. And he will continue to watch it to see what might develop."

I thought that approach was fascinating. On the way back to Second Command headquarters, I told the general, "Sir, thank you. That was a great education for me." Which it was in several regards. First, it educated me about how to read a battlefield. Second, the education came through people who thought about things differently, allies of ours with a different point of view. When I was first ordered to go to the Germans as a translator, I thought it was a slap of some sort. I wanted to stay with my platoon.

But it turned out to be an important experience; it helped me understand something about the strength that comes from working with allies not only to coordinate military movements, but to be exposed to different ways of looking at problems.

Those were remarkable lessons for a new second lieutenant to learn. When I came back to Germany as a battalion commander thirteen years later, I had partnerships with French, German, Canadian, British, and Belgian units. I welcomed those relationships with great enthusiasm in order to demonstrate to the officers working for me how important it is to achieve solidarity, mutual trust, and confidence and how fighting as a team multiplies each army's power. We all would train together and deploy in what we called the general defense plan, which governed how we would fight if the Soviets forced the issue. We had to be able to trust the people on our right and left. "Who's on your right?" DePuy had asked the soldiers in their firing positions. "Who's on your left?" "Do you trust them?" The same was true for the US military and our allies. You had to be able to trust each other and operate together.

When I eventually returned to Germany as a corps commander in 1989, the contacts and relationships I had made over the years proved crucial. My German counterpart when we both were colonels, Helge Hansen, was now a three-star general, as I was. And just as we had done when we were younger, we faced the Soviets opposite the famous Fulda Gap, but this time as commanders of major allied forces. Together we walked the line between his corps and mine. We figured out which units would take the lead in which areas. We overlapped and interlocked. And what we did was a signal to the Soviets because that's where they would attack if they could, along boundary lines and seams. And watching us deploy, the Soviets recognized that we weren't just separate forces out there—we were a coordinated, cohesive team.

And that was, without any doubt, an important deterrent factor.

These relationships with the Germans and our other allies weren't static; they had great significance for our national security, and they required nurturing. Facing uncertainty and danger demanded the ability for all of us to work together as an integrated, tied-in team. "One team," as I regularly put it to anyone who would listen, "one fight."

I left Germany for the army's Armor School in August 1965. Only a few months before that, the United States had decided to put combat troops on the ground in Vietnam. Up until then, America's war planning and training had envisioned fighting the Soviets in Europe; now we were engaged in a land war in Southeast Asia against a very different kind of enemy in a place we knew little about.

Even as I started the armored-warfare course, I knew I would be heading for Vietnam, and in June 1966 I received orders to report to the army's First Infantry Division in Di An as company commander in the Twenty-Sixth Regiment, the so-called Blue Spaders—a nickname that came from the spadelike arrowhead device on their shoulder patches. My former boss, William DePuy, now a major general, was the First Infantry Division's commander. Three other officers from my former battalion in Schweinfurt were with the Blue Spaders already. DePuy was loading up the regiment with the young people he had brought along in Germany, those of us who knew him and knew what he wanted.

In Germany, I learned the lessons DePuy and his successors taught about how to fight. DePuy in particular had taught the art of small-unit warfare, of leadership and maneuver, and of the integration of combat arms. In my time in Germany, I also learned the importance of coalitions and something about the requirements of building and sustaining them. Most important, I knew what we were fighting for. I had heard President Kennedy give his "Ich bin ein Berliner" speech. I had deployed in our forward fighting positions—that is, those units that would be the first to make contact with the enemy in battle—when it looked as if the Cuban Missile Crisis might trigger a hot war with the Soviets. I knew what America stood for and exactly why I was doing what I was doing.

3

Vietnam

I had spent four years in Germany thinking about a Soviet attack, planning for it and training for it. But now I was in Vietnam, a place that could hardly have been more different. Instead of Europe's highlands, plains, and open vistas, Vietnam featured dense tropical jungles and malarial swamps, sluggish rivers, canals, and rice paddies, all of it wrapped up in equatorial heat and seasonal monsoons.

The enemy in Vietnam was just as different as the landscape. The Vietcong and North Vietnamese didn't have the tanks, mechanized units, and heavy artillery. They didn't have the massed forces that could blow you apart if you weren't well prepared. Instead they had highly mobile, deadly infantry, adept at ambushes and surprise attacks, who could make themselves invisible and strike when and where they wanted. Many Communist soldiers were hard-core veterans who had been fighting more or less continually since their war against the French in the 1940s and 1950s. We didn't think the Soviets had much ability to improvise; they weren't agile. The enemy in Vietnam were masters of movement and elusiveness. Their guerrilla forces could strike and melt back into the general population or disappear into the vast networks of tunnels that honeycombed strategic areas. Their main forces were quick learners. They were expert at using the terrain and adapting their fighting methods to the strategy and tactics of their enemy—us.

I arrived there in June 1966, a little more than a year after two battalions of American marines had waded ashore in Danang. When I reported to the First Infantry Division in Di An, the number of American combat troops had grown from the initial fifteen hundred to more than a quarter of a million, a number that was spiraling upward as additional brigades and divisions poured into the country. They had brought with them all the heavy weaponry the US armed forces possessed, along with whole airmobile divisions fielding fleets of helicopters and air force tactical aircraft from jet fighters to gunships as well as B-52s flying out of Guam and Thailand.

But with all our immense buildup and overwhelming firepower, it couldn't be said that we were winning. The casualty rate was alarming.

Huge efforts to find and destroy the enemy frequently yielded nothing as Vietcong or North Vietnamese forces simply disappeared into the jungle. American units fell into small and big ambushes, took painful losses, and lost contact before reinforcements could come up to engage the attackers. Often the reinforcements themselves were ambushed. The initiative always seemed to be in the enemy's hands. In the first big-unit battle of the war, elements from the First Cavalry Division were badly cut up by three North Vietnamese regiments in the Ia Drang Valley in the Central Highlands before continuous runs by fighter-bombers and gunships and even carpet bombing by B-52s stopped the North Vietnamese and drove them into retreat. The lesson for Americans was that bringing immense firepower to bear was the key to victory. The North Vietnamese, looking for how to neutralize the Americans' advantage, decided that the way to do that was to close with their enemy as fast as possible and "grab them by the belt," putting themselves so close in that the Americans couldn't use their artillery or aircraft.

I got my first taste of action and my first lesson in Vietnamese-style warfare three days after I arrived to take command of B Company in the first battalion of the First Infantry Division's Twenty-Sixth (Blue Spader) Regiment. I had asked the battalion commander if I could have a week to train my new company in fire and movement techniques. He agreed, but two days later we were given a no-notice mission. Just as we were preparing to load up the helicopters, Major General DePuy himself, the First Division's commander, showed up, which brought me instantly back to my first day in Germany, five years earlier, when then Colonel DePuy had swooped in to my platoon by surprise. Back then he had wanted to walk my line. Now he talked about the kind of quick, decisive movements he expected. I understood what he meant. I had been practicing his fighting techniques the whole four years I was in Germany.

Our insertion point was a flooded rice paddy. As we set down, I jumped out of the helicopter along with my radio operator, who was shorter than average. When I looked around, he wasn't there; the mud and water had sucked him under. I pulled him back up by his harness, and the two of us struggled to where we found our footing. The company in front of me was in a firefight, and I was ordered to maneuver around them. But the sucking mud made movement difficult until we got to the berm separating our paddy from the next one over. With our artillery laying down high explosives and fighter-bombers roaring in for strafing runs, we made headway around the company that was engaged, but a few minutes later my lead squad came under fire. I moved up toward the point of attack so I could see what was happening when the platoon sergeant yelled, "Get your ass down, sir!" I hit the dirt just as a burst of machine-gun fire slammed over my head, straight down the berm. I crawled to the embankment and slid down, my radio operator on one side, my second company radio man on the other. I had the company net in one hand, the battalion net in the other when three bullets thunked into the mud right next to my ear. Holy shit, I thought. Welcome to Vietnam. My little operator was slumped over, dead. The other had been hit, too. A few minutes later a medevac helicopter hovered in under fire and perched down precariously on the berm just long enough for us to load the two men on.

We finally brought in additional air and artillery, which allowed us to move through the mud of the paddy and get to where we needed to be. It was a quick, hard lesson on how to use and not use the terrain.

Afterward I thought about what I could have done differently. I had thought the berm embankment would be protective. It wasn't. The radio antennas were sticking up, marking our position, a natural aiming point for the VC, not just to put the radio communications out of business but because they knew American commanders were always right there next to the radio sets. You had to get down to where you were really in defilade, which made communication more difficult, but you had to be aware of the trade-off. I didn't make the same mistake twice. After we got back from the paddies, I took a time-out and thought through what happens if we get under fire. I had been a commissioned officer for five years. I had been through Ranger school, airborne school, and Armor School. My units had faced off with the Soviets. But this was the first time I had ever been in live combat.

After that, whenever we went out, if I had the time, I would assemble every leader, from squad leaders on up. I'd explain: "This is where we are. This is my intent; this is what we're going to do. Let me tell you what's in support. We've got helicopter gunships, we've got artillery, and we've planned for their use. So that means at a certain point you may have to hunker down to allow the air to come in. I may have to bring them in close, so be prepared for that. Think through what your mission is. Pay attention to every detail. You're responsible. If you screw up, who's responsible? *You're* responsible! Don't mince words. Say that. Don't say, 'Well, the sergeant didn't do this, or the private didn't do that.' *You* are responsible!"

Guys would come up to me afterward and slap their chest with their right hand, meaning, "Yes, sir, I'm with you." That didn't mean they couldn't make a mistake. It meant they understood they were accountable for their decisions and that they were paying attention to detail, exactly what my own responsibilities were—DePuy's lesson number one and West Point's.

Toothbrush to the right, bristles up.

In 1966, the military as a whole was struggling to make the transition from anti-Soviet warfighting doctrine to an approach that would be effective in Vietnam. Senior officers had to get their heads around something they had no experience of. Although a few noncommissioned officers (NCOs) had fought in Korea, all the private soldiers were green, with no fighting experience. They had to learn on the job, which cost many lives. Like other American units, the First Infantry Division under DePuy's predecessor had had a rough time of it. They had lost a lot of people, both troops and officers.

My battalion commander in the Twenty-Sixth was Paul Gorman, a smart, imaginative lieutenant colonel who was facing the same problems everyone else was.

The unit was trained for Europe and hadn't yet adapted to its new enemy and new circumstances. Gorman was trying to fix that. He asked me about DePuy because he knew I had served with him in Germany and understood his methods. We got into the habit of consulting closely together, and Gorman later brought me onto his command staff as S-3 in charge of training and operational planning.

In fact, even though the enemy and battleground were so different from what we faced in Europe, the principles that governed how to fight were similar.

Security, for example. If you were moving, you needed to do it with security in place, in Vietnam especially because the jungle terrain was so ideal for ambush, the Vietcong's specialty. In essence, a main unit could move only as fast as its security detail—for a company, that meant two men on either side flanking the main unit. But you had to be disciplined. In the jungle with its limited vision, it was essential not to get in front of your security, no matter how fast you might want to go. Bounding and overwatch applied here just as it did in Europe: that is, in maneuvering, one element would take up a covering position while the second "bounded" forward, then the first would bound, covered by the second, and so on, leapfrogging toward the objective. We learned to do that with mechanized and tank units as well as with infantry. We learned to "cloverleaf," sending reconnaissance squads out in a cloverleaf pattern, one to the right, one to the left, each of them sweeping out, then curving back, then sweeping out to the next sector.

These principles were easy enough to articulate, but applying them consistently required discipline and lots of training. And even if you had absorbed them and been trained to them, the demands of battle could easily lead to mistakes. One of my best friends was Jim Madden. He and I had been at West Point together; then we had come in as second lieutenants at Schweinfurt under DePuy. DePuy had picked Jim out for the Blue Spaders, just as he chose me and several of our friends. I had B Company, and Jim had C Company.

Not long after I took over my company, Jim went out on an operation near the Cambodian border. The temperature that day was around 110 degrees; the air was thick with humidity. About half a mile past C Company's firebase, one of Jim's soldiers passed out with heat stroke. Jim called in a medevac helicopter to take him out, but it wasn't long before another soldier went down. Another medevac came in to get him. Jim then made the mistake of getting on a trail to make up time, hurrying to get to his objective, forgoing his security in favor of speed.

Several hours out he ran into a well-prepared horseshoe ambush. The medevac helicopters had told the Vietcong an American unit was on the move, and they had dug low firing positions around the trail and cut away a foot or a foot and a half of space in the jungle undergrowth at ground level. They were virtually invisible. When they opened up, their fire cut into Jim's company, hitting them in the legs and knees. C Company casualties were sprawled out along the trail as Jim worked to put together a defense.

I was monitoring Jim's net and was hearing everything that was going on. His voice was calm, collected, but it was obvious he was in deep trouble. I knew we were going to be sent in. I put out the order: "Get ready." I called all the leaders together; we went over our battle drills, our objective, the contingencies. We rehearsed, checked equipment, I detailed my intent. We were ready to move quickly, and, sure enough, thirty minutes later we got the order from battalion to move out.

Before long one of my platoons reported a heat casualty. I told them to pick him up and carry him. We weren't going to bring in a medevac and let the whole world know we were here. A little later a second man collapsed. "Carry him," I said. Everyone was keeping up, though I didn't know that the second casualty's squad was so pissed off one of theirs fell out that they just left him behind to fend for himself, figuring they would pick him up on the way back. When I found out somebody was missing, I asked the squad leader, "Where's So-and-So?"

"Back there," he said, "where he collapsed."

"Go back," I said. "Get him up here."

They did that. Then we moved in.

Halfway there we ran into a river flowing through a swamp, too deep to ford, but I had learned how to make a one-rope bridge in my Ranger training, and I had taught it to the company. My first sergeant got across and established a security perimeter with the other first crossers to give the rest of the company protection. We all got across, every man, including me, carrying a mortar round—I kept the mortar tube with us at all times. We made it across the swamp and the river with all our ammunition and equipment. But as soon as we were out of the water, we found to our horror that we were covered with blood-sucking leeches from the waist down. In an instant, almost the whole company had dropped their pants and drawers and lit cigarettes to apply to the leeches, which made them detach and drop off. Those who didn't smoke sprayed the leeches with mosquito repellent, which also made them detach. Meanwhile, Gorman, high up in his helicopter, saw white legs and skivvies and radioed down, "George, what the hell is going on down there?"

I gave people a quick minute to de-leech, then we picked up the pace, keeping security tight so that we wouldn't find ourselves in an ambush as well as C Company.

We came up on the enemy's flank as the firefight with Jim's company was raging. Jim had begun his withdrawal, and we did enough damage to cover him as he evacuated his casualties.

Jim was a hell of a soldier. In a later engagement, he was wounded badly (he was six-foot-seven, a big target), but he talked himself out of the hospital and got back to the battalion. Since he was in no shape to return to his company, he was temporarily assigned to the tactical operations center. I didn't know that. I was in the same battle and thought he had been killed. Then suddenly I heard his voice over the net, giving me orders. I was never happier to listen to someone telling me what to do.

DePuy was a devotee of movement. He had developed an effective intelligence network, and when we had something verified and actionable, he would move fast, often over long distances with armored cavalry and helicopters to disrupt the enemy, who had to move on foot and were slower. He got inside their decision cycle and used shock action—movement and overwhelming firepower—that inflicted severe losses time and again. Other times, he would use units to bait the Vietcong or North Vietnamese, and once they took the bait, he would have forces ready, including air and attack helicopters to spring his trap and hit them hard.

But given the characteristic aggressiveness of the VC and the NVA, or North Vietnamese army, it was inevitable that we were often fighting on the defense. In Germany, we had trained in techniques that would stop a Soviet regimental assault. Here DePuy needed us to figure out how to stop a VC or NVA regimental assault.

These were two different animals. A Soviet attack meant a bombardment by heavy artillery to blow a hole through you, followed by a tank and mechanized infantry assault to smash through the opening. Stopping such a thing meant bringing artillery and antitank weapons to bear, having maneuvering forces ready to flank the Russian thrust, and having a well-prepared line of defense in front of it.

That well-prepared line of defense centered on what came to be known as the "DePuy firing position," which was a foxhole of his own design. Typically it was a position for two riflemen, with a berm in front that afforded protection from direct fire and wasn't easy to target since from the front the men in the foxhole weren't visible and there were no muzzle flashes. The firing ports were instead at the sides of the front berm, protected by it and angled for diagonal rather straight-ahead fire. Each DePuy foxhole thus interlocked its fire with fire from the foxholes on either side of it.

An NVA or VC regimental attack differed considerably. In the first place, although they had little in the way of field artillery, they did have large numbers of mortars, including 82-millimeter medium mortars. Their attacks on American or South Vietnamese defensive positions were often preceded by mortar barrages. Because the jungle provided such thick cover, and because the Vietnamese Communist troops were capable of great stealth, they could often position their mortars close in to our defensive perimeters, which meant their accuracy was typically excellent.

An NVA infantry attack was like nothing else. Their sappers were expert at infiltrating, cutting barbed-wire defenses, and setting Bangalore torpedoes. With or without sappers, enemy infantry would come in as close to our perimeter as they could get, sometimes extremely close, then they would erupt in human-wave attacks, firing AKs and submachine guns as they came, throwing grenades, and dropping satchel charges in American foxholes and bunkers. Waves of attackers would come in, one after the other. They would suffer dreadful losses, but they would keep coming.

These were extremely brave fighters. Their objective was to penetrate our perimeters, cause havoc inside our positions, overrun us, and create total routs or total destruction. Against a Soviet attack in Germany, if a breakthrough happened, there was always a chance to retreat in some order to secondary defensive positions. In Vietnam, if you were overrun, there were few places to hide.

In order to confront this kind of attack, DePuy's foxhole concept needed to be changed, and he asked me to see if I could adapt it so that it would fit our new circumstances. We needed a firing position that could ward off human-wave assaults and would be effective even if our perimeter did get penetrated.

The answer here was that instead of arranging foxholes in a line, we should stagger the emplacements. That way, diagonal fire to the flanks could interlock, but also the foxholes that were staggered back could direct fire behind the more frontward positions. With all our firepower, including pre-ranged mortar and artillery fire, we could badly attrit an assault, even if we couldn't necessarily stop it dead at the perimeter. If the VC did penetrate and took one of our positions, they would think they were through the line, but then they would run into fire from other positions. But our troops had to be prepared for our own people firing behind them. That didn't come naturally. It took discipline. They had to train for it.

To protect against mortar attacks, we also beefed up the bunkers' overhead cover with a layer of logs and two layers of sandbags on top of the logs. We were the only unit in Vietnam that went into an air assault with chainsaws. With all of this—digging, cutting trees and hauling them, filling sandbags—building a DePuy firing position was a strenuous job, especially for troops who had been out in the jungles and swamps all day, maybe trekking distances, maybe engaged in firefights. The challenge was to get them to accept and believe in the concept and train hard so they were physically and mentally up to getting it done. They had to understand why this was so important, how digging in like this would save their lives and their buddies' lives, how it gave them a better chance of getting home alive. There was a lot of bitching and moaning—"Why are we cutting all these trees down when we're going to be moving out tomorrow?"—but we practiced and practiced and got very good at it.

DePuy would come down to see what we were doing. He would walk the line with me, the same as he had done years before in Germany. Being out in the jungle in a defensive perimeter, knowing there were people out there in the dark who had very bad intentions for you, was a scary proposition. It focused attention. I'd check the foxholes. "Who's on your right?" "Who's on your left?" "Do you trust the guy over there? How about over there on the other side?"

The question about trust was an interesting one. When you asked it bluntly to people whose lives were right there on the line, you could get some surprising answers. "Do you trust him?" meant "Is he on dope? Is he drinking? Is he going to fall asleep at night? Can you count on him?" And the platoon knew who was on dope, who had a drinking problem, who was not going to stay awake. Everyone's life depended on everyone else doing what they were supposed to be doing. I later wrote a pamphlet on the subject: *How to Dig In and Why.*

On one occasion DePuy told me, "I want to demonstrate our defensive tactics to the division leadership." He conducted the demonstration out in enemy territory—for the realism—with a platoon of my troops as demonstrators in front of all the command officers. I thought, "My God, if the VC only knew what was here."

DePuy also brought Moshe Dayan to look at what we were doing. Dayan, the one-eyed former Israeli chief of staff and soon to be defense minister, was getting a close-up look at the Vietnam War. He spent time with Special Forces, with the First Air Cavalry, with marines, and with us. DePuy introduced me to him so we could show him our thinking about defensive positioning. This was in August 1966, a year before the Six-Day War expanded Israel's borders. Dayan was an offensive-minded general, but Israel then had a very constricted area from which to fight off any large-scale Arab attack. Our fighting-position concept clearly interested him. He asked me pointed questions, got down in the foxholes with the soldiers, and asked them for their thoughts. It was fascinating to hear the level of detail he wanted to know about. His direct way of talking to troops reminded me a lot of DePuy. I got the impression he was an innovative, adaptive thinker.

With the First Infantry Division's intelligence regularly identifying VC and NVA operational areas and movements, and with an aggressive battalion commander like Paul Gorman, almost every time we went out, we found the enemy, though sometimes they found us. In late August, not long after Dayan's visit, a sister unit from the division's Second Regiment ran into the VC's famous Phu Loi Battalion, very tough guys operating near their home village.

I was with my company several kilometers away guarding a unit of engineers clearing a road of mines, but as usual I was monitoring the regiment and brigade nets, and I could hear what was happening. Then a call came in from Gorman. Charlie Company, commanded by my friend Jim Madden, was in a hard fight. They had been committed to the engagement with the Phu Loi Battalion to reinforce the units in it already. Madden was wounded, Gorman said. I didn't know then that Madden had been conferring with the battalion executive officer and Sid Berry, the brigade commander. Berry had just left the meeting when enemy fire killed the battalion XO. Madden was shot in the chest. Gorman said Madden was wounded, but from the way he said it, I thought my friend might be dead.

"Stop what you're doing," Gorman said. "Get up here with your company!"

With the engineer commanding officer's go ahead, I loaded the company onto the engineers' dump trucks and got up that road to Gorman as fast as I could.

"C Company can't move," Gorman said.

"What do you want me to do?" I asked.

He showed me the map. "The VC are getting out," he said. "We think they're going to pull back to here. You go there"—he pointed to a junction where railroad tracks intersected with a road. "Go there and hit them."

Another of our units had just come up, a cavalry troop commanded by Sam Wilder, a friend of mine from West Point and Armor School. We quickly decided to cross-reinforce: he'd take one of my infantry platoons and give me three of his tanks and an APC.

"They're going here," I said. I showed him the map. "You go down the railroad tracks. I'll swing around through the brush and hit them in the flank. You be the anvil; I'll be the hammer."

I was in the cavalry APC, crashing through the densest jungle I had ever seen, thick with biting red ants. Red ants were all over everybody; hundreds of them seemed to be crawling down my back. Gorman called; he was up in his helicopter now. "Change of mission," he said. "It's not good. They're not retreating. We're not holding the battlefield here. Come north."

By now I had climbed onto one of the tanks so I could see better through the trees and foliage, holding onto the barrel and directing the tank driver with a long stick, hitting his right shoulder—go right, or his left—go left.

When we got to the edge of the battle, Gorman's helo put down next to me. He jumped out, and suddenly my tank's main gun went off, a huge blast.

The tank crew had spotted a machine-gun nest about to open up on us. So now we were in combat, close range. I brought the rest of the company up for an assault as Gorman grabbed another of my APCs and one of my tanks and roared off to take control of the rest of the battle.

From outside the VC perimeter, we launched an infantry/armor attack. The tanks led, blasting their way through. My troopers came right in with them, and suddenly we were inside the Phu Loi Battalion's base camp. We were right in their knickers.

That was when I saw Tom Galvin, one of my lieutenants, get hit doing exactly what I had said time and again not to do. I had trained the platoon leaders not to fight but to lead. "Officers will carry .45s, not M-16s. Your job is to lead. You will think, you will talk, you will read your map. If you're out there, and you have to shoot, we're in very deep trouble."

But Tom had gotten his people to the trench line where the VC CP, command post, was, and a VC in front of him had jumped into a bunker. Instead of doing what I told him, Tom grabbed an M-16 from one of his troops and leaped in after him when a grenade went off and blew him out of the hole. When that happened, the attack stalled as Tom's men brought him to safety. I called in a medevac, telling a tank to pivot and provide protection for it as the pilot hovered low enough to get Tom on board. (Tom was a very lucky man; he survived.) Meanwhile, we were pressing the fight again, and in the middle of it Gorman called again.

"I need you to stop what you're doing and come around. We're in a tough place over here."

"I'm in their CP," I said. "I can roll them up."

"No," he said. "Come out. Follow my tracks to me."

I followed Gorman's APC and tank tracks. But I knew we were in trouble; we had penetrated their perimeter, now we were out on their edge, moving by them, giving them flanking fire at us.

When I found Gorman, he was up to his eyebrows. We weren't winning this thing; we were losing. It was a scene out of a movie. APCs were burning; tanks were burning; a forward controller's helicopter had been shot down and was turned over like a beetle. Gorman called in napalm, which was slightly off target, and he got some flame on him and the map he was reading.

I was taking withering fire, so I turned my tanks around and was ready to get into it. I told the tanks to load beehive rounds, cannister that spreads like buckshot. But there were some of our own troops in front of us, so I crawled up to them and found one of their sergeants.

"We're going to come in," I said. "Can you put fire into their flank as we come?"

He looked up at me. "Sir, we've got so many wounded and dead, we can't really help much."

"Just hug the ground, then, because I'm opening up with beehive."

The tanks turned in and let loose. VC were tied in the trees, firing from there, invisible, but we just blew them out, bodies dangling down from their rope harnesses. They also had the whole area tunneled and kept coming up from holes connected to their base camp, hitting us, then disappearing. But several rounds from the tanks got rid of some of them, too. All of this allowed us to gain momentum, though we were taking losses, too—my platoon leader, a cavalry platoon leader, an incredibly brave Hawaiian platoon sergeant, and others.

We again got into the trench line and bunkers, which was where we were when darkness fell. By that time, we were one of the few combat-effective units left in the division, but we knew we had inflicted severe damage on the VC. They were still occupying their base camp, but they were trying to pull out while they could.

That night I set three listening posts out a hundred yards from my CP, putting them all on the company net. I wanted to make sure everyone stayed awake and was listening. "No shooting," I told them. I knew other units had patrols out. "Hold your fire. Make sure you've got positive identification. We've got friendlies out there."

At about midnight I heard a whisper from one of the listening posts: "I've got movement in front of me."

I was just telling him to make sure it was VC and not one of ours when I heard a loud *bang*.

"Goddammit," I said. "We have friendlies out. How do you know it was a VC?"

"Sir," the soldier came back, "he's in the foxhole with me."

The VC was so close that when the trooper shot him, he fell into the hole. Our report of the battle included this incident, and early next morning a helicopter landed with Jim Hollingsworth, DePuy's assistant division commander.

"Georgie, where is he?"

"Where's who?"

Hollingsworth blew right by me and went out to the listening post, where he gave the soldier a medal on the spot.

With daylight it was clear that the Phu Loi Battalion, whatever remained of it, had pulled out. We were left to collect the dead.

After Phu Loi, we were in the thick of every fight in our area of operation, west of Saigon and up to the Cambodian border. DePuy was using us as his shock battalion. Then in February of the new year, 1967, a decision was made to go after the Central Office South Vietnam (COSVN)—the Vietcong headquarters that ran the war in the South. Intelligence thought it was operating up near the Cambodian border in Tay Ninh Province, where the border jutted out in what was known as the "Fishhook."

COSVN was sure to be protected by a main-force unit, at least a regiment. Other main-force elements were likely to be nearby. A three-division operation code-named Junction City was planned by Army Command to hit COSVN and flush out and destroy enemy forces in what was known as War Zone C. The Blue Spaders were designated to lead the strike on the enemy's headquarters, with our battalion out in front. It might have been said that we were the bait to draw out the enemy main force. But we didn't think of it that way. If their main force did come out, we would be outnumbered, maybe significantly, but once they committed, if they did, we would be able to hammer them with air and artillery. Moving to hit us, they would be drawn into a killing zone.

At the end of March, we moved up into northern Tay Ninh, a wilderness of heavy forest and open areas of three-foot-high elephant grass. There the First Infantry Division established Firebase Charlie, a massive artillery concentration of 105- and 155-millimeter howitzers, eight-inch cannon and heavy mortars, as well as a smaller firebase, Thrust—both bases positioned to provide targeted fire on any point within a many-mile radius.

By this time, Gorman had taken me from B Company and made me the battalion's S-3. I was flattered by the confidence he had in me, but it was wrenching to leave the company I had been in fight after fight with and was so proud of. These men had become everything to me. Telling them I was leaving was the toughest talk I had ever had with my troops or would ever have. A highly emotional moment for me and for them. Not that Gorman gave me any time to feel sorry for myself. "Turn your company over to your XO," he had said. "You're now S-3. I want our next tactical order out in four hours."

Not long after that, Gorman was promoted, and Lieutenant Colonel Alexander Haig came in as our battalion commander. I was at first concerned about Haig; he was an armor officer with little experience of infantry command. But in action after action he showed great tactical instincts and personal fearlessness. After our first encounters together, I thought, "I've got myself another warfighting commander."

At Firebase Charlie, the battalion dug in, as they had been trained to. The chainsaws ran for hours as they cut logs for their overhead cover. That first night, right on schedule, the VC hammered us with mortar fire, walking it right across the base and our CP. When the first rounds went off, Haig and I ducked into our bunker. As I scrambled in, I accidently dropped my map case, and when I reached to get it, two rounds hit right on top of us, blowing me into the back of the bunker. Haig grabbed me and shook me a little to help me clear my head. But other than being dazed for a few minutes, I wasn't hurt. Pure luck. Our tactical-op tent next to us had been shredded. We had been planning this operation for weeks, ever since the battalion had received orders giving us our mission. Now, at Firebase Charlie, we decided on a landing zone for our air assault, a big open area of wild grass surrounded by sparse jungle, then the typical heavy jungle. As usual, we did an air reconnaissance, and I had imagery of the area, but something didn't smell quite right. I wanted to get a close-up view, so I made a low-level helicopter run over it and saw things the air imagery hadn't picked up—mortar rounds and eight-inch artillery shells, all booby trapped, hanging in the trees all around our proposed LZ's border. I could make out freshly prepared firing positions, though I saw no one in them. I felt the VC had figured out where we were going to land and were back at their base camp waiting out the air and artillery preparation they knew would be coming.

After the prep, they would move in and hit us with the booby traps and everything else they had. It was obvious COSVN must be somewhere in the vicinity; they were going to make a fight of this.

After seeing what I had seen, I chose a different LZ area nearby, not as big, so it would take longer to get everybody in, but a lot less risky. The brigade called it "Landing Zone George," after me. Great, I thought, how appropriate, LZ George, possibly my last resting place.

Our assault went in on March 30. We put heavy air and artillery fire into the surrounding area, then landed the battalion, ten helicopters at a time, which was all the space the LZ afforded. As soon as we landed, I sent the companies out into our cloverleaf reconnaissance pattern to find out what we had around us. We found bunkers, but no VC. No contact, just an ominous silence. As we dug our DePuy firing positions, I thought, "For nine months we've been practicing for a regimental assault. Now we're going to get one." As darkness fell, we set listening posts and sent out ambush patrols, but the night was quiet, with no sign of the enemy.

The next day we sent out recon patrols again. This time they found signs in English hanging from low branches. "Go back, Americans, or die." The recon platoon surveyed the area around our original LZ and reported that they had found the bunkers and booby traps I had seen from the air.

I was up in a helicopter talking to the recon platoon leader, telling him to make sure his artillery cover was registered, when suddenly he said, "My lead's been hit. I'm going up to see."

"Get your artillery working," I told him. "I've got air ready to come." Then the link went silent.

After a minute or so the radio operator came on.

"Lieutenant Hill's been shot, sir. He's dead. We're being hit with machine guns and small arms. Mortars are coming in. I'm seeing VC in green uniforms and pith helmets."

Uniforms and pith helmets—not black pajamas—meant VC regulars or NVA. Intelligence was right; there were main forces here.

General DePuy had left the division by now, posted back to the Pentagon. Major General John Hay had taken over, with Jim Hollingsworth still as assistant commander. "Holly" was also up in his helicopter. He called. "I've got close air support and gunships stacked up. When do you want me to start dealing?"

The recon platoon radio operator was still on. "Do you have a smoke grenade?" I said.

"Yes."

"Throw that smoke as far as you can toward the VC. Then get your ass down."

He threw the grenade, and you could see the smoke.

"Can you see that?" I told the forward air controller, "As soon as you identify it, you hit that smoke grenade as close as you can with napalm."

A jet swooped in and did that.

"That's it, that's it," the radio operator shouted. "Right on target."

"Okay," I told the controller, "you've got your target."

Along with the air strike, we brought in artillery from Firebases Charlie and Thrust. Our battalion mortars integrated with the artillery. Cobra gunships flew under the artillery and joined the fight—just the kind of closely coordinated attack we had designed and practiced, then practiced some more.

Meanwhile, A and B Companies had moved in to try and get the recon platoon out. Haig tried to get up to the firefight in his little Loach helicopter, but as he closed in, the Loach was hit and crashed, though they were low enough so that Haig and the pilot were able to get themselves out and run for cover.

From my own helicopter, I could see the VC regiment maneuvering, closing in on our troops. But to do that they had to move through a relatively open area, so I directed everything we had at them—the Cobras, the artillery, the mortars, the fighter-bombers, all of it focused on that one area. That wasn't something they (or anyone else) could face. But we had to be exceptionally careful and precise. Our own people, including Haig, were down there, closely engaged. Before long, with all the fire going in, the VC broke contact, and we were able to extricate what was left of the recon platoon.

It wasn't until dusk that we finally got the entire battalion back inside the perimeter, carrying our dead and wounded under a hail of mortar fire. When I landed, I saw our battalion surgeon and our Catholic chaplain, Father Renee Ludee, out in the open ministering to the troops who needed attention. "Get your butts back to your foxholes," I told them.

"Listen," Ludee said, "you've got your job to do, we've got ours. Let us do ours." (Both Ludee and the surgeon received Silver Stars for their actions.)

We dug all night. We put out our listening posts. We set Claymores. All night our listening posts were reporting movement in the jungle. We knew what was coming.

At about 0445, a single mortar round impacted in front of B Company. Thinking it was probably a marking round, I woke Haig, who put the battalion on alert. Everyone hunkered down in their fighting positions, ready and waiting.

Fifteen minutes later it started. Mortars came first, positioned so close we could hear the rounds being dropped into the tubes. Then our positions were enveloped in explosions and plumes of dust and dirt. I was thanking God for the log-and-sandbag roofing—God and DePuy.

I listened to the listening posts calling in. They all reported troop movement; one reported towed machine guns; another saw a forward observer with a microphone around his neck, moving up to direct mortar fire. Other heavy weapons were coming through the forest.

"Just monitor," I said. "Discipline. Just monitor, watch, and report."

It was still dark when hell broke loose. The men in the listening posts blew their claymores and hustled back to our lines, though one post in front of Charlie Company didn't blow theirs in time to cover themselves, and a number of VC got through the perimeter with them. Our people still coming in, C Company wasn't able to fire until some of them were inside our positions.

But that was exactly the point where the VC main attack now hit, human waves sweeping up to our positions, guns blazing, grenades going off, Bangalores and satchel charges exploding. They broke through there, but Haig rallied the reserve—mainly the survivors of the recon platoon—and, together with Brian Cundiff, C Company's commander, counterattacked and drove the VC back. Cundiff was wounded several times, but he stayed on his feet, and in vicious hand-to-hand fighting he, Haig, and the troop they had gathered pushed the VC back to the perimeter. (Both Haig and Cundiff received well-deserved Distinguished Service Crosses for this action.)

But this was an enemy that didn't give up. They were taking terrible losses, but they kept coming, and when the sun rose, the fighting was fierce on B and C Companies' perimeters. We were on VC and NVA turf, and they felt they had the advantage. As the fighting raged, they kept pouring reinforcements into the battle. At one point, I went forward to a key C Company three-man machine-gun bunker holding the shoulder of that area. Our perimeter was so constricted that my CP was only fifty yards back. With the fighting all around them, one of the machine gunners was going back and forth for additional ammunition. A very brave thing. Outside their foxhole, enemy dead littered the ground. Inside it were two Chinese grenades that hadn't exploded. In the gun crew were one black soldier, one Hispanic, one white soldier. For an instant, the thought flashed—"That's America."

With daylight I was airborne again. Cundiff and his men, along with Haig and the recon platoon, had cleared the enemy from our positions and were readying a larger counterattack. Not far away came the *whump, whump, whump* of huge explosions. Even with all the other blasts and din, we could feel the ground shake. Hollingsworth had managed to divert a B-52 raid from wherever it was supposed to go in order to drop their bombs on the jungle near us. "I'm dealing them in," he said. "Where do you want them?" Now the VC were back on their heels; we could feel the tide shifting in our direction. I was orchestrating the artillery and air, and I had a cluster-bomb strike ready to go. "You know the big opening where we were initially going to land?" I told the pilot, "Put it right there."

The pilot dropped the munition and to our surprise caught an entire VC company crawling through the tall grass. They had been invisible. Had they made it to our perimeter, the outcome would have been a catastrophe. Our other assistant division commander, General Bernie Rogers, was in a helicopter at the time. "You know what?" he radioed. "There's a whole line of dead VC that goes on for a couple of hundred yards. I think you got everyone in the field." You need some luck in war, and this time it was on our side.

Finally, it was just too much for them. All the firepower broke the back of the attack. From my perch in the sky, I watched as hundreds of VC broke off and ran back toward the woods, our air and artillery pounding them as they ran. The force was overwhelming.

As they ran, Rogers called me again. In an open area north of our perimeter, he had spotted what appeared to be a wounded VC hiding in a shallow hole, trying to cover himself up with a US camouflage blanket. We were desperate to get intel on the rallying point for the retreating VC so we could pursue them there, and it seemed to me the wounded VC could likely tell us that. I told my pilot to put down next to the wounded man, and as we landed, I got out with my .45 drawn. But when I got up to him, it was obvious he was in no shape to offer any resistance. I told him in English that I wasn't going to hurt him. I don't know if he understood the words, but he got my meaning. He couldn't walk, so I lifted him out of the hole and put him into the helicopter, telling the pilot to drop him at the battalion landing pad.

Then I called ahead and told them to give him medical care, then interrogate him, and try to find where the retreating VC were going to be regrouping.

The helo took off, leaving me alone in the middle of the area where the heaviest fighting had taken place. I looked around to see if anybody else might have been left out here, thinking, "This is absolutely the dumbest thing I've ever done in my life."

The upshot was that we did get the rally point from the wounded VC. I wanted to go after them there, but division said no, so I used all the artillery and air we had to walk fire from our positions out to where they were supposed to regroup. Once everything had died down, the Sixteenth Infantry passed through us on our left flank and found in the jungle mounds and mounds of green VC uniforms, weapons, and other equipment. They must have had a graves registration unit along. Their usual procedure was to carry their dead with them whenever they could but to strip the bodies and use the clothing and equipment. They would come back later, after the US units were gone, and get the clothing and weapons left behind.

In the aftermath, we discovered that we had been facing the 271st Regiment of the NVA Ninth Division and elements of the NVA Seventieth Guards Regiment. These soldiers were not kids; they were hard-core, disciplined professionals. We counted 609 enemy dead. With all the blood trails leading off into the jungle, the number could have been higher. Or the count might have been exaggerated; I paid little attention to body counts. Our own losses, something of a surprise, were fairly minor.

A reporter who was with us wrote: "There were wounded men who wouldn't go to the rear but elected to stay with their buddies and keep the battalion strength up. There's a unique feeling of closeness between men in the infantry and these were some of the closest men I had ever seen. No one wanted to let the Blue Spaders down."

The fight was called the Battle of Ap Gu, after a nearby village. It was the last battle of Operation Junction City, the largest airborne operation of the war. At Ap Gu, we dealt the NVA and VC a tough blow, and we thought we had gotten near COSVN or maybe even right into COSVN: afterward we found large trench systems and deep bunkers, big enough to house many people. In one bunker, we even found a surgeon's light. But when all was said and done, we learned that the Vietcong headquarters was not a permanent complex of planning and administrative structures with large staffs and a hierarchy of war commanders, something like a Vietnamese jungle version of the Pentagon. It was instead a series of thatched huts and bunkers spread out in the Mimot Rubber Plantation straddling the Vietnam–Cambodian border, capable of moving quickly if it were ever seriously threatened.

We won the battle. The Blue Spaders had badly mauled a reinforced NVA regiment. But we achieved no important objectives other than the bodies we counted. After we left the area, the VC and NVA filtered right back in again, and Tay Ninh Province became the same dangerous place it had been before. The same was true of so many other battles we fought and won. Blood spilled, the enemy's and ours, but no permanent gains and little that could be called progress.

I left Vietnam two months after Ap Gu, bound for Loyola University in Chicago as part of the army's new civil education program. I was to get a master's degree there, then serve on the ROTC faculty. I knew that back in the States an antiwar movement was going on, with young people especially angry about what we were doing in Vietnam and about the military itself. But I wasn't aware of its extent or its vehemence.

As I left Vietnam, though, I had my own doubts. The entire time I was there, I had kept asking myself, "Where's the clarity? Why? What are we doing here?" To stop Communist expansion, we were told, and I sort of went with that. When you're fighting, you don't spend much time trying to figure the political angle. You're fighting to keep your people and yourself alive. But I came out of it wondering, "What the hell *are* we doing there?"

4

In Antiwar Chicago

I was fortunate to be selected for the US Army's so-called Option C, an experimental program that gave officers at my stage the opportunity to do graduate work and teach, enlarging their experience and integrating them to some extent in the world of university students and professors. The army wanted to see if ROTC couldn't contribute to the academic side of the institutions instead of just preparing cadets for commissions.

I welcomed that. I had questions about the military's role in Vietnam—how we had gotten there, why we had gotten there—and more generally about our military's role historically. Doing a master's degree would give me an opportunity to explore these questions. I was a professional soldier. What exactly was this profession I had gotten myself into? What was its purpose? None of my courses at West Point had addressed this subject, even briefly. I wished they had.

I was going to be in Chicago for at least three years—a year or a year and a half for my degree, another two years teaching. The best part was that I would have my family with me. I had met Karen when I was just finishing Armor School, between my European and Vietnam tours. She was from Orwigsburg, a little town just east of Pottsville. She was five years younger than I, but when I came back home on leave from West Point or on holidays, I would occasionally see her at a swimming pool I sometimes went to, a place where the local kids hung out. I had noticed her, but that was all. We had never said hello.

Five years later, in early 1966, I was home on leave. I hadn't yet graduated from Armor School, but I already had my orders for Vietnam. One day I was shopping at Knapp's Department Store looking to buy some gifts for my three nieces when I saw an extremely attractive girl working behind the counter. Not only was she great looking, but she also seemed vaguely familiar. "Haven't we met somewhere?" I said, thinking the moment I said it how stupid it must sound. The world's oldest pickup line. But to my surprise, she said, "Yes, we have."

Karen was working at Knapp's for the moment, she said, but it turned out she had graduated from Penn State. That was the start of a whirlwind.

Almost before I knew it, we had decided to get married. I just knew she was the right person, and to my lasting good fortune she felt the same way about me.

Both Karen and I anticipated a small wedding with just family and some local friends. I purposely did not invite any of my classmates from the Armor School. It wasn't that they weren't good buddies; they were, and I stayed close with some of them for many years, but they were young, exuberant armor warriors, not a good mix for a quiet, family ceremony at a staid, small-town Catholic church.

Of course, a group of them came anyway. They installed themselves in the Necho Allen, Pottsville's only higher-class hotel, named after the colonial-era hunter who, according to legend, had first discovered the region's coal seams. The Necho Allen had a huge chunk of anthracite installed in the lobby as a decorative memorial to the discovery. Somehow the chunk disappeared the night before the wedding. When the perpetrators were discovered (they weren't hard to find), they explained that they had wanted to give it to Karen and me as a wedding present. Their shenanigans didn't stop there. They treated the wedding rehearsal with less seriousness than it deserved, which didn't amuse the monsignor, and the fact that the Yuengling Brewery and its rathskeller were right next to St. Patrick's led to the inevitable, which didn't amuse Karen. She pulled me out of there early in the evening, telling me, "We have things to do tonight, and this isn't one of them!"

She forgave them, though. Karen knew them, and they knew her and couldn't have liked her more. They were just happy for us. When we left the church after the wedding the next day, they were on the steps in their dress blues with their sabers crossed for us to walk under.

While I was in Vietnam, Karen lived with her parents in Orwigsburg. She was pregnant with our first child while I was gone, which was on my mind whenever I wasn't in the middle of a firefight. But I wasn't worried about her. I knew her parents and my family would take care of her. Then during a lull in one engagement, I was sitting in a foxhole when one of my soldiers came up with a field telephone. "It's a MARS link," he said—the auxiliary military link used in emergencies. "Here, sir. Talk to your wife."

I couldn't believe it. Lieutenant Colonel Gorman had arranged the link. Karen was calling from the hospital. She had just given birth. Using the MARS system, you have to talk very loudly and use the same procedure you would for talking by radio hookup. You say something, then you say, "OVER," loudly, so the operators can switch from "talk" to "receive." The person on the other end does the same.

"WE HAVE A BEAUTIFUL GIRL," Karen said. "OVER."
"I CAN'T BELIEVE IT," I said. "OVER."
"THAT'S WONDERFUL! OVER."
"I LOVE YOU! OVER."
"HOW ARE YOU? OVER."

I was crouching in this foxhole, shouting into the phone, every soldier in the vicinity listening in. It was surreal. Wonderful but surreal.

Now, moving to Chicago, we would have a chance for a normal family life, at least for the next few years. How lucky could I be?

Of course, normal didn't mean tranquil. There was nothing tranquil about Chicago in 1967.

I knew that antiwar demonstrations were going on and that emotions were high, so I was expecting some of that. But I was not expecting the vehemence of it. I was certainly not expecting the personal attacks. When I walked through campus in my uniform, I heard, "Baby burner," "Murderer." Not regularly, but some students more radical than others were sure that I had committed atrocities or at the very least that I represented people who were committing atrocities. I saw the flag hanging upside down from some dormitory windows. A few times people spat on my uniform as I walked by. Some of the students, girls as well as boys, tried to grab my hat off, angrily, not joking around. After a couple of incidents like that, I stopped wearing it. Feelings were very, very raw.

These things were unsettling. Sometimes they angered me considerably, but even when I was first subjected to them, I felt that I had to temper my response. Getting pissed off was one thing, but duking it out with someone was another. I didn't want anybody to get hurt because of me.

I was studying for a degree in political science, so the courses I was taking typically had nothing to do with Vietnam. They were about the structure of government and the nature of international relations—the standard kinds of subjects you find in a political science curriculum. We had units on South American and European political history. Of course, no matter what we were talking about, Vietnam was always somewhere in the background. Given the situation, there was no way it couldn't have been. Even in courses that had nothing to do with the war, the subject would come up. The professor would ask the class how we felt about something that was in the news or about the administration's war policy. Then all eyes would turn to me, and the professor would say, "Captain, what do you think about this?" A couple of times it was even, "General, what do you think about this?"

Sometimes the questions were hostile. "Given the immorality of what we are doing, Captain (or General), how do you feel about it?" Usually they weren't, at least explicitly, but in either case I was faced with having to respond.

At first I would try to explain about my position and what I did, my experiences: that when you're at the platoon and company level in combat, you're not thinking about what the president is doing today, what the secretary of defense or the chairman of the Joint Chiefs of Staff is doing—you're struggling to get your troops through very difficult situations. I wasn't that smart about my response initially, but it grew on me that there had to be a way. I thought I needed to try to talk about all of this, not just describe what I might have been doing as a company officer.

I was trying to figure out, "How do I reach out here? What can I really say when they ask me about the atrocities they are hearing about?" And, of course, I wasn't that knowledgeable about the political and other ramifications of our involvement in Vietnam, but I started to educate myself on what was happening and why.

I also didn't think I needed to respond in a negative way. I didn't think that dissent was wrong or disloyal; I thought it was part of our history. What could be more American than dissent? And so my attitude was, "Let's have a dialogue; let's talk." And by responding that way, I could see that I was creating a sense that here's a guy who's willing to get into it, and he's not a rabid warmonger; he's really trying to explain what we're doing. And maybe this guy doesn't even believe we should be there either, but he's saying, "We're there. What do we do, how are we doing it, and what does it mean?"

I wasn't good at this at first, but after the first six months or so I found that I was really interacting with my fellow students. I wanted to listen, and the students understood that. I wasn't afraid to have a dialogue. I wasn't telling them it was this way or the highway. I don't think the answers I was giving were very sophisticated—I was trying to understand these things, too. But because I wasn't being strident or opinionated, people were willing at least to have a discussion. I talked about what I understood—the idea of trying to establish South Vietnam as a democratic country not tied down by communism, the desirability of stopping the spread of communism in Southeast Asia. But I found that was not the best way to address the issue of what we were doing there with what was by now almost half a million troops, a massive army. It begged that question. I had to look beyond that to engage in what I began to think of as a search for truth.

I also simply felt comfortable talking with young people—I was almost thirty, ten years older than most of them. The people I respected

most in the military—DePuy was the outstanding example—knew how
to talk to young people. I never forgot the way he would get down in the
foxhole with corporals and sergeants or how he interacted with me when
I was a brand-new second lieutenant. DePuy and the great commanders I
worked for later knew that listening was an important part of their job. I
always used to say to young officers after I became smarter and wiser that
to be a good commander, you have to be a good listener. You can't just be
in talk mode all the time; you have to be in receive mode sometimes. You
have to understand; you have to hear people out. By the time I got to
Loyola, some of that was already baked into my outlook, which helped a
lot as I was adjusting to the situation I found there.

This didn't happen just in my own classes; other faculty would invite
me to classes they were teaching. I started to think of myself as "the
stuckee." But after a while I began to relish it. It was stimulating to be challenged not just about the war but about my profession, in essence about
who I was.

Because it wasn't just Vietnam but often the military profession itself
that was being attacked. In a psychology class I was invited to, when one
of the students was saying I was a baby burner, complicit in the massacre
of innocents, this is what the military did, some of the other students said,
"Wait a minute, he hasn't even said anything yet. Let him speak."

I also understood that antiwar feeling wasn't all due to the idea that
the war was immoral or unjust; there was also a draft lottery in place,
and many young men were afraid they were going to be called up. They
weren't so much against the war as they were against getting drafted. I
didn't belittle that feeling. I understood there were complexities here that
required a lot of sensitivity.

I began to see that what I was really asking wasn't "Are we or are we
not justified in going into Vietnam and engaging in full-scale war there?"
The questions behind that were: "How are these kinds of decisions made?
How are they formulated? Whose responsibility is it to make them?"
That's what I decided to explore. I wanted to go back and examine the
roots of the military, how it evolved in relation to the political side in our
history. How could you judge the present without knowing what our
country has done through nearly two hundred years of existence? Where
have we been? What have we done? How did we respond to past events
that seemed to demand military action?

I was trying to explain for myself as well as for anybody else the two
experiences I had had: in Germany first, then in Vietnam. In Germany, I
had seen people killed trying to get across the barbed wire. There wasn't

any doubt about the enemy we faced on the other side of the East–West divide, who they were and what they stood for. In Germany, we were protecting our allies and ourselves. We were making an immense national effort to provide peace and stability in Europe. That was a fundamentally important undertaking, existential really. Almost everyone understood why we were there and what we were doing. And as I saw it, we were doing it successfully. The military in Germany had a clear mission with wide if not universal support. In Vietnam, we were also making a giant effort. But did we have clarity of mission? I didn't think so. Did we have universal support? Not judging from what I was seeing every time I went on campus or read the newspapers.

Yet both Germany and Vietnam were military endeavors undertaken by our democratically elected government. You couldn't condemn the military out of hand, as so many of Loyola's students and faculty were doing—"baby burners" and so on—and disregard the role the military has played in safeguarding our national life for two centuries—in Europe for the past two decades, just for example. No, you had to understand the relationship between the political and military leadership in a society structured like ours before you could start pontificating about what was wrong and what was right. I was at Loyola not only to take classes but to write a thesis and to teach. Now at least I was clear about what I was going to research and write about and what I was going to teach, too. And fortunately I was in classes not just with graduate students but with some top younger undergraduates as well, including the president of the senior class and the editor of the student newspaper. They were real militants; they were taking on not just the war but the military profession as well. But they were also open to discussion. They thought that was important. "You've got a way of talking to students," they said. "We'd like to have an alternative point of view. Why don't you come and give a talk at the Free University?"

This so-called Free University was basically a collection of courses in all sorts of things, open to everyone for no charge. They had a catalog and some publications, and they concentrated on alternative-type subjects from yoga and meditation to the evils of capitalism. The emphasis was on antiestablishment views and activities, especially antiwar topics. The student president and newspaper editor said they would like to include an alternative, and I was right there in their line of sight. I was going to be their alternative.

The Free University courses weren't housed on campus; they were held in a variety of settings—people's living rooms, church basements, coffeehouses. The course they wanted me for was in a coffeehouse near the university.

"Listen," I told them, "the army is nervous enough about what I'm doing here, but I'm interested. Maybe I'll do one lecture, but if I feel like I'm being set up, I won't be back again."

The fact is that I was intrigued by the idea. I didn't think the only people the students should hear should be antimilitary. But before I conducted a class, I wanted to do a recon, so I went to check out the coffeehouse.

I was in uniform when I went to see the place. When I walked in, a boy and a girl were in a tight embrace in the entranceway. They stopped what they were doing for a moment to stare at me. I must have seemed like an alien apparition. Inside it didn't look bad. There was a living-room-like space with sofas and chairs and some tables, okay for an informal lecture. But as I was leaving, the girl in the hallway grabbed my shirt. "You've got blood on this uniform," she hissed. Oh boy, I thought. I had decided I was going to give my talk in civilian clothes, but I changed my mind. "I'll be back here tonight," I said. "I'll be wearing this. Why don't you come and listen?"

That night there was quite the scene. The coffeehouse was crowded, mostly with antiwar students, but some of the ROTC cadets showed up, too. The place was wall to wall and loud. I stood at one end, in my uniform, but when I started to speak, I was shouted down. When it quieted a little, I started again, but again they began making so much noise, with hoots and all sorts of derision, that I couldn't talk. This went on for a while, but finally I was able to say, "Look, I won't judge you by your uniforms, so don't judge me by mine. We're all here to look for the truth." I told them that I wasn't going to speak about Vietnam; I was going to talk about the professional roots of the military and the role of the military in a democratic society. That deflected at least some of the animosity, and we ended up having an interesting discussion, even if it was a little raucous.

I went back the next week and the week after, again in uniform. But after the first few sessions I was much more relaxed and started wearing casual clothes. Not that the emotions the war provoked ever subsided. At one point, a young woman came up to me, barely managing to hold back her tears. She had been listening to all the angry antimilitary rhetoric. Her father was an air force pilot, she said. "He's involved in these terrible things that are going on," she said. "Why . . . ?" Her question tailed off as she tried to choke back the sobs that were breaking out. I didn't want just to defend her father; I wanted to explain what it means to be in the military. "In his situation he can't stand up and protest, like you're doing," I told her. "His situation doesn't allow him to do that." I was thinking of myself, too. My daughter was growing up. Was she going to have to go through the same kind of ordeal? And what would someone be able tell her about me?

I found a way to talk to people. But it didn't get any easier, especially after I was assigned to act temporarily as a survivors' assistance officer, the person responsible for notifying families that a father or brother had been killed in combat. An officer acting in one particular case had been relieved, and command wanted me to take his place. "Really?" I thought, feeling my heart sink a little. Not that I had any choice about it.

The case had to do with a Ranger who had been killed, possibly by friendly fire; it was unclear. The army wasn't saying. His mother was upset by that; she felt she was being mistreated. She was much more upset by the fact that she wanted his Bronze Star for valor to be buried along with him. The problem here was that there was no record that he had received a Bronze Star. Her son's buddies had told her he had, though, and, more to the point, she had a picture of Westmoreland pinning the medal on him. The officer whose place I was taking had apparently told her there was nothing he could do, but I felt the opposite. Who knew what might have happened with records coming out of the battlefield to the Pentagon? She had the picture. I made arrangements to bury a Bronze Star with him. At the funeral, I put the picture up on a stand next to the soldier's casket.

My second case was harder. The dead soldier was African American, and from the Cabrini-Green projects. A moment after I parked and stepped out of my car in uniform, I was surrounded by five or six little boys, all asking, "Mister, who got killed today?" As I got onto the rickety elevator to go up to the deceased soldier's apartment, the boys got on with me, still asking, "Who got killed?"

I found the apartment and knocked on the door, the little boys waiting with me. A woman opened the door, the dead soldier's mother, the father right behind her. The moment the mother saw my uniform, she collapsed. The father just managed to catch her before she fell to the floor. The hardest thing I had ever had to do in Vietnam was write letters to the families of soldiers who had died. This was worse.

I ended up teaching at the Free University every Thursday night for the next two years. I was doing research for my thesis at the same time, so my teaching helped focus my writing and vice versa. My lectures started with the American Revolution and went through the War of 1812, the Civil War, the world wars, the Cold War, Korea, the Lebanon Crisis under Eisenhower in 1958, and then Vietnam. I was able to draw a thread from Thomas Jefferson's commitment of armed forces against the Barbary pirates in the early 1800s all the way through Vietnam, looking at how the Constitution's definition of war powers was interpreted and how the president acted as commander in chief.

By now I was far better educated about Vietnam than I was when I was in the country fighting. I knew about the overthrow and assassination of Ngo Dinh Diem as well as about the train of coups that had brought various inadequate governments into power and the bind that put the United States in. But I tried to get the class to think above that. I felt I needed at least to impress on them that the military has played a major role and will continue to have a major role in the development of our country. "Vietnam," I said, "is the here and now, and we'll talk about that. But the idea of trying to provide for the common defense is something that's going to be with us on into the future. You need to understand that, so don't throw the baby out with the bathwater."

My course was entitled "The Military Instrument." It was listed in the Free University catalog between "Marxism" and "Free Love."

As I finished my degree, I started teaching essentially the same subjects in the ROTC program. My initial course there was "The Foundations of National Power." But the university administration arranged for the course to be cross-listed with political science courses so that non-ROTC students could take it for credit. I considered that a compliment. It meant that in the midst of all the antiwar turmoil the university thought it important to include a different voice. One of the goals of the army Option C program was that ROTC needed to contribute to the intellectual life of universities, not just recruit students for service. I felt I was doing that. I began team teaching with professors from other relevant departments: psychology, history, business. The courses were so popular that I was even given the Teacher of the Year Award. That was a real honor. In my last session in 1968, the final assignment was to examine America's military treaties: NATO, the Southeast Asia Treaty Organization (SEATO), and others. I had the usual mix of students in this class: Students for a Democratic Society, Black Panthers, cadets, as well as regular political science majors. For this assignment, I had divided the class up into four-person committees. On each committee I put an ROTC cadet, a Panther, an SDS member, and an "unaffiliated" student. Their assignment was to write a paper on one of our treaty commitments, analyze the commitment, and present recommendations for changes the United States should make.

It just so happened that a massive student strike was called for the day the class was to have their papers ready. The campus was shut down, and all classes canceled. But I told my class that I intended to show up, and I did, in uniform. The paper that was going to be presented that day was on SEATO—that is, Vietnam. Every student in the class was eager to hear what was going to come of this. They all were present; the room was packed.

The SEATO working group mimeographed copies of their paper and handed them out. They had chosen the SDS member to make the oral presentation. The US "Vietnamization" policy had started up by now, which called for the measured withdrawal of American ground forces but also for continued full-scale air support and material assistance to South Vietnam's army.

In their presentation, the group agreed with current American policy and specifically with Vietnamization. You would have thought a hand grenade had gone off. This was the policy of the hated Richard Nixon and his accomplice Henry Kissinger. There was an explosion of shouting and arguing. The committee, led by its SDS spokesman, argued back just as loudly. "Let us give you the facts," they said. I sat back and watched this unfold. It was astonishing. An antiwar strike was going on outside, and in here the SDS and Panthers, at least some of them, were defending American policy in this loud, vigorous debate. I couldn't have been prouder of the entire class.

What with my Free University talks, the always interesting dialogue in my classes, and my relations with the faculty and administration, I felt as if I were on a continual, exhilarating high—stoked up by the confrontational edge the war gave to almost everything. Not completely everything, though. In September 1968, Karen gave birth to our second daughter, Chris. We now had a new baby to go with our two-year-old, Jennifer, whose birth I had learned about in a foxhole. Fortunately, some of my students were eager baby-sitters, including one or two of the SDS "bring the troops home now" kids. I don't know what the Fifth Army (to which I was assigned) would have thought about that—or what other SDS militants might have thought, either. But to all of us the situation seemed just natural and friendly.

The times couldn't have been more volatile, though. In April 1968, not long before the end of the semester, Martin Luther King Jr. was assassinated. Chicago, like so many other cities, exploded in riots. Two months later, at the beginning of June, Robert Kennedy was murdered. At the end of August, the Democratic National Convention opened in Chicago's International Amphitheater. The city braced for the worst, and that's what it got.

Most of my classes were at Loyola's Lake Shore main campus, but I was also teaching at the downtown campus, which was where I was on the afternoon of August 28 when antiwar demonstrations kicked off in Grant Park around the equestrian statue of Civil War general John Logan. The statue was set at the top of a hillock there, and what looked like a sea of protestors gathered around it, even on top of it—many thousands of protestors in demonstrations organized by the Yippies (members of the Youth International Party) and the Movement to End the War, an umbrella organization that included SDS, the Women's Strike for Peace, and others. Demonstration leaders had promised that hundreds of thousands of protestors would descend on the city, which didn't happen, but the gathering looked like an army of them anyway (later accounts said between ten thousand and fifteen thousand participated). Meanwhile, the city mobilized all its police and coordinated with the Illinois National Guard. City officials were afraid of what might be coming. They were prepared for battle.

Around Logan's statue there was a din of shouting and some attempts at speeches, which I couldn't hear. Then the march started. The scene was unlike anything I had ever imagined. The crowd were carrying signs that read "Babies Are Not for Burning," "End All Capitalist War," "Victory for the Vietcong," and dozens of other slogans and demands. Above the shouting I could hear the chants, "Ho, Ho, Ho Chi Minh, Vietcong is going to win," and "Hell no, we won't go." The tear gas was so thick it seemed to me the police must be firing hundreds of cannisters. They were also swinging clubs and beating protestors. Protestors were throwing bottles and stones. Ashtrays were sailing out of the upper-floor windows of the Hilton Hotel, aimed at the police, like bombs. It was a brutal, brutal scene. One demonstrator walked by me in full beard, full head of hair. He had camouflage fatigues on, a gas mask, a web belt. He obviously saw himself as a revolutionary, ready to bring as much chaos as he could to the situation and take on the "pigs" in open combat.

I just shook my head, thinking, "Is this the revolution they're talking about? Is this what it looks like?" These young people were getting hurt not by the military, not by the draft, not by Vietnam—but by the cops right here. They were provoking the police, and the police all too obviously weren't trained to handle this kind of thing.

The riots left the city shaken. The aftermath—court charges against protest leaders for inciting to riot and against the police for civil rights violations—was big news for many months. Antiwar momentum ratcheted up even higher than it had been; the whole country seemed to be inflamed. Demonstrations and marches disrupted city after city. And then on May 4, 1970, at an antiwar demonstration at Kent State University in Ohio, National Guardsmen, who had been called in to assist local police, shot into a crowd and killed four students. That truly ignited the powder keg. Student demonstrations kicked off all over the county. University after university was shut down, Loyola included. A nationwide student strike was called. At Loyola, students were going to march on a nearby National Guard armory. I knew the soldiers in the armory weren't the best-trained troops in the world. Most of them were there because they didn't want to go to Vietnam, so they had joined the Guard. I was very afraid of what might happen; it was a high-risk situation for the student marchers.

To try and keep people safe, I got the Rangers from the ROTC program—the elite group among the cadets—gave them walkie-talkies to communicate with each other, and sent them out in regular clothes to do what they could to guide what was going on and keep the demonstrators from getting hurt.

All we needed was another Kent State.

The armory demonstration went off, loud and angry, but there were no dangerous confrontations; nobody got shot or even hurt, and the students dispersed safely.

That wasn't the end of it, though. Not long afterward there was another protest event in the Loyola basketball arena. There must have been five or six thousand people packing the place. The student organizers had asked me to speak, along with a number of others, including Staughton Lynd, one of the country's leading peace activists, who was scheduled to go on last. They thought I was going to say, "I'm Major Joulwan, and I'm against the war" (I had been promoted from captain). Instead I got up and began talking about the proper way to protest and bring change and about the role of the military in our government. I don't know how many in the crowd wanted to hear this; the emotional level after Kent State was through the roof, and a group of forty or fifty radicals from off campus weren't going to have any of it. They came after me, yelling curses and slogans; they were going to physically throw me off the stage. But they were surprised when the Loyola students, who recognized them as outsiders, stood up and blocked their way, then forced them out of the arena. I went on to say that the university stands for the search for truth. "That's what Loyola is about. Let's pursue that, not let people prevent anyone from speaking." I told them that if anyone wanted to ask questions I would meet them in Mertz Hall, an academic setting, not here in the gymnasium. As soon as I was finished, I stepped off the stage and left the arena before Lynd came on. Several hundred students came with me.

While all this was going on, I was finishing up my thesis. My focus was on Article 2, section 2, of the US Constitution: "The President shall be the commander in chief of the Army and Navy of the United States, and of the militia of the several states, when called into the actual service of the United States."

I was primarily concerned to explore the chief executive's use of war powers in undeclared wars from 1945 up through President Nixon's Cambodian incursion, which was going on as I was writing. But I began by tracing the history of the relationship between Congress, which has the power to declare war, and the president, who has the power to command the armed forces, going all the way back to the debates on ratifying the Constitution.

Not all the prominent figures of the revolutionary period were in favor of granting the president that much authority. In Virginia, Patrick Henry spoke against it. "Your President may easily become king. . . . If your American chief be a man of ambition and abilities, how easy it is for him to render himself absolute. The army is in his hands." Elbridge Gerry of Massachusetts spoke against, as did George Clinton of New York.

I found that until Abraham Lincoln's presidency, presidents, with few exceptions, were wary of using the armed forces in any significant way without a congressional declaration of war, though the exceptions were interesting: Washington's suppression of the western Pennsylvania Whiskey Rebellion (of course, the rebels were not a foreign government) and Jefferson's use of the navy against the Barbary pirates. Lincoln, though, changed the ball game. After the attack on Fort Sumter, he assumed what he termed "war powers" and put the Union on a war footing, calling up troops, blockading Southern ports, and suspending the writ of habeas corpus.

It's still debated as to whether or how far Lincoln exceeded his constitutional authority, but he stood his ground against challenges and declared that he was authorized to do things on military grounds that the Congress couldn't do. He assumed these emergency powers after the attack on Sumter, when Congress was not in session, and when it did reconvene, he requested and received approval. His actions after the Sumter attack initiated a historical movement that progressively enlarged the president's authority to commit troops without congressional consent.

In the post-1945 period, which was my main interest, President Harry Truman sent an army to fight a war in Korea and other large contingents to Europe to strengthen NATO. President Kennedy blockaded Cuba to prevent Soviet missile emplacements—an act of war meant to prevent war. Neither Kennedy nor Truman had congressional approval. Eisenhower did ask approval to commit troops to Formosa, if necessary, during the Quemoy and Matsu stand-off with China, though he believed he had the authority to do it regardless. In the end, he didn't send troops, but he did send American aircraft and naval vessels and heavily reinforced the Chinese Nationalist military capacity in the air and artillery war between the two Chinese sides.

My study concluded that for a variety of reasons historical precedent was on the side of the chief executive with regard to deploying the military without congressional approval. President Nixon was doing just that, sending troops into a foreign nation, Cambodia, without the legislative branch's approval, which was just then creating a firestorm of public reaction.

By the time I finished writing, I had a grasp of the historical contention between the president and Congress with respect to waging war. I also had at least a partial answer to the question that had been bothering me throughout my own Vietnam combat tour: Where was the clarity of mission?

I looked at the Gulf of Tonkin Resolution, which had given President Johnson a blank check "to take all necessary steps, including the use of force," in Vietnam. I saw that resolution as part and parcel of the progressive congressional retreat from its constitutional responsibility to commit or not commit the nation to war. The incidents that had triggered the resolution, the attack on our destroyers in the Tonkin Gulf, were unclear. Of the two days of attack, the first day's incident might have happened. The second apparently hadn't taken place at all. But even if it had, were those grounds enough for Congress to have passed an open-ended war-powers resolution? Did those incidents justify the kind of war that I had fought in and that we were still fighting, a massive national commitment of the nation's military, with all the blood and treasure that entailed? Those were shaky, shaky grounds, and the resolution had been passed hastily, with only two votes in the Senate against and none in the House, and with almost no measure of reasonable prudence and scrutiny. This wasn't a national emergency that required immediate action, like the attack on Fort Sumter or the Cuban Missile Crisis.

There was time in this case for consideration and forethought, but nothing like that had taken place.

And so where was the clarity of mission in all this? A rhetorical question. Given the nature of the process, where could it have been?

When I left Chicago in June 1970 to study at the Command and General Staff College at Fort Leavenworth, I took with me the conviction that for a military undertaking to be successful, clarity of mission is a rock-bottom necessity. I was also thinking that, given the military's subordination to the political leadership, it was the job of the senior military to engage the political order at the highest level beforehand to ensure the clarity of the goals the nation's armed forces were expected to accomplish.

5

An Army in Retreat

I left Loyola in the early summer of 1970 on a high. I felt I had accomplished some important things. I knew the university valued the courses I had taught; they had contributed to the school's academic life, which was what the army had intended. So that was a satisfaction. In my research, I had learned a great deal about the relationship between the political and the military in American life and about my profession as a soldier as well. Just as important, for three years I had been in the middle of a social upheaval that was challenging the stability of fundamental American institutions: political, military, and educational.

Chicago had been a scene of chaos and disarray—rioting, strikes, outrage, and violence—and I had managed to find ways to navigate through the turbulence (very helpful for the future; before long I would find myself in the White House during Watergate). Dealing with these disruptions had helped enlarge my sense of how to approach the breakdown of norms. I knew that when the world looks as if it's coming apart, you can't just sit back and point fingers; you have to interact.

Of the feedback I received, I was proudest of a letter from a student who identified himself as a "leftist," one of "Agnew's bums" (Vice President Spiro Agnew had repeated President Nixon's attack on student dissenters as "bums").

> Dear Major Joulwan,
> I find myself in the perplexing situation of addressing a benevolent note to you, a military man. I was actually moved by your remarks and answers, the more so because I never expected anything like your candor . . . to come from the mouth of a "brainwashed" military officer. While I condemn the heinous acts which American leaders have forced you and the men with you in the service to commit in Vietnam, your reasoned statements were an epiphany for me. . . . Everyone knows how you gave the strike leadership your time. . . . Actually it blew a lot of minds, including my own.

I took the hyperbole with a large grain of salt, but I was still moved by the letter, especially when the writer attached a "personal note." He had just received his induction letter, he said. He hadn't yet decided whether to "submit" or escape to Canada. It sounded to me as if he was deciding to stick it out.

I arrived at Fort Leavenworth's Command and General Staff College in June 1970. The Staff College is a rung in the ladder—from the basic courses you take as a lieutenant to the advanced courses as a captain and then as a major or lieutenant colonel to Leavenworth, where the focus is on higher-level staff work. Now you immerse yourself in study and discussions about how to handle divisions and corps, what your responsibilities are, how as a division or corps officer or commander you have to be able to read the overall battlefield so you will know how to bring into play the elements of warfighting—reconnaissance, maneuver, integration of combat arms, and others—that you have learned to handle at smaller-unit levels.

At Leavenworth, we studied the nuts and bolts of high command, but Vietnam had put enormous stresses on the army, with dangerous consequences: a confused sense of purpose, deteriorating morale, performance breakdowns, and worse. Shortly after I arrived, the Staff College circulated an in-depth analysis of the state of the army as perceived by the officers corps. The *Study on Military Professionalism* emphasized the lack of idealism, an absence of moral courage in acknowledging responsibility, a breakdown in discipline, and the frustration of subordinates, who typically found their superior officers unwilling to listen to them. It painted a picture of an army in trouble.

The faculty and students at the Command and General Staff College tried to come to grips with that. After all the tragedies in our country and setbacks in Vietnam, where were we going with our military? How should we go about remedying such profound problems? And now that Vietnamization was well along and we were drawing down our forces there, how could we switch our focus from the jungles of Vietnam back to the plains of Europe? For years we had been embroiled in an infantry war in Vietnam, and while we were occupied there, the Soviets had been modernizing and bulking up their armored and mechanized forces across the dividing line in Europe. To cope with that buildup, the US Army was in serious need of reorganization and a redefinition of its warfighting doctrine.

Those projects were already in the works back in Washington, where a team led by William DePuy, now assistant vice chief of staff, was quietly determining how to revitalize a badly damaged institution. Meanwhile, at Leavenworth there was a great deal of discussion and tension about who was going to be assigned to Vietnam at this point. Some, like me, had already served a tour or two; some hadn't been to Vietnam at all and didn't feel as if they were being treated fairly.

In any event, I received orders to report to the 101st Airborne Division headquarters at Camp Eagle, which was up near the border with North Vietnam. On the flight over, I met Colonel Bob Arter, whom I had known earlier in Europe. He was going to take over the division's First Brigade from my old boss Paul Gorman. "I want you to be my S-3," he said, which sounded fine to me.

I thought I might have some time to get acclimated, but when we flew up to Camp Eagle, I was quickly disabused. While I was having dinner in the division mess hall, Gorman came in. "Joulwan," he shouted, "where are you?" He spotted me. "There you are. Good. We need to talk." When I heard that, I right away excused myself to use the bathroom; I just knew I wasn't going to see another flush toilet for a while. Gorman obviously wanted me for something other than brigade S-3, and he wasn't someone who believed in wasting time.

All night he briefed me on the military situation, the state of the division and the First Brigade, and the problems, which were many. We were an army in retrograde, military for withdrawal or retreat. Morale wasn't good. No one wanted to be the last person killed in a war the army didn't want to fight any longer. Soldiers weren't motivated. There was a lot of drug use. In some places, conflicts between blacks and whites had become a problem. So had insubordination. Many officers were dispirited and not doing an effective job commanding their units.

Just as I suspected, Gorman had something other than the brigade staff in mind for me.

"You're going to be the S-3 of the 2/237" (Second Battalion, 237th Infantry), he said.

"Okay. Why there?"

"We had a unit overrun at Firebase Mary Ann," he said. "Lots of casualties. The battalion that was supposed to be providing defense was asleep at the switch. The bad guys got inside; we lost half our people. We think this battalion I'm sending you to could be next. They've got problems. You look at it and fix them."

We drove up to Firebase Birmingham by Jeep. By now I was practically asleep on my feet. No sleep on the marathon plane ride from the States, no sleep since I arrived at Eagle—I had been up for forty-eight hours.

I arrived and met the battalion commander. Operating on pure instinct, I told him I was going to walk the line—DePuy's conditioning at work.

The first position I came to was an unbelievable mess. Guys in half uniforms, guys in no uniforms. I was pulling soldiers out of foxholes reeking of marijuana.

"Let me see your weapon," I said to the first soldier I pulled out. I couldn't open it; it was rusted shut, the ammunition rusted as well. Other rifles were the same. I walked the entire perimeter. There were gaps in the line, no interlocking fire, no fire plan, no range cards. Nothing.

I went to the mortar platoon. They were in disarray, confused. "Where's your platoon leader?" I asked.

Out came a second lieutenant. "Form up your platoon," I said.

They formed up—one white squad and one black squad. "What the hell?" I thought.

I yelled out, "Fire mission!" looking to see how they managed their fire plan. But they had no fire plan. It looked like a scene out of the Keystone Cops.

"You've got a problem," I told the platoon leader. "I'll be back at 1700 this evening. You start training. Be in the right uniform, helmets, and flak vests. Your platoon is in direct support for the battalion. If you can't do your mission, everyone here's in big trouble!"

When I went back, they all were in their full uniforms. And when I gave them the fire mission, they executed it—not well but at least decently.

When I reported what I was finding to the battalion commander, he told me I better be careful. "Don't try to do what you're doing," he said. "We've got a lot of fragging going on here."

"Listen," I said, "these soldiers' lives are in jeopardy. You've got a disaster waiting to happen here!"

The next day I went to see the recon platoon. The platoon leader was a big, heavy-set guy wearing a boonie hat. All of his troops were out of uniform. I had been told most of these guys were on drugs.

"If we get any good intelligence, your platoon will be the first to go in," I told him. "You need to be ready to answer a fifteen-minute alert. I'm not seeing that, are you? I want you to prepare to be out for three days. You need the ammo, water, rations, everything. For three days. Is that clear?"

The next day the battalion intelligence officer reported, "We've got a radio fix on a VC headquarters. They're in our area."

I alerted the recon platoon. Helicopters came in to take them out, but the platoon didn't show. Forty-five minutes later they came sauntering down to the landing pads.

They inserted near where we had traced the VC radio transmission. But half an hour after they went in, the platoon leader called: "Dry hole. We're ready for extraction."

"Negative," I said. "You're in there for three days."

"We don't have water or food for three days. We don't have additional ammunition."

I left them out for three days. When they came back, we relieved the platoon leader.

At this point, I had been with soldiers for ten years. I understood the problem at Firebase Birmingham wasn't the soldiers; it was their leaders. It wasn't the soldiers who were failing; it was their officers. The leadership needed to get its act together. In short order, we replaced the battalion commander and four of the five company commanders. I tightened up the perimeter, closed the gaps, and set fields of fire. With new officers in place, we set standards. We had frequent weapons inspections and personal-appearance checks. We trained hard, including patrolling technique. I told the soldiers, "I know no one wants to be the last person killed in Vietnam. I've heard that. But if you don't do what I'm telling you to do, that's exactly what you will be. You'll be one of the last people killed over here because the enemy is not letting up, and he's getting bolder and bolder. So we have got to be on our toes."

There were low points, but there were more high points. We had some deep-seated difficulties, but we had to take them on head to head. If we wanted to survive this, it had to be as a team. "Who's on your left? Who's on your right? Do you trust them? Can you trust the guy who's supposed to be on guard when you're sleeping, whether he's white, black, Hispanic, or whatever? If you say no, then you better figure out how to get that guy bucked up to where you can trust him." This is what I tried to inject into the battalion's mentality. And the soldiers responded; they started performing as they should have been.

I was with the 2/237 for a month. Bob Arter had now replaced Gorman, and as he had told me he would, he called me up to be the First Brigade S-3. Shortly afterward we decided to build a new firebase across from Birmingham but at a lower elevation. In the hill country south of the Demilitarized Zone, the fog and clouds would roll in and the North Vietnamese would infiltrate underneath, invisible to our eyes and ears at Birmingham. The new firebase, Apollo, would prevent them from doing that.

Arter and I went out to inspect Apollo, which was being defended by the same battalion I had spent the first thirty days with. As luck would have it, just after we landed, a VC mortar attack came in. The mortar platoon quickly returned counterfire, right on target—the same platoon that a month earlier hadn't been in uniform or able to execute a simple practice mission. When they saw me, they were all smiles. They gave me a shouted "uuh ah" that made my day. I couldn't have been prouder.

The attack on Apollo came down on Firebase Birmingham as well, and in the middle of it I received an order from the 101st Airborne Division to pull out a particular company and have them take a urine test. "You've got to be kidding," I told the division command post. "I'm not taking them out; we're in the middle of a fight here."

"Listen," I heard, "we got this straight from Washington. This is the unit they want tested. Right now!"

I thought for a moment about simply refusing to carry out a direct order and quitting on the spot. I didn't. I argued some more, fruitlessly, then I pulled them out. The entire company stood in a line next to the Firebase Birmingham air strip peeing in bottles. It was awful. "Talk about destroying morale," I thought. "The problem's not just the leadership here; it goes all the way up."

None of the higher officers had the moral courage to stand up and say, "No, we simply will not do this." I did what I could, but I didn't have the weight to make it stick. That incident left scar tissue that didn't fade. More than forty-five years later, it is still vivid in my memory.

This was a tough time for everyone. During my first tour in 1966, morale was high as a kite. We were going to establish ourselves, dominate the battlefield, and drive the Communists back to where they came from. Even when the enemy showed how good they were, we still wanted to beat them down and were sure that we could. Now we were an army in retreat. I thought about my soldiers then and now. Was there a difference?

At bottom, I didn't think so. Once the battalion shaped up, they acted professionally. They trained, they rehearsed their missions, they went into battle determined to accomplish what was asked of them. I often spoke with the men personally before they loaded onto the helicopters for action. I listened to their squad leaders give them final instructions. I felt their anxiety beneath their readiness, exactly the same anxiety I and the men I led into battle had felt during my earlier tour. But they also showed the same dedication and courage. As Arter put it in one of his day orders, "No tougher mission has ever been given to the soldiers of the First Brigade. You must be more alert, more responsive, and more dedicated than the soldiers who preceded you." Later, when my tour was over, I wrote to Gorman, my former commander: "When the leadership problems were solved, the soldier problems were greatly reduced. I found the soldier today every bit as eager and responsive as the soldier in the 1/26 Infantry [my first-tour Blue Spader battalion]." A few months back the division's mission was still to search out and destroy the enemy. Now we were being told the mission was "mobile defense." But that wasn't so. In a memo I wrote, I argued that in defense the objective is still to destroy an attacking enemy. This division is not fighting in defense, I said. We had to formally recognize that we were in retrograde posture. The mission now wasn't to destroy the enemy; it was to withdraw in good order. Saying we were in retrograde wasn't palatable to many officers; it gave at least the impression of retreat in the face of the enemy. But I felt that once we understood withdrawal as our mission, we would find it easier to extricate ourselves. We would be clear on what we should or should not be doing. In withdrawing, we wanted to avoid any decisive engagements; we wanted to minimize casualties and keep all of the division's resources intact.

But that didn't mean we couldn't be innovative.

The A Shau Valley was a major infiltration route for NVA troops and material coming in from the Ho Chi Minh Trail in Laos. One of our patrols ambushed an NVA recon team there and captured the patrol leader. From the interrogation, we learned that the NVA Sixth Regiment was preparing to establish a forward base to launch offensive operations against us once the dry weather set in. Being in retrograde, we couldn't put troops in to block this offensive, so I developed a deception plan that I hoped would do the NVA damage while not risking any American lives.

At an abandoned A Shau firebase, we set up a dummy battalion headquarters and brought troops in on helicopters, which gave the impression the battalion was conducting an airmobile operation into the valley. The helicopters set down and off-loaded the soldiers. The second wave of helicopters came in and did the same, except they also took the first wave of troops out with them. Then another wave did the same, then another, until it looked for all intents and purposes as if we were conducting a battalion insertion. We simultaneously kept up radio traffic that indicated the same thing. My thinking was that the NVA Sixth would take the bait, shell the hell out of our apparent LZ area, and then attack. We planted listening devices all over so that we could pinpoint their movements and location. Meanwhile, we preplanned airstrikes and artillery fire. The NVA Sixth did take the bait and attacked, pouring in to destroy the

American battalion, which, of course, wasn't there. When they did, we hit them with everything we had lined up. We were tuned in to their radio net, so we were able to monitor their casualty reports. We knew we had hurt them badly. The deception was so successful that we did it again, this time a three-battalion fake insertion farther to the south, which drew a larger NVA attack. The second action was more successful than the first, high enemy casualties without a single American life lost. We even learned from radio intercepts that the NVA unit commander had been relieved.

This was heady stuff. We were restricted on what we could do—we didn't want to lose any men—but that didn't mean we had to sit on our duffs and stare at the jungle. We could be innovative and try to take the fight to the enemy, so we wouldn't just be hunkered down waiting to be assaulted. The two deceptions did great things for morale. When I described the results to the men, it was amazing how they responded. You could feel the First Brigade getting a sense of mission again. Our patrolling became more active. Our training took on a greater sense of purpose.

I could see the change. From battalion to brigade, the vigilance stepped up rather than falling off. "You can't sit on your ass," I said. "You've got to get out. You've got to fix the enemy. If we don't keep him off guard, we're going to be more and more vulnerable. They can mass more troops than we can, and they can do it effectively." I appealed to the men's sense of self-preservation but also to their sense of duty and their pride in who they were.

What they wanted was leadership. They needed someone to tell them this was no time for hand-wringing; this was what had to be done, and they had to be up to doing it. "You want to keep your asses alive," I said. That was my primary purpose. I hit that theme at the battalion level; I hit it at brigade level. "How to keep your ass alive" was my mantra.

Firebase T-Bone nearby was the home of an Army of the Republic of Vietnam (ARVN, the South Vietnamese army) regiment that trained and fought side by side with us. These ARVN troops had great leadership. They patrolled well and ambushed well. They did all the things we were hesitant to do in 1971 and 1972. They were a tough, disciplined unit, part of the ARVN First Division that had defended the central Vietnam city of Hue against the best the Communists had to offer in the desperate fighting during the Tet Offensive in 1968. Leaving them behind as we withdrew was an emotional experience. One day especially engraved itself on my memory.

We were scheduled that day to turn over our forward firebase between the A Shau Valley and Hue to this ARVN regiment as we moved

out. Firebase Bastogne had a history in support of several large operations. It had been established in 1968 and named for the World War II
Battle of Bastogne, in which the 101st Airborne Division had heroically
defended the surrounded city although heavily outnumbered and outgunned by German armor. (This was the battle in which the 101st commander, General Anthony McAuliffe, had famously answered, "Nuts" to
a German demand to surrender.)

The ARVN were supposed to come in by helicopter at 1000 hours,
but rain and heavy fog made flying impossible. We were ready for the
turnover, but given the conditions I had no idea when the South Vietnamese regiment would make it, if at all. "This just isn't going to happen," I
thought. But at 1000 hours, out of the mist and fog the ARVN regiment
marched in through Firebase Bastogne's front gate, colors flying. They
had started early in the morning and had moved by truck and then by
foot to make sure the handover went off exactly as scheduled. When they
all were in and facing our units, the two commanders, American and
South Vietnamese, stood next to each other.

They lowered the American flag and raised the flag of South Vietnam.
Music played as the commanders saluted each other, then the units
saluted each other.

I watched this scene, feeling the poignancy of it. It was such a sym-
bolic moment. This was Vietnamization. We weren't leaving behind a
bunch of ragtag summer soldiers afraid of their shadows. They were fighters. I told our troops, "These are the people who are taking the fight to the
enemy. They're our partners, they're our buddies as we go through this."

The proof of who they were came just as we were in the last stages of
withdrawing. The Tet Offensive of 1968 had been a disaster for the Vietcong, who sustained so many casualties that many of their units were
more or less incapable of doing any more fighting. North Vietnamese
troops also suffered severe losses then. Now, four years later, in the spring
of 1972, the Hanoi Politburo was ready for another try. Already in February, American and ARVN forces were watching the North amass armor,
artillery, and materiel and concentrate fighting divisions for a full-scale
invasion. We knew that at least one thrust of the attack would come
across the DMZ right at the bases we were abandoning, which shielded
the city of Quang Tri and, south of that, Hue. Another thrust was likely
to come in from the west through the A Shau Valley, where we had
ambushed the NVA Sixth Regiment not much earlier.

It was noon of March 30 when the dam broke. Two NVA divisions
with artillery and additional tank regiments stormed across the DMZ.

Others struck through Route 222 in the A Shau toward the coastal city of Quang Tri. The shock rolled into the South Vietnamese forces and knocked them back. But they recovered and stiffened; they counterattacked and took back territory. Our partner regiment fought like hell there, and eventually they and other South Vietnamese forces, with massive American air support, stopped the northern onslaught in every region where they struck, in the North, the middle, and the South of the country. The offensive lasted months before it ran out of steam, its manpower depleted and much of its equipment in ruins. It was a bloody affair that tested the Vietnamization policy—and the test showed the policy to be a decisive success.

We watched as the early stages of the attack flooded toward our old bases. Firebase Bastogne itself was the scene of ferocious fighting that went back and forth. But the 101st was all but out by that time. A unit's withdrawal will normally be covered by a different unit, but we covered ourselves, sending a cavalry squadron up into the A Shau Valley, which allowed us to redeploy from Firebases Apollo and Birmingham, then from Camp Eagle and the huge base at Phu Bai, the cavalry hitting northern forces as we pulled back. The Second Battalion, 327th Infantry, was the last unit out, the same men I had spent my first month with, the "No-Slack" Battalion, which now had the distinction of being the best unit in the division.

We came down Route 1 through the Hai Van Pass, the so-called Street without Joy, the cavalry and other combat elements covering us as we moved. Finally we came to China Beach, where we staged for our departure. Directly north of China was Red Beach, where seven years earlier US marines had waded ashore—kicking off America's ground war in Vietnam.

We departed in good order on ships and planes, moving all our helicopters, weaponry, and other materiel with us. It took another three years before the North recovered sufficiently from its defeat to launch another all-out conventional attack on the South, which, deprived by then of American support, could not stand before the onslaught. But in 1972 I didn't think that the United States would pull the rug out from under our allies like that. I didn't foresee the last helicopters taking off from rooftops, leaving crowds of desperate people below them, the image most Americans have in their minds when they think about how the Vietnam War came to an end.

What I did see was that we, the 101st Airborne Division and my brigade, had carried out a difficult retrograde movement and withdrawn successfully, which was our final mission. And I saw that we had left behind a South Vietnamese army that fought sometimes poorly but often with courage and sometimes heroically. So I did not leave thinking of Vietnam as a failure. I saw it as a war we fought with an inadequate strategy and without a clear, well-thought-out objective. Clarity, I thought, was not there either at the beginning or later. But as we left, I felt that we had done our job well and that we were leaving behind, at least in our area of operation, an ally who was determined to stand up and had proven they damned well knew how to fight.

6

In the Watergate White House

The 101st Airborne Division left Vietnam for its home base at Fort Campbell, Kentucky, but I didn't go with them. Instead I got a request from General Sam Walker, the West Point commandant, to come to the military academy as a tactical officer. He wanted me to start training a Beast Barracks company of newly arrived plebes during their summer introduction to army life, then take over as tactical officer for a regular company of cadets.

I couldn't have been happier with the assignment. I knew General Walker. As a colonel, he had been one of DePuy's successors as head of the Third Division battle group I started out with in Germany. Walker was one of the finest soldiers I had ever served under, and I knew he was determined to instill his sense of professionalism and pride in West Point's post-Vietnam cadets, all of them products of the awful turmoil of the nation's recent past. I loved West Point. My own time there had been a great inspiration for me, so I was eager to get back and impart some of what I had learned over the years.

A tactical officer's job was tailor made for that, and after two combat tours in Vietnam and a different kind of combat tour at Loyola I was more than ready for some quiet time. A tactical officer assignment at West Point was always locked in for a minimum of three or more normally four years, so at long last I would be able to settle in with my family, our two daughters and Karen, now pregnant with our third child. At West Point, we moved into nice, spacious quarters. Karen's father came up to help me wallpaper our three bathrooms and panel the basement as a playroom. We had wonderful neighbors; many of my old classmates and friends were there.

Everyone was happy. "This is really going to be good," I thought.

Good but a challenge. Not long after I arrived, I was invited to a cocktail party where there was a mix of faculty and graduating senior cadets. Talking with a number of these students, all of them cadet corps leaders, I asked what branch they had decided to go into—armor, infantry, artillery, engineering—remembering having to make my own decision as a graduating cadet. But what these cadets really wanted to talk about was their second career, what they had in mind for their professional lives once they were finished with their military commitment. These young men were just days away from being commissioned officers, supposedly the army's future leaders. I tried to be polite, but it was a struggle. That kind of emphasis just seemed terribly wrong. I knew it was a consequence of the times, the anti–Vietnam War, antimilitary atmosphere they had grown up in, but it told me something about the kind of job I had in front of me.

A tactical officer at West Point is different from a faculty member in one of the academic departments. A tac officer is given a company of cadets, maybe 100 or 120 drawn from all the classes, plebes through seniors (Firsties). Tac officers train, advise, and lead their charges as they transition from civilians to army officers. The professors teach the cadets law, political science, psychology, and so on. Tac officers evaluate and write reports. If someone doesn't have the potential to lead troops in battle, isn't physically or morally fit, or isn't up to it psychologically or intellectually, the tac officer's job is to identify that person. The tac officer takes a personal interest in his (or her) cadets, in their families; he does his best to understand whatever issues they might have. He counsels them, mentors them. He makes sure they learn the ways of their profession.

My company was G-1, and I was fortunate to have a wonderful group of young men. The cadet captain was John Abizaid, who eventually rose to four-star rank and headed the US Army Central Command, overseeing forces in the Middle East and Central Asia. His cadet executive officer was Karl Eikenberry, who reached three-star rank and later served as ambassador to Afghanistan. "I've run three companies," I told Abizaid and Eikenberry. "I'm not going to run this one. You are. For the first month I'll show you the standards; I'll be all over you. But after that I'm going to step back. I expect you to provide the leadership."

Given the attitude I had seen among some of the graduating seniors, I had a "Come to Jesus" meeting with the company first classmen early on. I laid out my expectations. I described some of the elements of their lives I felt were most important, whether they were going to be in the army three years or thirty years, including displaying moral as well as physical courage, taking responsibility, being accountable. "I'm concerned about attention to detail," I told the Firsties, who were complaining about the Blue Book that spelled out all the regulations governing cadet life. The Blue Book included many more rules and requirements than when I was a cadet, and many of the first classmen considered some of the details "chickenshit," as they put it. They were adults, they said, not children. Why did they have to arrange their medicine cabinets a specific way or fold their clothing in the prescribed manner?

"These things train you to pay attention to detail," I told them, "and there's nothing more important. In a fight, if you're on a tank and your track goes off, and you don't have the right wrench to fix it, you're a sitting duck." I told them about some of my Vietnam experiences, how the troops liked to hang hand grenades on their harnesses as if they were John Wayne. "I had standing orders for everyone to carry grenades in their ammo pouches. But no one checked, and two soldiers were killed when their grenades caught on vines in the jungle, and their pins were pulled out.

"Imagine what a soldier's chest looks like when a grenade goes off. That's not something you ever forget. In Vietnam, I ordered the men to pull their sleeves down and use insect repellent at night. I put that out to the lieutenants and sergeants, but again no one checked, and at one point I lost almost half my company to malaria. Whose fault was that? Mine, because I didn't pay enough attention. You have to discipline yourselves to always attend to details. That's why you fold your clothes a certain way. That's what 'toothbrush to the right, bristles up' means. It's meant to ingrain in you discipline and attention to detail. This isn't chickenshit. This is how you learn to keep your men alive. And this is where you learn it."

Abizaid and Eikenberry were magnificent. They were quick learners and showed exceptional leadership ability. I loved the way the company was coming along. (At the end of the year, it won the Superintendent's Award as the best company in the Corps of Cadets, though I was out of the picture by then.) I felt strongly that I was passing along to them lessons I had learned from people such as DePuy, Gorman, and Haig. Another pleasure was that two of my own classmates were coaching the West Point 150-pound football team, and they asked me to assist. The 150-pound cadets were fired up; their morale was over the top. I worked with the defense, which had superb players that year. Unfortunately, I had to leave West Point halfway through the season, but for the last game, against navy's 150-pounders, the team asked me to join them. I drove to Annapolis for that and sat on the bench with my defensive linemen, in my uniform, in front of four thousand midshipmen. In that game, our defense made five goal-line stands. The final was 41–0. There was nothing I didn't like about being a tac officer at West Point.

Late that November, though, I got a call from Rick Brown, an armor officer who was with us in Vietnam, a friend. Rick had been working with Alexander Haig, who earlier in 1972 had been promoted to major general. Haig had been working in the White House as Henry Kissinger's military assistant and had been in Vietnam various times to assess progress and coordinate with the South Vietnamese government.

Rick had been doing studies for him.

"General Haig would like you to come to Washington with him," Rick said. "He's expecting another assignment and wants your help."

Haig and I had kept in touch periodically since our time in Vietnam together. After that, he had commanded a brigade, then had been at West Point as a tactical officer under the previous superintendent. I knew he was working with Kissinger, but nothing more than that. "He specifically wants you," Rick said.

"You know," I said, "I've just come back from Vietnam. I've only been here a short time. We've got nice quarters here. We've got two young children; my wife's pregnant with our third. We're settled in. Please tell General Haig I'm flattered, but no thanks."

A few days later Rick called again.

"George, he really wants you. It's important. He'd like you to reconsider and come."

"Rick, I'm just not coming. I've moved around too much. I've got responsibilities to the cadets and to General Walker. I'm enjoying myself. It's a three- or four-year commitment, and I've only been here six months. Please give him my regrets. I'm sure he can find someone else."

Finally, Haig himself called.

"George, I wouldn't ask if it wasn't important. I have a new job coming up, and I need someone I can absolutely trust. I trusted you completely in Vietnam. I know for sure I can trust you now. I need you to be with me in this."

This was a tough one. Haig was my battalion commander, the man I had fought battles with and shared a foxhole with, the man who had held me when I got blasted to the back of our bunker at Firebase Charlie. The decision was wrenching, but I thought I really didn't have a choice. So I saluted.

Haig hadn't told me what his new assignment was. I thought he was probably going to go from the White House back to a two-star army posting, possibly to command a division. But two weeks after I went down to Washington, I was on a plane with him to Vietnam. Haig had been made a special envoy. This was on December 18, 1972, the day President Nixon started the so-called Christmas Bombing of Hanoi. The Paris Peace Talks had broken down; the North Vietnamese negotiators had pulled out. The Christmas Bombing was Nixon telling them they would either get back to the table or suffer the consequences. The newspaper headlines read, "Haig Lands in Saigon, Bombs Fall on Hanoi."

That was when I found out that the president was going to promote Haig from two stars directly to four stars and appoint him army vice chief of staff. I had apparently enrolled myself as assistant to the vice chief.

Karen was nine months pregnant when I left, so now she was there by herself at West Point with our two little girls. On December 1, she called me. The dishwasher in our apartment had flooded, she said. And also . . . her water had just broke. She was going to the hospital.

It was snowing up and down the Middle Atlantic that day. I caught a flight to La Guardia, where an army car picked me up and raced through the storm to West Point. The hospital then was down by West Point's South Area (it moved and expanded later). We drove in on the road just above and parallel to Thayer Road, the academy's main street. And just as we were coming in, the army football team was marching down to the main gate, where buses were waiting to take them to their annual game with navy. The entire Corps of Cadets was marching with them, tanks up front, flags flying, the band playing, the whole corps singing "On Brave Old Army Team," and I was thinking, "My brand-new son is being born, and the first words he hears are 'On brave old army team.' What a great football player he's going to be." (This was before parents knew whether they were having a boy or girl, but I was absolutely certain.)

When I got to the hospital, I flew up the stairs to the maternity ward. "I want to see Karen Joulwan," I said. "I'm Major Joulwan, her husband."

"You're her husband?" the nurse said. "We were wondering. Someone else came in with her, then another officer came to see her. You're the actual Major Joulwan, the father?

"Yes, can I please see her?"

"Of course, and congratulations, Major Joulwan. Your wife and new daughter are doing just fine."

Haig received his appointment as army vice chief in January, with me as his assistant. It was February before I was able to move the family to Washington, where we were given the vice chief's aide's quarters at Fort McNair at the confluence of the Potomac and Anacostia Rivers. Over the next months, I traveled with Haig to South Vietnam several times and went with him to Fort Knox, Fort Benning, and Fort Bliss to review procurement, research, and other systems. I had the opportunity to hear army leadership discuss how we were going to come out of Vietnam and what the new army should look like. I was getting insight into inner workings of the army I had known little about before.

Meanwhile, the political situation in Washington was reaching the boiling point. In June 1972, a security guard had noticed a burglary in progress at the Watergate complex. Several people associated with Nixon's Committee to Re-elect the President had broken into the Democratic National Committee's offices there. The scandal had been escalating ever since, getting closer and closer to the president himself. In February 1973, the Senate established a committee to investigate the affair. Under huge pressure, at the end of April President Nixon had fired Robert Haldeman, his chief of staff, and John Ehrlichman, his senior domestic adviser. Two days later he asked Haig to come to the White House as his new chief of staff.

To say Haig was conflicted is the understatement of the year. He was back in the army, which he loved, after spending three years in the White House working as Henry Kissinger's military assistant, then as deputy national security adviser to the president. Now, only four months later, Nixon was asking him to leave the army and come back to the White House—into a maelstrom. Haig wrote in *Inner Circles,* "I knew this could mean the end of the life I had chosen for my family and myself. Given the poisonously anti-Nixon mood prevailing in Washington, the personal consequences were incalculable."

Haig told Nixon he did not think he was the right man for that job—he didn't have political experience, he didn't know domestic policy, he knew almost no one in Congress. Also, he thought it was a bad idea to have a military person in the chief of staff's role, especially at such a volatile juncture. He asked Nixon to reconsider.

Nixon did. A day later his press secretary, Ron Zeigler, got back to Haig, telling him the president understood his reservations, "but he wants you to do this."

Haig took that as an order from his commander in chief. So he bit the bullet.

When Haig told me that he was going to have to retire from the army and go to the White House as chief of staff, my first thought was, "Okay, see you later." When he asked me what I would like to do, I said, "I want to go back to the troops; I'd like to do that in Europe."

"Okay," Haig said, "but why don't you first get me over to the White House and get me settled in?" I couldn't exactly refuse to get him settled in, so I agreed. As far as I was concerned, this was a temporary assignment. I was going to get Haig "settled in," whatever that meant. I was given a commission as special assistant to the president and assigned a small office in the White House next to Haig's, sharing the space with Rick Brown. I was two doors down from the president, which was heady stuff. I had never set foot in the White House before this. It's an exciting place to be, the beating heart of the government. But I wasn't comfortable. Haig had had to resign from the army before coming on as the president's chief of staff, and here I was, an active-duty major, as his assistant. It didn't seem exactly right; I didn't think anything like that had been done before. But there I was.

In a situation like that, you either sit there and suck your thumb or get on with what needs to be done. I decided to get on with it. I wrote up an analysis of what I thought a chief of staff's assistant's job entailed, which Haig liked. Then I started doing the staff work for him that I had outlined.

I arrived in the White House in June. Haldeman and Ehrlichman had been fired at the end of April. On May 17, 1973, the Senate began televising the Watergate Committee hearings, which glued people across the country to their television sets. A few days after that, Archibald Cox was appointed independent special prosecutor. As the pressure mounted on Nixon, Haig spent more and more time on Watergate. He kept me away from that side of his activities, but that meant the preponderance of the organizational work of running the executive branch of the government—that is, the chief of staff's job—began falling to me. Haig would meet with the administration's principals, then give me his guidance, which I would then promulgate to the midlevel staff, the people who actually did the work.

I assumed that Rick Brown, my office mate, would be staying in the job and that at some fairly near point I would be leaving, which was what I wanted to do. Rick was extremely smart and motivated, a hard worker. He later rose to three-star rank and earned a PhD. He was the obvious person to carry on, but Haig had different ideas.

My family and I were still living in the Fort McNair aide's quarters, but Haig wasn't army vice chief any longer, and I was no longer the vice chief's aide, which meant our quarters at Fort McNair were needed by someone else. Karen wanted to know what we were going to do and where we were going to live. She was ordinarily imperturbable, but it was her business to take care of the family, and she had to know where she, our two older daughters, and the baby were going to live. She wasn't happy that I hadn't worked that out.

One day I was in a senior staff meeting with Haig when his secretary came in with a note for me from Karen. "A moving van is at our door.

What do you want me to do?" When I asked Haig what he wanted, he said, "You are staying where you are!" Right after that I wrote "Memorandum for the Chief of Staff. Subject: Me." In it I explained that I wanted to go back to the troops. At the end, I put a decision box: "For Action." I put the memo at the top of his in-box, but Haig kept switching it to the bottom. I'd then put it back on top.

This dance went on for a bit, but finally he couldn't put it off any longer. "I want you to stay," he said. "The country's in tough shape. We work well together. I want you to do the same thing you did for me in Vietnam. I need straight talk. You aren't afraid to disagree with me. I trust you to do that. I don't know how long this is going to go on, and I don't know what the outcome is going to be, but I'd like you to serve."

I'm not sure what Haig expected when he accepted the position as White House chief of staff. He certainly wasn't under any illusions about it. Of course, no one could have predicted the course this thing was going to take. In July, Alexander Butterfield, who had been Haldeman's assistant, told the Senate Committee about Nixon's taping system, which triggered a no-holds-barred battle between various investigators and Nixon's attorneys for possession of the tapes. Then in October Vice President Spiro Agnew resigned. Investigators had found that as Maryland's governor he had taken bribes in return for granting contracts, and he had continued taking them even after he became vice president. Shortly after that blow, the battle between Nixon and Special Prosecutor Cox came to a head, which led to the "Saturday Night Massacre," when Attorney General Elliot Richardson and Deputy Attorney General William Ruckelshaus resigned after refusing Nixon's order to fire Cox.

The White House was coming apart. The vice president was a corrupt bribe taker. Most people believed that President Nixon was engaging in a cover-up, lying, and obstructing justice. And Haig was right in the middle of all this, struggling to help Nixon and keep the executive branch running at the same time.

I thought about it. I considered the potential consequences of working with this administration. No one wants to be on a sinking ship, especially a notorious one. There was the chance I'd be marked by the ongoing scandal in some way. I thought that if I took the job, it might be my terminal appointment. One of my friends looked at me thoughtfully and said, "It's the kiss of death."

The other side was that there were loyalties and then there were loyalties. I had those deep ties to Haig from Vietnam. He and his wife, Pat, were godparents to our daughter Jessica.

He needed help getting through this very tough knothole he had gotten himself into. The White House was like another battlefield. In Vietnam, we had been in a bunker together; we were in another one here. Grenades were exploding right and left. Do you just cut and run when the flames are coming up? If everyone left because they didn't want to get muck on them, how was the business of government—the country's business—supposed to get done? What bills had to be researched and vetted? What laws had to be signed? Who needed to be appointed to do what? Who were the right people, and how could you get them in? "This place is like a battalion that's been overrun," I thought, "all of whose officers have been killed." Haldeman, Ehrlichman, Dean, John Mitchell, Charles Colson, Attorney General Richard Kleindienst, Richardson (Kleindienst's successor), Agnew—all gone, fired, or resigned. In that kind of situation, somebody has to stand back up and rally the forces.

I didn't feel qualified for any of this, but I was in the position. When I talked to Haig about where he thought this might be going, his answer was, "We just have to let the Constitution work," which made sense to me, especially after I had spent so much time studying the Constitution while I was at Loyola. That was his refrain with others, too: let the Constitution work.

I thought about the situation. I thought about Haig, how tough it was on him and his family. I thought about what it meant to serve. I remembered my grandfather's words when I was a cadet at West Point. "America's been so good to our family. It's very important that a grandson of mine is going to serve in the military of this country"—my grandfather, a Lebanese Christian who emigrated from a very hard part of that region. Whatever thinking I was doing, that memory was wrapped up in it.

In the end, I told Karen the country was in bad shape and General Haig wanted me to do this. I was going to agree. We would just have to suck it up. As always, she was a rock of support. I was saluting, but she was saluting along with me, and I knew that her salute was harder than mine. When I told Haig I'd stay, he said, "Now you're really going to know what duty to the country is all about."

The first item on the agenda was to bring in people to replace those who had been fired or resigned. It wasn't just Haldeman, Ehrlichman, and the other principals who were gone; their staffs were gone now, too. Many of the brightest young people who were still on board were getting ready to bail, all of them thinking about how best to serve their futures. I was afraid that David Gergen, the thirty-one-year-old head of the speechwriting and research group, was going to leave, but he decided to stay, and he kept his group of fifty pretty well intact. Later in his life, after serving in three more administrations, Gergen wrote that Watergate was a crucible that allowed him to understand which moral values were fundamentally important.

Haig took the business of recruitment in hand, bringing in some true heavyweights to fill positions or advise. One was Bryce Harlow, a senior Republican figure who had previously worked for both Eisenhower and Nixon. Others included George Schultz, Bill Simon, and Mel Laird, all of them strong, determined figures.

This wasn't the first time I found myself in a chaotic situation where critical norms had broken down, though nothing I had experienced earlier actually compared to what we were facing here. When I was at Loyola in the late 1960s and early 1970s, it sometimes seemed as if the whole country were coming apart. On a smaller but more deadly scale, the battalion I was assigned to at the beginning of my second Vietnam tour was a unit where coherence, discipline, morale, and resolve had fallen apart in the face of a lethal enemy. These situations may have been apples and oranges, but they had in common the fracturing and disintegration of accepted standards and norms.

Maybe the most powerful tool you can use to counter that kind of breakdown is to establish a sense of purpose or mission that people find compelling. It wasn't easy dealing with the problems in Vietnam—the drugs and racial divisiveness and indiscipline. But as I worked to bring the soldiers to concentrate on their mission, which was to protect their own and their buddies' lives by training, patrolling, and persevering in battle as we withdrew, they responded. Against the forces of disarray, a shared sense of purpose can work wonders. I was in no position at Loyola to do something similar, but I was able to shift the conversations I was part of away from partisan anger over the war and toward the military's crucial role in the country's life. That went some way toward easing the rancor and encouraging dialogue. If you can instill a sense of common purpose or even just point it out, positive things happen by bringing people out of their obsessions with their own needs and emotions. Focusing on fundamental requirements or values puts personal and intergroup problems and conflicts into perspective.

Haig met with the senior staff every morning at 8:30. I followed up with the deputies, telling them what needed to be done and overseeing their work. On the great consuming issue of Nixon's unraveling presidency, I told them, "The president's the president, but the bigger picture is the people, the soldiers and sailors and the everyday regular citizens, whose lives are impacted by what we do here. This is a rough time, but we aren't here to wring our hands. We're here to serve the country. We have work to do, and we need to get it done. We need to keep our eyes focused and keep the wheels of government turning."

Patriotism has become an old-fashioned term, but that's what I wanted to emphasize. As I saw it, my job was to say, "Serve your country." That was Haig's message as well. The people who stayed and the new people who came on understood that.

This wasn't a fun time, but we could find bits of humor here and there that weren't just gallows humor and eased the tension. The press kept referring to the "bunker mentality" in the White House, that everyone working there was "hunkered down." Bill Timmons, the president's legislative assistant, had an old World War I gas mask and helmet. One day he came into my office wearing them, saying nasally through the mask, "I understand there's a bunker mentality here." In retrospect, that might have qualified as gallows humor. The fact was that I had nicknamed my little office "the Bunker."

Henry Kissinger was now wearing two hats, national security adviser and secretary of state. I would see him walk by my office on his way to see Haig or Nixon, and once or twice he stopped in to say hello. On one of these occasions, he told me he was proud of the fact that he had been an infantry private crossing the beaches in Normandy with the US Army Fourth Infantry Division. He was a rifleman at first, but when his unit took the German city of Krefeld, he was put in charge of the city's administration due to the lack of better-qualified German speakers. After that, he was assigned to army counterintelligence and rose to the rank of sergeant.

Twenty-five years later, in 1997, when I was supreme allied commander, I introduced him at a conference and mentioned that he had been a sergeant in the US Army during World War II, at which he interrupted me. "I wasn't a sergeant," he said. "I was a *staff* sergeant." He didn't want me undervaluing his service.

As the Watergate case moved toward a climax, almost all of Haig's energies were engaged in trying to find ways to save Nixon's political life. Although most Americans may have turned skeptical about the president's denials, Nixon continually reassured Haig and others close to him that he had done nothing wrong, and I think Haig believed that until it was proven differently. Haig and I often drove to the White House and back home together, and when he had had an especially bad day, he would want to talk. I usually thought that the last thing he needed at those times was gratuitous advice, so I mainly listened, though when he wanted my opinion, I didn't hold back. Sometimes we agreed, and sometimes we didn't. He had told me, "You're not just here to be an aide; you're here to give me the same sort of advice you gave me in combat." This was very much a combat situation; he saw it that way, and I shared his perception.

But whether Haig was getting something off his chest or considering a decision he had to make, he invariably related the issue back to what was best for the country. That was his litmus test. Adhering to that principle gave him great resolve and strength. He especially treasured a letter he received from General Matthew Ridgway, who had led the Eighty-Second Airborne in World War II, had reorganized the US Army in Korea into an aggressive and potent force after its retreat from the Chosin Reservoir, and had served as the army chief of staff from 1953 to 1955. There wasn't a more revered figure in the US military. Ridgway wrote to Haig: "Your contribution can be of tremendous importance in helping to restore the public's confidence in government at the highest level; in enlarging public recognition of the competence and integrity of our senior officers; in grasping and dealing with the full dimension of major national problems; and, by your personal example, in demonstrating the unswerving adherence to the code of personal honor which governs the members of the Corps throughout their lives."

Despite the looming debacle, there were events along the way that spoke to Nixon's very significant capabilities as president. Few questioned his great effectiveness in foreign affairs: his initiation of détente with the Soviets, his opening to China, the first round of the Strategic Arms Limitation Talks and its aftermath, his efforts on Israel's behalf during and after the Yom Kippur War.

Watergate didn't stop him from pursuing international issues and relationships. I accompanied him and Haig on visits to the Soviet Union, Iceland, and the Middle East. I was in France with them for the ceremonies marking President Georges Pompidou's funeral. In Paris, Nixon was staying at the ambassador's residence and at one point was scheduled to meet with France's interim president. The French Presidential Palace was directly adjacent to the ambassador's residence, and the two properties were connected by a gate in their elaborate back courtyards. It was arranged that Nixon would go to the palace through that gate to avoid the crowd that had gathered out in the street. But when he got there, along with fifty or so staffers, security people, and others, the gate was locked, and after a flurry of confusion and searching no one could find the key.

I was watching all this from the ambassador's patio, along with a number of reporters, including the young Tom Brokaw. When Nixon couldn't get through the gate, he spun around and whizzed past me, though the front gate, and to the main street, the Secret Service and others scrambling to keep up, briefing books and all.

Outside, hundreds of people were shouting, "Vive Nixon, vive les États-Unis," as he walked down the middle of the street to the palace. Whatever Americans thought of him, in France he was greeted with admiration and respect. As we watched, Brokaw said to me, "Listen, George, you may not be Deep Throat, but I'll take anything I can get."

On that visit, several heads of state wanted to meet with the president. Each of those meetings took place in the US embassy, and I was able to sit in on a few of them. Nixon dominated those meetings. He was gracious, remembering details about his counterparts' families and asking about them. More to the point, he had complete control of the issues and engaged in important, substantive discussions. This was in April 1974. The House of Representatives was going to start impeachment proceedings in less than a month. Given the immense pressure Nixon was under, his performance in France was simply remarkable.

Shortly after the president returned home, the tape issue came to a head, which moved events toward their end. First, the House Committee subpoenaed the White House recordings. When Nixon didn't fully comply, the special prosecutor (Leon Jaworski, Archibald Cox's successor) also subpoenaed them. When Nixon still didn't comply, the Supreme Court required him to. When the tapes were analyzed, one stood out, a recording from June 23, 1972, five days after the Watergate break-in. On it Nixon could be heard instructing Haldeman to initiate a cover-up. It was the smoking gun.

The day the investigators found the June 23 tape, I was with Nixon, Haig, and the presidential party in San Clemente. A call came in about the tape's discovery very early in the morning, while the president was still sleeping—in California it was three hours earlier than in Washington. Shortly after that, I began fielding calls for Haig from people anxious to know what was going to happen now, what the plans were.

Jim St. Clair, Nixon's lawyer, was up with me, but it was only about 5:00 a.m., and Jim didn't see any reason to wake the president, so instead we went for a ride in a golf cart down toward the water. When we got to the beach, though, the cart got stuck, and St. Clair and I found ourselves pushing the thing out of the sand and up the hill. We finally got it back up and walked together across the property near the Coast Guard station and toward the house. It was a stark moment. Both of us understood the importance of what had just happened, and Jim was preparing himself to talk with the president—to inform him and no doubt to advise him on his options, all of them bleak.

Nixon went back to the White House on July 28. On August 9, after the tape's revelation had all but eliminated the last of his support in Congress, Nixon resigned the presidency. Head speechwriter David Gergen and his group prepared four different wordings for his resignation letter. They finally decided on the simplest and most succinct, one sentence: "I hereby resign the Office of the President of the United States."

Haig was with Nixon in the second-floor Lincoln Sitting Room when I took the letter up, knocked on the door, and went in. "The president needs to sign this," I said, putting it down in front of him. Haig and Nixon talked about it for a moment, then Nixon signed. I then took the letter to Henry Kissinger, the secretary of state, to whom it was properly addressed. Kissinger initialed the letter, and the resignation took effect.

That afternoon Nixon gave his farewell speech in the East Room in front of his family, Vice President Gerald Ford and his family, the cabinet, the White House staff, and many of the wives and husbands. The room was packed. Many were emotional.

Some of the house staff were weeping. Karen was there with me. She had lived through all of the drama and deserved to witness this historic moment. "We think," Nixon said, "that when someone dear to us dies, we think that when we lose an election, we think that when we suffer a defeat, that all is ended. We think that the light has left his life forever. Not true. . . . Only if you have been in the deepest valley can you ever know how magnificent it is to be on the highest mountain." By then, many in the room were crying openly.

Afterward, Haig and I walked with Nixon and Ford and their families to the waiting helicopter. Nixon went up the steps, turned, smiled, and raised his arms to the crowd. Then he was gone.

The subsequent transition was smooth. Gerald Ford had been vice president ever since Spiro Agnew resigned ten months earlier. Haig and Ford got along well, and Haig had kept him closely informed as Nixon's hold on the presidency became increasingly tenuous. When the time came, Ford was well prepared to move into the Oval Office.

At first, Ford wanted to keep the kind of routine he had developed as a congressman, with an open door to anyone who wanted to see him. It didn't take long, though, for him to recognize that he needed a chief of staff who could control visitors and organize the work flow. As effective a chief of staff as Haig was, Ford wanted him to stay on, but Haig decided against it. He had had to resign from the army to take the job under Nixon, but generals can always be recalled, and Haig wanted badly to get back to his army life.

I was just as determined to get back. But then Ford's White House counsel, John Marsh, asked if I would stay on. I had briefed Ford on a few occasions, so he was aware of who I was and what my function was with Haig. The first time we met was immediately before Nixon introduced him as the new vice president taking Agnew's place. Ford and Mrs. Ford had been brought to the White House secretly to avoid any media prior to Nixon's announcement. I met them at the back door to the National Security Council meeting room and escorted them up to the East Wing. Ford had been a center on the University of Michigan's national championship football team, so both of us had football in our pasts. Ford was down to earth, an easy person talk to. "You're a lineman," I told him. "That's good preparation for what you're about to go through."

Now Ford was president. "He'd like you to stay in your job," Marsh told me. "Thank you," I said. "I'm flattered, but I think I've served my time here. I've done the best I could helping General Haig, but it's time for me to go back to being a soldier." Shortly afterward, Ford appointed Don Rumsfeld to take Haig's place and Dick Cheney to take mine.

Haig probably would have been appointed army chief of staff, the job he would have loved, but he had been so closely associated with Nixon that both Ford and he knew his confirmation hearings would be full of contention and a platform for those who wanted to pursue Nixon further, especially after Ford's quick decision to pardon the former president. As an alternative, Henry Kissinger suggested that Ford appoint Haig supreme allied commander of NATO and of American forces in Europe.

When that happened, Haig said to me, "George, you know I'm being appointed SACEUR. I'd like you to come over there with me . . . just to get me settled in."

7

The Post-Vietnam Army

As President Ford's team was taking over at the White House, I checked in with the US Army Military Personnel Center, responsible for assignments. I wanted to see what kind of troop slot might be available for whenever I would be able to leave my new (hopefully temporary) job with Haig.

"Joulwan," they told me, "your name is mud around here."

"Really?" I asked. "Why is that?"

"We've been trying to assign you, but we keep being told, 'No.' That's why. The good news, though, is that you're on the list for a battalion command."

"I can't do that right now," I said. "But what's coming open around June?"

"In June? First Battalion, Twenty-Sixth Infantry in Göppingen, Germany."

"Really!" First Battalion, Twenty-Sixth, my old Blue Spaders. "Put me down."

They did, but I didn't tell Haig. I wasn't sure exactly when or how I was going to do that.

Haig and I left for Europe in November. In his new position as supreme allied commander—SACEUR—he would be wearing two hats: commander of NATO military forces and commander in chief of US forces in Europe, or CINCEUR. The full acronym was SACEUR/ CINCEUR.

Haig was replacing Andrew Goodpaster, who had been in the position for four years. Goodpaster was an old-time warrior, a highly decorated veteran of World War II. After the war, he had earned a doctorate from Princeton in international relations and had been Eisenhower's deputy when Eisenhower himself was SACEUR. When Eisenhower was elected president, Goodpaster had gone to the White House as his adviser. Later he was third in command of forces in Vietnam and served as military adviser to the US delegation at the Paris peace negotiations. Goodpaster was extremely senior and widely admired. He was not pleased to be leaving the post.

89

Goodpaster's own predecessor, Lyman Lemnitzer, had served as SACEUR for six years, and Lemnitzer's predecessor had served for seven. There was no set time limit for the assignment. Goodpaster was scheduled to retire in June, only eight months away. It made sense for him to retire from the position, but now he was being told his command was being cut short, giving him much less time than he would have liked to say farewell to his international contacts, tie up loose ends, and move out of his residence. The word was that he considered the hurry an affront. I understood that Goodpaster had expressed his displeasure all the way up to President Ford. It didn't make for a smooth transition.

The SACEUR/CINCEUR change of command takes place in two ceremonies. The CINCEUR ceremony is at American headquarters in Stuttgart, Germany, followed by the NATO SACEUR handover in Mons, Belgium. Goodpaster chose to be absent for the CINCEUR ceremony, which Haig took as a slight. Goodpaster did come for the NATO ceremony, though. Haig's speech there was highly laudatory. "You have met each challenge with dedication and skill," he said to Goodpaster. "You have been both a brilliant leader and articulate proponent of allied strength and solidarity." He said he had long admired Goodpaster as an international commander. After Haig's speech, Goodpaster gave him a hearty handshake.

That alleviated some of the tension, but not by any means all of it. With Haig and Goodpaster sitting next to each other afterward, the reporters at the changeover asked Haig pointed and embarrassing questions. "Why were you selected?" "Are you a political general?" A *Stars and Stripes* photo of the Mons ceremony illustrated the unhappiness. The photographer had shot it so that Goodpaster looked like he was seven feet tall, towering over a diminutive Haig, which gave a sense of what the view of the changeover was in some quarters. Haig was very aware of the deprecation. "I would like you," he said, "to judge me by what I do now, not for what you think I may have done in the past."

Goodpaster's staff had worked with him for a long time and were extremely loyal. It's normal for there to be some friction between outgoing and incoming staff, but the perception that Goodpaster was being treated shabbily exacerbated that.

In terms of Haig's incoming staff, I was it. At that point, I had just been promoted to lieutenant colonel, which meant I was far junior to many of the officers Haig and I would now be working with. Haig, of course, had been Nixon's chief of staff, so now here this person associated with Watergate had abruptly arrived, along with his henchman. Since Haig had in some sense been connected with the scandal, the assumption was that he might have also had a hand in Nixon's pardon, so it was easy enough to conclude that President Ford had given him the SACEUR/CINCEUR job as a reward. In addition, Haig had gone extremely rapidly from one star to two stars to four stars, so some saw him as a political rather than a fighting general, which of course wasn't true, but the perception was there.

I found myself in the middle of all this friction, and I was a far easier target for resentment than Haig. So when we got to NATO's Supreme Headquarters Allied Powers Europe (SHAPE), I stepped back. "I'm not here to make waves," I said. "I'm here to help." Haig had a very particular way of doing business. "Let me give you a hand in understanding the way General Haig likes to work," I told the two-star SHAPE executive officer, and I prepared a memo that outlined the staff and office routine Haig preferred. The response was that they didn't work that way in Mons. General Haig would have to get used to the way business was done at SHAPE.

That wasn't a good response. A week or so later I was in my office in a back room when I heard Haig shout, "George!" When I got into his office, he was yelling, "What the hell is this? What are they giving me here? Why aren't they doing this right?" Not long afterward, SHAPE had a new executive officer, Joe Bratton, who later became army chief of engineers. I was appointed special assistant to the supreme commander and moved into Bratton's office. It didn't take long for the staff to start doing business Haig's way.

What Haig wanted was a briefing report every morning that brought him up to speed on what had happened in the previous twenty-four hours in his area of operation (in the Pentagon this report was called the "Early Bird"). With the NATO and US commands together, Haig was responsible for ninety countries, including all of Europe, Africa, and the Middle East. He wanted to know the major events that were taking place in these countries and to be informed of any significant intelligence.

If there was a coup in Somalia, an assassination in Algeria, an incident on the Israel-Lebanon border, he needed to know. He had to understand what the Soviets were up to and whatever might be going on with the Warsaw Pact countries. Haig was a voracious reader, and he wanted a wide view of what was happening in his segment of the world. Preparing a daily report for him was a gigantic job, but we had a large staff, and once they understood his requirements, they got into the rhythm of it.

Goodpaster had been Eisenhower's assistant, and the Germans were comfortable that he was knowledgeable about their postwar history and problems. By the same token, they were wary of a brash new commander who might not have the same familiarity. But Haig got up to speed quickly on the Germans, as he did on the other NATO countries. He spent the first thirty days or so getting intensive briefings. Then, because that "political general" aura was still hovering around him, he wanted to get out and be seen with the troops, which was my strong advice as well.

No one knew better than I what a canard the "political general" accusation was. I had been in firefight after firefight with Haig, in addition to Ap Gu, where he had won the Distinguished Service Cross. Haig was a real leader of troops, and we wanted to show that. So after he was thoroughly oriented, we went out to the main North German training area. The German brass there were hard-core, most of them holdovers from World War II, when they had been junior officers. Among the Germans, Haig looked youthful, his dark hair contrasting with the gray heads around him.

The German commander was a crusty old four-star, a legend in the German army. He and Haig introduced themselves, then the two of them jumped into a Marder, the new German fighting vehicle similar to our Bradley, and took off like bats out of hell, their security details racing to catch up. Both of them were standing up in the hatch, zipping through the area for twenty-five or thirty minutes. The press loved it.

There is a great picture of Haig sitting on the ground eating field rations with the troops when we visited the American training area at Hohenfels. The press covered him discussing the Fulda Gap, Berlin, and other strategic hot spots. They followed him as he toured the forces of each of the NATO countries. Before too long there was a shift in how he was being perceived, not just among the NATO partners but among the SHAPE staff. People began to understand that this was a person who was going to focus on warfighting, war deterrence, the strength of the alliance, the readiness of American and other forces. Instead of speculation about Haig's Watergate involvement and his political ties, there were now articles about his work with the National Security Council, his involvement in Vietnam negotiations, and his grasp of geopolitical issues. In his first couple of months as SACEUR/CINCEUR, he set a clear direction and highlighted the role of NATO in keeping the peace.

Haig's first visit to American forces was to the First Division headquarters in Göppingen to see our old battalion from Vietnam, the Blue Spaders. Brigadier General Wally Nutting, the First Division commander, picked us up in his helicopter to take us there. The three of us had headphones on as Wally laid out for Haig what was going to happen when we landed. I was monitoring the conversation.

"We're going to be met by the command sergeant major," Nutting said to Haig. "He'll take you through the honor guard, then we'll go into the headquarters, and you'll sign the visitors' book. After that we'll take you out to the field to see some of the training. Meanwhile, the sergeant major will show Colonel Joulwan his new quarters."

"What?" Haig said into the mic. "What do you mean, his new quarters?"

Nutting was startled. I could see the color draining from his face. I went on the intercom.

"Look, boss, I want you to know that before we left Washington, the Infantry Branch offered me command of the First Battalion, Twenty-Sixth Infantry. Our old unit. You commanded it. What a privilege for me to take command here in Germany. But that won't start till June. I didn't tell you before because you've had a lot of other things on your mind."

When Haig told the story later, it varied a little from the facts: when we got to Göppingen, he said, he went off in the rain and mud up to his knees to be with the troops, while I got into a big limousine to look at my new quarters.

In the course of my career and our marriage so far, Karen had moved at least six times in nine years. Now she and our three children were moving again, this time to Germany. At this point, we had a dog, a big Airedale named Max. Our three girls loved this dog, so I said, "Sure, bring him over." To prepare Max for the flight, they were supposed to give him a couple of animal tranquilizer pills. But somehow he ended up eating the whole bottle. He probably thought they were treats. The whole flight over he was out like a light. When the flight landed, they offloaded the baggage, including Max, conked out in his crate. I was overjoyed to see everyone, and when the kids emerged from the plane, I squatted down and waited for them to jump into my arms. They made a beeline, then flew right by me to find Max and see if he was okay. He wasn't; he was out to the world. It took almost three days for him to slowly come out of it.

I took command of the First Battalion, Twenty-Sixth Infantry at the beginning of July 1975. Saigon had fallen to the North Vietnamese only two months earlier, a sad moment, particularly when I thought about the courageous South Vietnamese soldiers I had fought next to and how Congress's withdrawal of support had made their last fight a futile one.

The war had ended up a catastrophe for the South Vietnamese. It also had terrible consequences for the US Army. The last American combat units had pulled out of Vietnam by 1973, but in 1975 the army was still struggling with the aftermath. Haig wrote in *Inner Circles* that when he began visiting our post-Vietnam troops in Europe, he was appalled by the drug use, the alcoholism, the indiscipline, and the potentially disastrous lack of combat readiness. If the Soviets had chosen to attack then, he said, the consequences could have been dire.

I too found myself worrying about how the Soviets might be interpreting our situation. The United States had just gone through an unprecedented presidential crisis. We had an unelected and therefore weak new president in the White House and a conflicted turnover in the SACEUR position. We were in a vulnerable moment.

With respect to our troops' state of readiness, I was every bit as appalled as Haig. As I left SHAPE to take command of the Blue Spaders, it seemed to me that the army was at the low point in its history. Drug use was rampant, as was alcohol abuse. There were racial conflicts. Everywhere you looked you could see the lack of discipline and the below par training standards. In a way, the army was reflecting what was happening in society generally at that time. But there were other reasons for its poor condition, too. When we went into Vietnam, we had had a solid NCO corps, but many NCOs had been killed in the war, and many had left the service. The NCO corps had been decimated, which showed in the troops' carelessness and indifference.

What was true for the army as a whole was also true for my battalion. Deterrence was our first mission, and if deterrence failed, we were supposed to be ready to fight and win. But to do that we needed disciplined, motivated troops and leaders focused on their missions. We simply didn't have that. The fighting quality of our units had deteriorated to the point where building it back up was going to be an enormous task.

The day I assumed command it was raining hard; mud was everywhere. With that weather, instead of the traditional ceremonial change of command outside, with guest dignitaries, band music, formal inspections, and so on, the troops were lined up, and we passed the flags in the big motor pool garage area at Hohenfels, with all the battalion's tanks, APCs, and trucks right there. As far as I was concerned, the setting was perfect. The battalion didn't need ceremony; it needed to get down to business. After the brief handover of command, I marched the whole unit out to the maneuver ranges. I wanted them to get the idea right off what kind of work I was going to demand of them.

I also attacked the drug and alcohol problem head on. The primary way of doing that was to get the troops to understand the mission and buy into that. What was our purpose in being where we were? Getting that across would give us cohesiveness. Getting the soldiers to focus on our mission would help them understand why they had to sacrifice and train as hard as I was going to train them. They needed to understand that to be ready to fight they couldn't be addicted to anything except the job we were there to do.

So that was my challenge. Here was a battalion really feeling the pains of Vietnam. They had to be weaned from the destructive habits that had developed out of the purposelessness that had pervaded the army in the course of its engagement there. I talked to them. I made sure they saw me and the other officers all the time. I remembered so well DePuy always talking, always explaining. I did the same, not just about how to fight but about why we had to know how to fight. I explained the importance of our job in facing a real, immensely powerful enemy just miles away across the East–West German border. I talked to the families as well as to the soldiers, explaining why the army was in Europe, why American leadership was so important. I started Friday-night officer get-togethers, where we discussed our mission and the business of learning and teaching how to fight, all in a relaxed setting. We invited the wives, too, and after the officers' session we would have drinks and social activities, which built the sense that everyone was part of one team. I also started a full-court press against addiction, with counseling, urine testing, and disciplinary action where we needed it. We got rid of soldiers who couldn't stay away from drugs. It wasn't long before I was seeing real progress.

The key was training; that was the glue that held the unit together. First, physical training to get the soldiers into shape. I had the whole battalion out running at 0600 every morning, including myself and all the officers. Men who dropped out had to do remedial PT. We also began right off training in warfighting skills from squad to platoon to battalion level. Digging in properly, maneuvering, bounding, overwatching—all the combat lessons I had learned over the years, readjusted now from how to counter the Vietcong to how to fight the Soviets.

Because we were a mechanized battalion, soldiers had to know how to operate together within a tank or APC—how to fight mounted as well as on foot. I was especially concerned about maintenance. When I took over, the maintenance rate was poor. But if your vehicle breaks down in battle and you can't fix it, you're in deep trouble. I hammered on the essential importance of maintenance, not one of the more exciting elements of military life. I worked hard to impart that awareness. It caught on, but it took a year before I was happy with our performance. The troops had to internalize that they were going to be measured not only by how well they could shoot but also by how they maintained their vehicles.

When we came back from field training, we would note how many vehicles had lost a track or had broken down and how good or bad the response by the crews and maintenance people was. We might have been out for thirty days, so that everybody was dead tired and eager to get back to the barracks or families. But first they had to go through postoperational checks: washing the vehicles down, cleaning headlights and reflectors, checking fluid levels, making sure they would be ready to go at a moment's notice with no prep time.

Everyone had to do that before they were released. That caused a lot of bitching the first time. But by the third time, they all understood and got right down to it. There was a fence around the motor pool, and wives and kids would be there passing sandwiches through the chain links. I put the battalion through long motor marches that were rough on the equipment, especially in the winter snow. The Germans used to laugh at Americans because units would litter the roads with broken-down and disabled vehicles—except for us. I got a kick out of our allies' amazement.

We had major trainings two or three times a year, but they were scheduled, so everyone knew and got ready for them. But being ready for occasional training wasn't the same as being ready to fight on day one of a war if the Soviets were to cross the border. So I instituted unrehearsed exercises, what I called "shock training." Without any advance notice, I would load a platoon's or a company's tanks on carriers and get them up to our gunnery areas. The crews had to maneuver and shoot just like they would if war suddenly broke out. We taught the gunners to fire their tube-launched, optically tracked, wire-guided (TOW) antitank missiles at their maximum effective range of three thousand meters, beyond the range of the Soviet tanks. The tactic was to create an engagement area for the Soviets by emplacing mines, then hit them with artillery to get the tanks to button up, then knock them out with the TOW missiles. When you challenge soldiers, when you give them a tough mission, they will respond. The troops loved it; they loved being capable of doing these things, and they loved competing against their sister platoons and companies. They wanted success, and we gave them success.

At our Grafenwöhr range, I ran exercises meant to get everyone to understand combined arms and how to maneuver under fire. I put all the men in bleachers first and had our S-2 (intelligence officer) wear a Soviet uniform and tell them exactly what the Russians were going to do to them. Then, with the "Soviets units" dug in on a distant ridge line, I sent the companies into action, one company at a time while the others watched from the bleachers.

First, our artillery and mortars came in, huge explosions rocking the area. Then the maneuver started, the engaged company's tanks rumbling up in front of the bleachers and letting loose. Then the infantry in their APCs raced forward, dismounted, and bounded, units leapfrogging each other as they had been taught. All of a sudden the A-10 Warthog ground-support planes roared in under the artillery and mortar arcs, all the fire converging on the enemy positions.

It was a loud, heart-pumping scene. It was also dangerous. We had units moving forward under all that massed live fire. I didn't want anyone to be hurt or killed, but this was the combined arms design I had worked out at Ap Gu and other battles, and I wanted the troops to understand what was meant by "fire and maneuver." I wanted them to have both a visual and a visceral feel for it. When during the company rotations my S-2 in his Soviet uniform came out to brief the men, they booed and jeered; they were fired up. Then the one-star general in charge of the training area showed up and said, "What the hell do you think you're doing out there?" I think he believed that since I had been in Washington with Haig, I must be a political soldier, too. He understood, though, when I told him I would take responsibility for anything that might happen, but this was the way I needed to train my battalion. I was lucky he was a hard trainer himself.

Our regular training regime took us into the field for thirty to forty-five days at a time, which was hard not only on the men but on their wives and families. To address that, we called all the wives in together with the chaplain, the doctor, the commissary officer, and the PX (post exchange) officer to make sure everyone knew the services that were available to them.

Karen took that a long step further. She organized the officers' wives as a support group for all of the American women and children. Many of the enlisted men's wives were quite young, some of them teenagers right out of high school, some not having even finished high school. They could easily feel lost, especially since we didn't have enough housing on base. With the army building up in Europe now, we had more than nine hundred men in the battalion rather than the more typical seven hundred, so quite a few families were living in apartments in the local German community. The wives, some with infants or young children, didn't speak the language and could easily feel isolated and helpless in dealing with whatever problems they might be facing. Karen arranged for the officers' wives to visit every one of the families while the men were away to make sure they and their children were okay and to help with any problems.

Generally speaking, the families were doing well, but of course Karen and her group did find difficulties. Sometimes husbands feared for the safety of wives living off base and told them not to go outside. The fears were unnecessary, but these were youngsters with no experience of foreigners. A few young husbands had strong jealous streaks and took their wives' ID cards so they couldn't go on post, where they might possibly meet someone else. Of course, without ID cards the wives couldn't access the PX, where they did their shopping, which meant if they were running short of necessities, they couldn't get them.

Karen's group—one company's wives called themselves the Mama Bears—found one young woman whose husband had ordered her not to leave the house and who was now panicked about how to feed her baby. The Mama Bears took care of that, but that incident started Karen thinking that family support meant more than responding to problems. With that in mind, the Mama Bears began organizing activities for the wives and kids. Among other things, they chartered a big bus and took the wives out on shopping excursions. At one point, I brought the battalion back from a long field exercise and found the base more or less deserted. Everyone was out on the bus. When they got back, one of the wives asked me, "Colonel, how soon will you be going out again?" There's an army saying: "We enlist soldiers. We reenlist families." Karen proved the truth of that. The battalion had exceptionally high reenlistment rates. Now, forty-five years later, the military has extremely good service organizations that support deployed families, but Karen created a family-support service before the army thought of such a thing.

Along with tough, realistic training, I put a lot of emphasis on the partnerships we had with units from other countries. We needed to be as proficient as possible with our weapons, but it was also essential to understand why we were in Europe. I made a point of conveying that message from the beginning of my command, talking about it, explaining it, giving the men and the wives, too, a feeling for our mission and its importance. Partnering up with other countries' forces showed the soldiers the broader aspect of their mission.

When we trained with the British, Belgians, French, and Germans, it expanded our troops' understanding of why we were in Europe; it exposed them to different ways of doing things. Not least, it built a sense of trust.

The units we trained with were going to be right alongside us if it came to fighting.

We trained with German mechanized-infantry battalions, the so-called Schützenpanzer. Our soldiers liked this training because they could see who their partners were going to be—who would be on the right, who would be on the left. They gained confidence in the professionalism of the German forces and in their equipment. To help cement the bond, we had social activities together. A couple of times a year the Germans would come up to Göppingen, or we would go down to their base at Neu Ulm. My philosophy was that the more a commander could get soldiers to understand the wider environment, the more effective those soldiers were going to be and the more invested each soldier would be in the importance of his or her role. Partnership was a way to reinforce mission, essential not only on the political level but also on the troop level.

Later, when I was a brigade commander, I established a program in which German merchants volunteered to take a few solders for a half day or a day to let them work in their shops. We had soldiers in a *Backeri* baking bread and a *Metzgerei* making sausages. We placed others in a winery and on farms. Our own farm boys loved driving the tractors and helping out with the harvests. When we saw the ongoing friendships these interactions created, I thought it was one of the best things I had ever done. American soldiers and German civilians got to know each other as real people, which greatly contributed to our troops' understanding of why we were there.

We went on field exercises with Canadian and French units as well as with our German partners. We got to know a British elite unit called the Green Jackets, who visited when they passed through Göppingen. Their history went back to American units that fought on the British side during the Revolutionary War, specializing in ambush, fighting from cover like Indians and American frontier militia, and wearing green instead of marching in field order wearing red uniforms like British regulars.

All these relationships were significant as I went up in rank. When I commanded a brigade and then became chief of staff of the Third Infantry Division, they helped cement combat relationships as we faced the Soviets in sometimes volatile circumstances. When I became NATO supreme commander, they were of inestimable value in bringing an end to the Bosnian wars.

In the fall of 1976, I was just finishing a REFORGER (Return of Forces to Germany) exercise with my battalion. REFORGER was the annual exercise bringing NATO forces together to practice the rapid deployment that would be necessary in case of a Warsaw Pact attack. As we were wrapping up, I got a call that General DePuy was at corps headquarters and wanted me to come up and brief him.

After Vietnam, DePuy had gone to the Pentagon as army vice chief of staff; then in 1973 he had been appointed first commander of the army's new Training and Doctrine Command (TRADOC). My former chief Paul Gorman was working with him there, as was my friend Jim Madden.

"I'm in the field with my battalion," I told the caller. "Please tell General DePuy that I have to stay here until we're done with everything." I knew what DePuy's response to that would be; he'd get in a helicopter and come down to see me, which is what he did. I briefed him on what we had done and learned in the REFORGER exercise, spreading out the maps on the hood of my Jeep. Afterward we did what DePuy always did; we walked the line, DePuy stopping to talk to my TOW gunners and others about antitank tactics. As head of TRADOC, DePuy was developing new doctrine that was in the process of transforming the US Army. But here he was, still talking to soldiers about their own jobs and missions.

At TRADOC, DePuy and his staff were formulating and implementing new warfighting procedures for the post-Vietnam army. Many of the army's systems were working poorly. Training was inconsistent and deficient. Procurement systems were antiquated. Weapons needed to be modernized. The wartime system of conscription had been replaced by an all-volunteer army, with all the problems of how to manage this new kind of force. As head of TRADOC, DePuy was the chief architect of a vast restructuring and revitalization of an army that in many ways had been devastated by its experience in Vietnam.

The planners' consensus was that the army needed to turn its focus back to Europe. That was where the chief threat lay, and the debate was about how to defeat the Soviets in Germany, the same problem that had challenged the West for decades. NATO forces were still facing daunting odds in terms of numbers and armor and stood to be crushed by the successive hammer blows the stacked Soviet tank armies could launch. DePuy had been thinking about that from at least as far back as his time as a brigade commander opposite the Fulda Gap, but now he was looking at the problem with new eyes.

The Yom Kippur War between Israel and Egypt in 1973 was a catalyzing event for him. The great surprise of that war was the appearance of new, lethal antitank weapons. The Egyptians had shown that modern infantry armed with guided antitank weapons could inflict massive damage on tank forces. In the first week of the Yom Kippur War, Israeli tank units had suffered severe, demoralizing losses against Arab armies they had always dominated.

DePuy's TRADOC digested this new factor and concluded that it would be possible not just to delay a Soviet advance but also to stop it in its tracks, fix it, then bring enough firepower to bear to destroy it. The problem, as always, was how to do sufficient damage to the successive Soviet tank echelons to prevent the buildup of unbearable pressure on Allied forces.

To address this need, the army was developing and bringing on line a variety of new deep-attack weapons: tactical missile systems, the Apache attack helicopter, precision-guided long-range artillery. Other moderniza- tion was in the pipeline as well, including the Abrams tank, the Bradley Fighting Vehicle, and advanced night-vision equipment that would give us significant tactical advantage.

All of these modernization programs coincided with TRADOC'S development of a new doctrine called "AirLand Battle," which empha- sized close coordination between agile, maneuver-oriented ground forces, on the one hand, and air and deep-attack elements designed to break up follow-on Soviet forces, on the other. DePuy and his successor, Donn Starry, saw the introduction of new doctrine as a lever for rebuilding the US Army according to this vision. DePuy felt that implementing an aggres- sive, offensive-minded, combined-arms warfighting doctrine would help us get the army out of its post-Vietnam doldrums.

In my time as Haig's deputy at SHAPE and as a battalion commander, I saw the bottoming out of the army and a new energy take hold. I felt that I was on the leading edge of the turnaround since I had known and worked for DePuy and Gorman and had been able to anticipate where we were going. They had mentored me years earlier, DePuy from the time I first arrived in Germany. As a result, I was already utilizing the tech- niques they were now infusing into the army at TRADOC.

The US Army had been, as one senior officer put it, "flat on its ass." I gave up my battalion command in the spring of 1977. By then, DePuy's innovations were taking hold. We could already see what the rebuilt army was going to look like.

8

Brigade Commander

I turned over command of the Blue Spaders on April 1, 1977, the anniversary of the battalion's big fight at Ap Gu, which made leaving even more emotional than it ordinarily would have been. I had been selected for the Army War College at Carlisle, Pennsylvania, one of about two hundred lieutenant colonels and colonels in the War College's new class, which included for the first time a number of foreign officers as "international fellows."

The Army War College is an academic training ground for officers the army believes may at some point go on to higher command. The courses focus on strategic understanding, national security issues, leadership, the army's place in society, and other essentials that officers need to function at higher levels of command. The War College had been established by Theodore Roosevelt and his secretary of war, Elihu Root, in 1901. Its alumni included a large proportion of army officers whose careers had brought them to national prominence.

Almost all our class members had led units in Vietnam as well as at least briefly in the difficult postwar environment. Everyone—students and faculty—understood that the army was emerging from the depths, but there was still a lot of uncertainty about where we were going, not only as an army but as a society. We were only two years past the war, and the national conversation was full of assessments and reassessments of how the war had affected the country, what it all meant, and where we were going to go from here. The army was having the same basic discussion. We—my War College class—had fought the war, and now we were being prepared to lead in the postwar period. Lieutenant colonels and colonels now, at least some of us were headed for higher rank. We were going to be the key link in the army's transition.

I had come to Carlisle feeling great about what my battalion had been able to accomplish in Germany, but some of my classmates had had more difficult experiences. Among us there was a common eagerness to discuss what we had experienced. We plunged into classroom debate after debate and discussion after discussion about what the future army should be, how to fix what was broken, and how to refocus as a professional fighting force. We asked ourselves how we should relate the issues we faced as young leaders in Vietnam to the new challenges we were encountering against a more sophisticated and more capable Soviet Union.

Some of the discussion was strictly military: how best to match the necessities for deterrence, or battle, with the available resources; how to manage large formations in open landscapes rather than smaller units in constricted jungles; how to go about achieving clarity of mission, which had been such a vexing problem in Vietnam.

But the war had opened a subject that hadn't been so fraught earlier but was now: What was the relationship between the military and the larger society it was part of? How should the army think about that, and how should it prepare its leadership to engage with a more complex world? The war had created a serious tear in the fabric that knitted together the military and the nation. I had had a front-row seat for that when I was at Loyola. The antiwar movement had targeted not only the war but the military as well and had raised questions that ten years later still hadn't been answered.

The War College responded to this problem in several ways. One was by taking the entire class of two hundred plus officers to New York City for a two-day tour, capped off by an address by the American ambassador to the United Nations. Since I was at the college for two years, I got to go on two of these annual trips and to help organize and run them. These visits were planned to maximize the students' exposure to as many significant areas of New York civilian life as we could squeeze in. We visited financial companies, retail outlets, real estate firms, and media companies. We saw upscale New York and spent time in poor neighborhoods. We wanted the officers not only to see something of how the city worked but also to look at the social needs, so they could understand that when the military pushed for more funding, it had to be extremely well justified. Other social demands—education, housing, health care, and more— were also urgent and were competing for slices of the federal budget. Some of our officers were from poor urban neighborhoods, but others had rarely if ever seen a city like New York. Almost all had been in the army since their late teens or early twenties, and their careers had taken them from base to base, often without much exposure to mainstream life. To some, these trips were nothing short of a revelation.

The college also responded by organizing a series of very well-attended seminars on the military and the media. In the army, a strong current of distrust had arisen in reaction to much of the media reporting about the war. Vietnam had been the first televised war. Clips of firefights and all-out battles were seen by millions of viewers, and how these scenes were interpreted by television newsmen and commentators made all the difference. By the time the war's initial stages were over, many media anchors and leading journalists had concluded the American engagement was a mistake or worse. They laid the onus for failure on both the politicians and the military, which colored their reporting in sometimes momentous ways.

The Tet Offensive of 1968 was a prime example. A disastrous loss for the Communists, the fighting had decimated the Vietcong and nearly ruined its ability to recruit. But the press had portrayed Tet as a demonstration of Communist resilience and power. A month later Lyndon Johnson announced he would not run for a second term. The battle for Khe Sanh was similar, a drawn-out, bloody siege that badly tested the surrounded marines but ended as a graveyard for the better part of an attacking North Vietnamese division. The brutal realities for the isolated and tormented marines were extensively reported, but very little if anything about the debacle the North Vietnamese had suffered.

The military's reputation sustained terrible harm during the war. Its victories went underreported, the occasional atrocities stained its record, the cruel nature of its totalitarian enemy went virtually unnoticed. Two big lessons came out of that. One was the magnified significance of the media's attention and opinions. Another was the significance of the military's role as an institution in national life. To help students understand these realities, the War College invited many journalists and other lecturers to come and speak to us. Following the lectures, we would get together in small groups to discuss the issues in greater detail. That stimulated us to go well beyond the curriculum's emphasis on leadership, tactics, and other military subjects to explore the broader aspects of the army's role in society and the forces, such as the media, that affected it.

The media course helped us recognize the essential importance of reaching out, particularly to young people, to discuss the war and to create dialogue and understanding about the military's place in the country's life. One result was that the War College formed the Current Affairs Panel. Five of us were selected for the panel. We traveled all over the country, speaking at colleges and universities. There were powerful residual feelings about the war at many of these institutions, not only among students but among faculty. The questions we fielded were often blunt, but even though some of the discussions were charged, they were almost always respectful, nothing at all like the shouting and jeering that marked events during the war years.

I took these presentations as occasions to put back on my professor's hat from Loyola and talk to students about the function of the military and its role as an integral and essential part of national life as well as about their own obligations, not necessarily to join the army or navy but to find a way to give back to their communities, to their country. That was an important responsibility, I told them. That might not have been a controversial message, but I don't think it was one university students heard very often.

My classmates on the panel gave responses that came out of their own experiences. The five of us were from different branches—infantry, armor, and so on. Two of us, David Maddox and I, eventually became four-star generals. Later in his career Maddox took over the army's European Command. Cal Waller rose to three-star rank (lieutenant general); he was Norman Schwarzkopf's deputy in the Gulf War. I think each of us considered that speaking to these student and faculty audiences was an eye-opening, important part of our education as commanders. These tours took us to every section of the country. In the South, Cal Waller, who was African American, sometimes drew special attention. Our usual format was that the five of us, in uniform, would sit in a row up on stage. A faculty person would open the evening, then we would introduce ourselves. One of our stops was the University of Mississippi in Oxford. "Ole Miss," as it was affectionately called, had been a bastion of white supremacy until James Meredith integrated it in the early 1960s in a series of events that brought the school national attention.

Meredith's initial application was rejected, even though he was highly qualified and a retired air force sergeant. It took a Supreme Court decision in 1962 for the university to agree with great reluctance to admit Meredith, and even then Mississippi's governor, Ross Barnet, intervened to stop him from enrolling. In the end, Attorney General Robert Kennedy mobilized the Mississippi National Guard and sent them with federal troops to stop the rioting by students and other protestors.

Two people were killed in the melee, though not by the army. When Meredith graduated, he was still being protected by military units. A few years later, in 1966, he was wounded in an assassination attempt while he was on a freedom walk to the Mississippi state capital.

We were there fifteen years after these events, but racial tension hadn't disappeared either in Mississippi or at the university. On the stage that evening, Cal stood out. There was a lot of murmuring coming from the audience. Cal was big; he looked like a football player. I think he *was* a football player. When his turn to introduce himself came, the tension level was rising. "You know," he told the crowd, "I had an offer to come to the University of Mississippi." He paused. Cal was a jovial guy; there was a big smile on his face. "They offered me an athletic scholarship."

This wasn't likely. There were still very few black athletes at the school. Back when Cal graduated high school, no black kid had ever stepped over the Ole Miss threshold. The room was hushed.

"Yes," said Cal. "I had an offer to be the designated javelin catcher." Today that remark would be inappropriate, to say the best for it. Back then it was hilarious. I almost fell off my chair. The audience completely broke up. The tension disappeared, and we got on with the evening.

After the event, the five of us went back to our rooms, changed into casual clothes, and went out to dinner with our faculty host. At the restaurant, we were seated at a round table looking at our menus and talking about how the presentation had gone. At some point, I noticed that three older men at another table were staring at us, at Cal specifically. We all stopped to look back. I could sense Cal getting a little uneasy.

"Cal," I said. "I'm going to go talk to those guys."

"No," he said, "I'll handle it."

Cal walked over to the table. The three guys looked like crusty old-time farmers.

"Lieutenant Colonel Calvin Waller, United States Army," Cal said, introducing himself. "Nice to meet you. It's a pleasure to be here in this great town. I'm here talking to the students at the University of Mississippi."

Well, that diffused the tension. Instead of confrontation, there was interaction. "Exactly," I thought. "You don't just sit there fuming and wringing your hands. You take it on." And that was Cal. He no doubt had experienced a lot of this kind of thing in his life. He knew how to manage.

Toward the end of my year as a student at the War College, I was promoted to full colonel, and my name was included in the brigade-command list, although a slot wasn't going to open up for a year. Carlisle was a stimulating experience, but I was eager to get back to soldiering. I could have gone to a staff assignment, but that wouldn't be getting back to the troops. I had to decide what to do.

The War College solved my problem by offering me a one-year faculty appointment. That seemed perfect. I loved teaching, and being an instructor would give me the opportunity not just to teach whatever curriculum subject was required but to design a course around a topic I felt would be essential for upcoming officers, something that would get them thinking about tough subjects like clarity of mission and moral courage.

Almost nine years earlier, the War College had circulated an in-depth analysis of the state of the US Army, commissioned by then army chief of staff William Westmoreland. When the study was released, I was a student at the Fort Leavenworth Command and General Staff College, thinking hard about my first combat tour in Vietnam. The *Study on Military Professionalism* painted a troubling picture. Based on wide-ranging interviews with officers from every branch, it described an institutional climate characterized by a lack of moral courage and commanders' unwillingness to listen to subordinates or take opposing points of view into account. That hadn't been my experience, but I knew I had been exceptionally lucky in the commanders I had.

In 1970, the year the study was published, the army was well into its withdrawal from Vietnam. Morale was headed downhill. Officers then were involved in combat situations, where there was always the incentive to hide their mistakes and embellish their accomplishments. At the same time, officers as well as soldiers were affected by the desire not to be the last man killed in a war we were leaving. People were anxious about what was next, where their careers might be going in that climate. The times weren't conducive to standing up and accepting accountability.

That was then. Now we were completely out of Vietnam, an army recovering from its low point. Officers now had opportunities to look forward to instead of the uncertain prospects they faced back then. So what was the prevailing state of the officer corps now? Where did we stand now in relation to where we stood nine years earlier? I thought it would be fascinating to repeat Westmoreland's study, to see what, if anything, had shifted, knowing that the project would reveal to my students and others—future leaders—some of the problems that required addressing. And whatever we might find, the process itself would focus my seminar class on the central importance of moral courage in a commander's life. The *Study on Military Professionalism* was classified confidential, but I got permission to use it for a seminar project that would duplicate it. "This is what I want to do," I told the department head. "The study is nine years old. We need to know where we stand today."

This was going to be a large undertaking, but the seminar members took to it enthusiastically and got to work. They put together questionnaires, duplicating the questions the previous study had used. They distributed these questionnaires at the same institutions—the same war colleges and career courses—the previous study had surveyed. I also wanted to include the NCOs, so we sent it out to the Sergeants Major Academy as well.

I don't know if I was exactly shocked when we reviewed the answers we got, but I was surprised. The results of the 1970 survey and ours were very similar. One finding that particularly stood out was that the officers in our study were very hard on their commanders for the same deficiency the officers nine years earlier had been. They didn't think their senior leadership had the moral courage to stand up and be counted on tough issues.

The results led to a series of long, in-depth discussions in the seminar. Could we assign reasons for what we had found? Given all the differences between the US Army then and the US Army now, did the same results suggest the problem of moral courage was systemic, that officers were always going to find their leaders lacking in this regard, whatever the circumstances?

These issues had been on my mind a long time. I believed that moral courage was the bedrock of who we were as the military of a democratic political system. My position was that we officers owe it to our senior leaders, military and political, to give clear military advice. We need to have clarity of mission in order to be successful. To achieve clarity of mission, we have to be able to question our superiors' judgments. We have to be willing to stand up and be counted on tough issues. We have to have the personal wherewithal to question and assert our judgment, whether in the end that judgment is accepted or not.

That's a large part of having moral courage. Officers need that, and we need to figure out ways to assert our judgment effectively.

As subordinates, we need to be proactive, not reactive. We can't ask questions and provide advice after we have gone into a situation; we have to do that before we go in. The other side of the coin, just as significant, is that as leaders we need to be open to input from our subordinates. Disagreement is not disloyalty, any more in the military than it is in politics. Once a decision is made, everybody must be on the same team. But differing opinions need to be welcomed, not shut off.

The seminar members were midlevel officers, a year or so behind me, but doing similar things. They were on track to be future leaders. I told the class: "We need to incorporate these principles in the way we function. They have to be part of our kit bag going forward. Many of us are going on to brigade and division command. I hope someone does this same survey ten years from now and that we'll see different responses then."

At the end of the seminar, pretty much all of the students came up to tell me how much insight they got out of this exercise. We then briefed our study to all the other seminars. The reaction of the entire class was strongly positive. These issues resonated with them.

For me, Carlisle was a watershed. The school allowed me a period of reflection on the thread that connected my experiences from second lieutenant on. It gave me a chance to sharpen my thoughts about where I was going. As students, we had to write about national security strategy and lay out what we believed to be the priorities of our national interests. This was a cathartic exercise for us because we were able to talk with complete candor about the issues that were uppermost in our minds, from Vietnam to our latest assignments. Then we had to offer solutions about how to fix what was wrong. This was where my thoughts about the need for a clear strategy and doctrine began to take shape. It gave me the opportunity to pull together the ideas and beliefs I had accumulated over the sixteen years of my career.

Carlisle was important in other ways, too. Many of the friendships I made there lasted through my career and beyond. At Carlisle, we lived together, close in. We had social functions and sports teams. I got to know and exchange ideas with peers who were going to be part of the army for another twenty or more years, some of them in the highest leadership positions. Six of us in our War College class made four-star rank: Gordon Sullivan, Binnie Peay, Dave Maddox, Gary Luck, John Shalikashvili, and me. Cal Waller was promoted to three-star rank. Our experience at Carlisle was a bond. We all agreed that the army had to focus on mission and that this mission focus would come through doctrine. At the War College, we examined and argued out these issues together.

It would take another several years before AirLand Battle doctrine, embodied in the new *Operations Field Manual* (FM 100-5), would have a full impact on the way the US Army functioned in everything from training to planning to warfighting strategy and tactics. It was this War College class that carried that doctrine through and transformed the army from what it was in Vietnam to a modernized force focused on deterrence in Europe, setting the army's compass for the next fifteen or twenty years.

In June 1979, my year teaching at Carlisle was up, and I took command of the Second Brigade, Third Infantry Division, in Kitzingen, Germany, the same "Rock of the Marne" division I started with as a second lieutenant in 1961.

The very first thing I did was call in the brigade command sergeant major to let him know about my training expectations and to get the lay of the land from his perspective. "Your experience is what we have to build on," I told him, just as a battalion doing physical training ran by my open window. I jumped out the window to join them; Command Sergeant Major Ramirez jumped out with me. That was my introduction to my new troops.

The great challenge for the Second Brigade was that of its four battalions, two were in Kitzingen, one was based sixty miles away in Wildflecken, and the fourth was one hundred miles away in Augsburg. Getting the brigade focused on training and mission was similar to what I did as a battalion commander, except that with four battalions scattered all around Germany, the task was more of a challenge. The most effective tool for helping the brigade achieve mission focus was the so-called General Defense Plan. This was the war plan that told each unit where it would go in the event of a Soviet attack and how it was expected to fight in the opening hours and days. The intent was that we would know the terrain intimately, far better than the Soviets, which would give the defense its biggest advantage. Each unit, right down to platoon and squad levels, had a battle book that provided terrain analysis, battle positions, artillery targets, and minefields marked on maps. The prerequisite here was to master the terrain. To ensure that mastery, my commanders regularly took leaders and troops on hikes and terrain walks so that they knew every hill, every depression, every road, and every trail.

Each soldier needed to know exactly what to do and where to go on day one of a conflict. As a result of this focus, both leaders and troops knew the territory, and the mission was always front and center in their minds.

My brigade's sector extended north to the town of Coburg, famous as a vacation spot for nineteenth-century European crowned heads. Queen Victoria's husband, Prince Albert, had been born there, and his family was linked with much of Europe's royalty. Coburg was a beautiful, picturesque place. The city had sustained little damage in World War II, so its many historic buildings going back to the sixteenth and seventeenth centuries gave it a classical German look. But Coburg was located smack on the border with East Germany. My brigade's position was southwest of there, on the Main River, a hundred or so kilometers away. That meant we would be giving up substantial territory at the very beginning of a fight. I saw no reason we should do that.

When we opened up the map and did the analysis of Soviet strategy and deployment, it seemed clear that few Soviet divisions would come straight at us through the Meiningen Gap. Most would instead come through the Fulda Gap to our northeast. If they came through Fulda, they would have an exposed flank, which would give us an opportunity to counterattack. If we and our NATO allies were going to conduct a defense at Fulda, no matter how agile we were, we were going to take a pounding. Instead of sitting back in defense, then, why not attack?

As I developed that idea, I asked and received permission to move my area of the General Defense Plan so that it could cover Coburg more easily. When we did that, the mayor of Coburg gave us a plaque of appreciation. Under our initial war plan, he feared his city would have been abandoned.

My counterattack proposal caused some anxiety in the army. Any talk about crossing the border was politically volatile. General Frederick Kroesen Jr., head of the US Army in Europe (USAEUR), had heard about my planning and came for a briefing on what I had in mind. I showed him on the map that there was a salient on the east side of the Fulda Gap and that our intelligence was telling us that the Soviets would fill that salient with artillery and supplies in support of their main thrust through Fulda.

Our troops defending the gap would be subject to heavy flanking fire. My plan in the event of a Soviet assault was for a brigade attack along the shelf of the Werra River that would cut that salient off and hit into the flank of the Soviet main attack. "Why can't we nip that salient off and cut off the Soviets' artillery and supply?" I asked Kroesen. I called the plan "Nip the Nipple."

For years, the US Army wasn't thinking outside the box, so to speak; all the planning in Europe had been devoted to building the most effective defense we could. "But should we not," I asked Kroesen, "anticipate and at least plan for a counterattack if the conditions are right rather than just sitting there and taking a punch?" Kroesen was intrigued and told me to continue my planning but not to trigger anything without his permission, whatever the circumstances.

If we weren't going to counterattack, we had an excellent defense plan in place. But my favored option was counterattack, and that is how we trained.

Counterattack was what I wanted the brigade to be very skilled at. The troops loved it. I learned when I was a battalion commander how important it was to be able to go on the offensive; it made a great difference in the troops' enthusiasm for the mission. So in the REFORGER exercise in 1980, we put all our effort into attack. In the course of the exercise, we launched five night attacks against a cavalry regiment playing the Red forces. By that time, we were getting good night-vision equipment, and I wanted to demonstrate our attack capabilities and show that the night was ours, not the enemy's.

Moving at night is difficult, even with night-vision goggles. My experience in Vietnam was that whenever we stopped for a brief rest during night movements, soldiers would fall asleep. On our first REFORGER night attack, I noticed that the company I was with had no NCOs assuring security. Command Sergeant Major Ramirez grabbed a senior NCO, took him to the back of the line, and told him, "Every time the column stops, you start walking forward. Make sure the men are oriented properly, one pointed this way, one that, so that we've got alternating fire. And make sure everybody gets up as soon as we start moving!" Ramirez's Spanish was better than his English, which made him a little self-conscious, but he was a hard-driving soldier who was responsible for making the NCOs into the backbone of the brigade. I had great respect for him, especially since I remembered all too well the deteriorated state of the NCO corps after Vietnam, which was largely responsible for the lack of discipline and even some of the racial conflict.

Most of the lessons I took away from the brigade command reinforced what I had learned from my company and battalion commands as well as from my stay at Carlisle. I was, if anything, more attuned to the importance of the commander's personality in how a command functions. A good commander doesn't have to be everybody's buddy; I was a tough trainer and set a high bar for discipline. But at the same time a good commander must be accessible and must value feedback in order to instill trust and confidence. The more commanders have a human touch with their troops and leaders, the more they will listen as well as talk. If commanders are willing to accept blame and take the heat for their own errors, that sense of responsibility will permeate their command.

At the brigade level, I was especially conscious of the need to take a serious interest in the well-being of wives and families. I did this at the battalion level, where Karen and her Mama Bears had done so much to support the women and children. I did that here, too, on a larger scale. But our brigade units were spread out over three cities, and our challenge was to create a sense of unity among the families as well as among the fighting men. On this occasion, too, Karen and the other officers' wives were extraordinary.

Karen understood the need for unit cohesion as thoroughly as I did, and the women organized family-support groups in each of the battalions. In my former battalion, we had had the highest reenlistment rate in

Europe. We achieved that in our brigade as well. A brigade commander is responsible for the proficiency and combat readiness of the command, but he's also the caretaker of a large community. Schools have to be important to him, as do medical facilities and recreational opportunities. A great unit is one that is tactically and technically proficient, has great cohesion, and feels good about itself, its leaders, and its families. That was what we aimed for in the Second Brigade, Third Infantry Division, and it gave me great satisfaction to note our successes.

Another lesson the brigade command emphasized was the significance of multinational operations. I had seen this when I was a lieutenant with a platoon, then again when I was a captain commanding a company, and yet again when I was a lieutenant colonel running a battalion. In each of these situations, I found myself working with allied partners.

Defending western Europe would simply not be possible without these partners, which meant that America's own security was at stake as well. Americans have a tendency to think that they are the only players in the game. It's a prejudice that doesn't match reality. My own experience was that we learn from our allies. I began understanding how to read a battlefield when I was liaison with the German Second Corps just months after I first arrived in Germany in the early 1960s. Later I saw the Germans employing a reverse-slope defense—that is, digging in on the reverse slope of a hill that may come under attack and thus sheltering troops from heavy artillery barrages and waiting to ambush attackers as they crest the hill. The Germans had been doing this long before we knew the phrase *reverse-slope defense* in the US Army.

The difference now in working with allied partners was scope. Situations I had participated in at the company and battalion level, I now saw through a wider lens that emphasized the significance of joint action. Our partners—Germans, Belgians, French, and others—employed different tactics, techniques, and procedures. I learned from them. I also saw the problems in joint maneuvers more distinctly. Equipment differences were a special frustration. Our combat field radio, for example, couldn't completely interface with the Germans' radio. At the brigade level, I also saw with more immediacy the need to harmonize NATO operational doctrine with US doctrine. If you were organizing to fight, you would want to know that the units on your right and left have the same general orientation you have.

After two years commanding my brigade, I was called up to be chief of staff of the Third Division. The Third Division's commander, Major

General Fred Mahaffey, was an unusual individual, one of the brightest officers I had ever known. Brilliant, easy to get along with, courageous—he had won three Silver Stars as a battalion commander in Vietnam—he had all the prerequisites for higher command.

Mahaffey was a born leader. When I worked for him, he was forty-seven years old. By the time he was fifty-one, he had risen to four-star rank, one of the youngest full generals in US Army history. He was considered a potential choice for army chief of staff or for chairman of the Joint Chiefs of Staff, but his career was cut short by cancer that was diagnosed when he was commander in chief of the army's Readiness Command. In college at the University of Denver, he had been an All-American running back. On the far side of forty, he was still nimble and agile in his movements. His early death was a great loss, mourned by the army but especially by those of us who knew him.

Mahaffey had worked with DePuy in the army vice chief of staff's office and was highly attuned to the transformation the AirLand Battle doctrine was effecting throughout the army. For Vietnam, the army had been tailored as an infantry force. But during the years the army's attention was on that task, the Soviets had been modernizing and bulking up their armored forces in Europe. The urgent need to switch gears in order to counter their buildup had led to the development of new weapons systems, some of which had begun to flow into Europe when I was a battalion commander. Now, in 1981, the Third Division was receiving shipments of the new Abrams M-1 battle tank and the Bradley Fighting Vehicle, the first unit in Europe to field these weapons.

The challenge was to bring the new equipment into service, with all the training necessary, and to maintain a high level of readiness at the same time. Both the Abrams and the Bradley as well as other equipment we were receiving were sophisticated systems. They employed new weapons and munitions as well as new sensory and aiming mechanisms; their capabilities dictated changes in the way we would fight. New equipment training could take a year, and units going through the training would be at low levels of fighting readiness. While I was Third Division chief of staff, we developed a highly detailed campaign plan that would get us through the training rigorously but also quickly.

By 1982, I felt the units I had been serving in were ahead of the power curve of the army's transformation. By that time, too, the army was well advanced in institutionalizing methods of organizing and fighting that we in our units had already been doing. I felt that was a sort of validation of what I had done as battalion and brigade commander and now as the Third Division's chief of staff. I was eager to go from the Third's chief of staff to assistant division commander, which I knew could very possibly be my next assignment.

General Mahaffey and I were briefing European commander General Kroesen in the Third Division war room when an aide came in saying that I had a phone call. My first thought was, "Why is he interrupting me in the middle of a meeting like this? Is there some family emergency?"

"It's General Vessey," the aide said. "He wants to talk to you."

General John Vessey was vice chief of staff of the army, but the word was that newly elected President Ronald Reagan was going to appoint him chairman of the Joint Chiefs of Staff.

Both Mahaffey and Kroesen looked at me. "George," Kroesen said, "take the call."

I knew Vessey only by reputation. I had never worked with him or even met him. It wasn't clear what he might be calling me about, but once I was on the line, he got right to the point.

"I'm being appointed chairman," he said. "I'd like you to come to Washington as my XO."

My immediate instinct was to decline the offer. "Sir," I told him, "normally for an XO you want someone who's worked with you, who knows your habits and the way you like things done. I don't think I'm that person. I'm very happy here with the division, and I'd really like to try to finish what we're doing. I think I'm making a difference here."

"Well," Vessey said, "I understand that. But why don't you come to Washington, and we can talk about it?"

9

The Chairman's XO

I was pretty sure what was going to happen once I got to Washington. But I really did want to stay with Mahaffey and the division, and General Vessey's aide, Bill Nash, was well suited to take on the executive officer's job. He knew Vessey's likes and dislikes; he knew his work habits. He was an armor officer who understood tactics. He was devoted to Vessey. He would make an excellent XO for him. I was going to reiterate my desire to stay in Europe, and I would make an argument for Nash, but I also knew Vessey wouldn't have me fly over unless he had more or less made up his mind already.

When I landed, Vessey brought me up to his quarters at Fort McNair. We had dinner, then sat out in his sunroom overlooking the Anacostia River. I told him where we stood with the Third Division in Germany and why I thought I should stay there. I told him again that he really needed someone who knew him well, knew how he worked and how best to facilitate that. I mentioned Nash. None of what I said had any noticeable effect.

"I have it on good authority that you know Washington," he said. "That would be extremely helpful to me. I know your field record. I've also heard you're not reluctant to give candid advice. I want someone I can count on for that. You come highly recommended. Besides, it's only for two years. I've told Avis [his wife] it won't be more than that; she wants to go back to Minnesota."

I had been through this kind of thing before. There really isn't much you can do. Whatever you might want, you think about your commitment to serve, and in the end you salute. Besides, even though I would have liked to stay in Germany, this was a highly interesting opportunity. Vessey's influence was going to be central to what was developing in Europe. He also hinted that I had been selected for brigadier general, and the XO position was a brigadier slot. "I want you to come with me," he said. "I think you can help." So I saluted. Then I went back to Germany to close up my work with the division, and while I was there, General Mahaffey told me he had in fact been planning to assign me as his assistant division commander. That would have been a great assignment. But you can't look back, and by then I was eagerly anticipating working with Vessey.

I had also learned more about Vessey in the interim. When he was sixteen years old, he had enlisted in the National Guard as a motorcycle driver, then had fought through North Africa in World War II, receiving a battlefield commission at Anzio. Like DePuy, he knew warfighting from the ground up. One telling situation had taken place when Vessey commanded US forces in Korea in the late 1970s. Apparently, President Jimmy Carter was planning to appoint him army chief of staff, but when he interviewed Vessey, the president told him he intended to withdraw troops from Korea. Vessey told Carter that he opposed the idea, that in his view our forces provided stability as a hedge against whatever might eventuate from an unpredictable, aggressive North Korea and against any attempt by either China or the Soviets to build influence inside South Korea.

That rang the death knell for Vessey's appointment as army chief. Carter instead selected General Edward "Shy" Meyer, a much younger man. Then Carter offered Vessey the vice chief's position, under Meyer, and Vessey agreed. Nobody expected him to do that; most senior generals would not have, but Vessey was such a soldier. Taking that job under Meyer said a lot about him and sent a strong signal across the army—a message about the obligation to serve, which he did, and it wasn't always easy. Shy Meyer could be volatile at times, and Vessey was on the receiving end of some of that, but he served. When Davy Jones retired as chairman of the Joint Chiefs in late June, President Ronald Reagan appointed Vessey to succeed him.

I became Vessey's XO on day one of his tenure. During our earlier discussion in Washington, Vessey had said all the right things, but we hadn't discussed any of the details of his plans or what he might be expecting of me. With my experience at the White House and at SHAPE, I understood something about how high-level staff ought to work, but I knew the first order of business was to understand Vessey's thinking. I had seen enough to know that a subordinate, however experienced he might be, shouldn't try to impose everything he might think on a principal. If a subordinate wants to be good at the job, he will work to understand the principal's priorities and try to figure out how he can best help get the principal where he wants to go.

To Vessey's credit, he understood what I needed. He didn't just leave me to figure things out for myself. We sat down together in front of an easel with butcher paper. "Let me tell you where I think we're going," he said, and he began to sketch what he wanted to do and his philosophy behind it. After two or three pages, I didn't have any doubt about his priorities. He was thinking first about the CINCs, the commanders in chief of forward-deployed combat forces in the world's various regions. "The staff here," he said, "support the CINCs. That's their role. Every time a CINC comes into town, I want to be able to see him. I want you to make that happen. This is an open door for them."

He wanted to build trust and confidence with the chiefs. He wanted my advice whenever we found ourselves in situations where that could help him. "You're not just an aide," he said. "I'm going to count on you for that advice." He wanted me to set up a rotation with the chiefs of service—the army, navy, air force, and marine chiefs—so that when he traveled, which would be often, one or the other would serve as acting chairman, so there would be uninterrupted continuity. "It's your job to set up a rotation," he said. "Establish a duty roster for them."

"A duty roster for all those four-stars," I thought. I was still a colonel, and I was going tell these guys what they were supposed to do. An interesting thought. "Boss," I said, "you're putting me in a tough situation."

"Don't worry about it," he said. "You'll know how to make it work."

The chairman of the Joint Chiefs is the principal military adviser to the president, the secretary of defense, and the National Security Council (NSC). When it came to affecting national security policy and strategy, Vessey could best make his influence felt in his daily 11:30 meeting with Secretary of Defense Caspar Weinberger and in his attendance at NSC meetings. The clearer the military advice the chairman could give, the greater the chance to achieve political clarity.

The prerequisite was to enable the chairman to give the clearest possible advice, and that meant organizing staff work effectively to support the chairman's objectives. To do that we established a staff operations and intelligence briefing each morning where Vessey could give guidance to the staff and debrief them on his meetings with the secretary of defense, the NSC, and the CINCs.

I also set up a quarterly "duty roster" for the chiefs to rotate as acting chairmen when Vessey was away. That meant organizing schedules a year in advance so that a chief knew he would be acting chairman for a particular quarter and thus would be able to coordinate his schedule with the chairman's. In the past, when the chairman was away, the XO would have to contact all the chiefs to find someone who could temporarily take over. That approach was haphazard, and if there was an emergency, it could be nerve wracking.

The chiefs joked about the "duty roster" business, and they bitched and moaned about being forced into it, but the fact was that they came to enjoy the role. More important, they learned from it. Vessey intended the arrangement not just as a way of covering his absences but as a strategy. It was one of the best things he did. Each quarter an acting chairman would have the opportunity to meet with Weinberger and with the NSC. I would bring the staff in to brief the acting chairman before those meetings to make sure he was well versed on Vessey's positions. At those times, the chief involved would become a *joint* chief. He would see that these national and international issues didn't involve just his particular service; his job was to speak for the entire armed services.

Vessey made it clear to the chiefs in this and other ways that they were not simply representing their own services. They needed to think what was best for the military as a whole, not just for the army or navy or air force or marines. Given the long history of fierce, often intractable intraservice rivalries, this task wasn't easy. Thinking like that didn't come naturally to them; they had to be conditioned to it.

Vessey was bent on making his point understood. When we started talking about weapons systems and funding allocations, everyone couldn't have everything they wanted. The chiefs needed to look at decisions in terms of what was in the best interest of the entire military rather than of each one's particular service. We urgently needed to have a cooperative rather than a confrontational approach. The joint part, the "purple part," as we put it, was essential, and the chiefs had to learn to think in those terms. That was the point Vessey was striving to make. And the change in thinking did happen. After a year or two of this, the chiefs became far more accustomed to taking a joint perspective. They understood the wider view of "what's best for the country, what's best for all the services." That hardly meant that all the rivalry went away; budget decisions were a zero-sum game, adversarial by nature, with every chief trying to protect and expand his share of the pie. But under Vessey the chiefs became much better at complementing rather than fighting one another.

Every morning when both were in town, Vessey would meet with Secretary of Defense Weinberger in Weinberger's office. Vessey took the assistant to the chairman with him. When I first came to work with Vessey, the assistant was my former battalion commander Paul Gorman, who had just left TRADOC, which gave me some inkling of where Vessey had come up with the idea to tap me as his XO. The other attendee was General Colin Powell, Weinberger's military assistant. They would sit around a table and discuss key issues, including the NSC agenda for its next meeting.

In order to make these meetings substantive, I provided Vessey with a three-by-five card with key points to discuss. Afterward I would get Gorman to debrief me and the staff so that we would have continual communication and everyone would be on exactly the same page in terms of the chairman's needs. In a large organization, sometimes the troops don't understand clearly; they're drilling away, thinking they're working on the right things, when in fact they're not. I wanted to make sure the staff's energies were harnessed together and focused on the same goals.

With their daily meetings, Weinberger and Vessey were almost always in close sync regarding their views. They also hit it off extremely well personally. The result was that they would go into NSC meetings and speak with one voice on issues, which meant they were often able to wield significant influence on political decisions. Ordinarily at these meetings, the CIA director would give an intelligence update; then Secretary of State George Schultz would review current diplomatic issues. Then Secretary Weinberger would speak, after which he would turn to Vessey for his presentation. We tried to make sure that Vessey was provided with all the information he needed regarding whatever issues were being discussed, along with maps and charts that would illustrate possible courses of action.

President Reagan liked visual aids, so he often focused on them. In one NSC meeting, the issue was a possible deployment of troops in Iran. We made a map for Vessey that showed the distances, routes, and timelines for getting troops into that region. We determined that it would take months to transport a sizeable force—which was borne out later during the first Gulf War. Vessey was able to show this map to the president. That was clear military advice about the challenge of getting a force into the Middle East. You can't beam troops into Iran. You need time. You need a buildup; you need air and sealift. The president looked at Vessey and Weinberger. "You mean it's going to take that long? Months?" Vessey wasn't saying we didn't want to do the mission; he was providing clear military advice to help shape a correct decision. But after that there was no more talk about going into Iran.

On October 14, 1983, Maurice Bishop, the Marxist prime minister of the island nation of Grenada, was overthrown by a harder-line Marxist group within his own party. He was arrested and several days later executed by firing squad. Grenada had been a British protectorate until 1974 and was still part of the commonwealth; Paul Scoon, the British governor-general, was placed under house arrest at the same time Bishop was arrested, although he wasn't harmed.

The Reagan administration had been watching Grenadan developments for some time. Under Bishop, the Grenadans were building a new airport with an especially long runway, capable of handling the biggest Soviet military transports. Bishop had been close to Fidel Castro—as was the coup leader, Bernard Coard—and six hundred plus Cuban engineers and construction personnel were working on the airport project.

Bishop had signed military agreements with the Soviet Union and North Korea, and in the opinion of some analysts Grenada was setting up to be used as a transshipment point for weapons bound for Angola, Nicaragua, and El Salvador. A wild-card factor was that eight hundred American medical students were studying at Grenada's St. George's University Medical School. The chaos in Grenada was exacerbated when coup leader Coard was arrested and replaced by an army general, who declared a shoot-to-kill curfew. The administration felt that in such a violent, unstable situation the students were in danger. The Iran Hostage Crisis had ended only two years earlier.

After Bishop's execution and the ensuing unrest and violence, the Organization of Eastern Caribbean States asked the Reagan administration to intervene and restore order. These states feared that an aggressive Communist regime linked to Cuba and to revolutionary movements in Nicaragua and El Salvador with weaponry supplied by the Soviets and North Koreans would pose a serious threat to their own stability.

Reagan and Secretary Schultz agreed, and planning quickly got under way for an invasion.

The invasion plan, put together by the Atlantic Command under Admiral Wesley L. McDonald, went through several iterations before the Joint Chiefs approved it. At the meeting where Reagan gave his final approval, Vessey was away, and Admiral James Watkins was the acting chairman. The meeting was held on Sunday, October 23, a day of explosive pressure. Just hours earlier in Beirut, a truck loaded with explosives had crashed into the US Marine barracks at the Lebanon Airport, killing many marines.

The initial count was more than a hundred. There was no doubt it would go much higher.

I picked Watkins up at his residence and briefed him about what to expect regarding Grenada. I updated him on the students, whom we believed were in jeopardy, and on the Cuban "engineers" on the island. We had video of a man in civilian clothes getting off a plane from Cuba and being greeted by the Cubans, all of whom saluted him. We believed he was a high-level colonel sent to organize a defense (he did, and he did it well). The construction people, we were fairly certain, were soldiers, combat engineers. "Given what's happened in Beirut," I told Watkins, "the president may think he doesn't need another large number of casualties right now. He may want to postpone an invasion. But we need a decision now in order to be able to go in on Tuesday." If we were going to do this, we had to do it quickly to avoid any leaks, which would jack up the chances that the Grenadans might round up the students as hostages.

When Watkins came out of the meeting with the president, he told me President Reagan had approved the plan. Given the circumstances, it was a courageous presidential decision. We had taken a major blow in Beirut; the anguish about the loss of so many young marines was palpable. In Grenada, we faced the possibility of losing more people, but Reagan was convinced this was something that had to be done.

With the signal to go, the war plan went into effect. It was complex, and there was a great deal we didn't know about what to expect. There were no detailed maps available. Later, when Weinberger and Vessey briefed the press, we couldn't find one until someone came up with a gas station tourist map. We cut it out, mounted it on a white poster board, and that was the map they used to brief the press and the nation. The invasion plan included army Ranger battalions, SEALs, Delta Force operators, air force units, and elements of the Eighty-Second Airborne. Their objectives were to take the old airfield, the new airfield under construction, the British governor-general's house, where Scoon was being held, neutralize the Cubans, and find and safeguard the students. Lots of elements and lots of units that hadn't trained for such an operation and had never worked together.

The evening before the invasion, Vessey's J-3 operations chief invited Weinberger and other senior security people to a briefing at 5:30 a.m. so they could have a real-time view of events as they unfolded. When Vessey heard that, he cancelled the invitations. "I'll be in at 0800 as usual," he said. "They can come then." He didn't want anyone interfering with the operation. There were many elements in play, any one of which could go wrong, and he didn't want anyone, the secretary of defense or anyone else, interfering. "Let the commander do his job," he said.

In fact, a lot did go wrong. Members of SEAL Team Six were being sent in surreptitiously the night before the operation to invest the new airfield and set beacons for the Rangers to drop the next day. In the dark, they parachuted into heavy seas, and four drowned. The rest of the SEALs piled into a Zodiac rubber boat, whose engine refused to start, and they had to be picked up by rescue craft. They were sent back the next day, which put a crimp in the timing, but they weren't able to make it ashore then either. The marines, though, helicoptered in and took the old airfield against scant resistance.

The Ranger drop on the airfield under construction didn't quite go as planned, either. The lead air force plane carrying the Rangers missed its glide path, but the Ranger captain, John Abizaid—my cadet company commander when I was a West Point tac officer—told the pilot, "Come around, we're going to drop. But we're dropping at five hundred feet instead of twelve hundred." The Cuban colonel had organized quad and antiaircraft guns on the high ground above the airport. They peppered the Rangers as they parachuted, but jumping at such a low altitude saved many lives. The Rangers' parachutes were full of holes, but they didn't lose anyone. Had they jumped at twelve hundred feet, the story would have been different. On the ground, Abizaid secured the airfield against two armored vehicles that had rolled up to attack the Rangers on the ground and those still in the air. Putting the vehicles out of commission, the Rangers then stormed the high ground, driving a bulldozer at the front of their charge. Before long, that fight was over, too.

From there, two companies of Rangers headed for the Medical School to rescue the students, taking fire from the hilltops and frustrated because they couldn't talk directly to the marine attack-helicopter pilots. It turned out the marine and Ranger radios operated on different frequencies. General Norman Schwarzkopf had been pulled out of his division command to take up a position aboard a navy ship off Grenada with army radio equipment so that he could make sure army and navy could talk to each other. It was a clunky fix for an astonishing problem.

While the Rangers were herding Cuban prisoners onto the tarmac and heading to the Medical School, a SEAL unit fast-roped down onto the governor-general's house and rescued Scoon, his wife, and the staff. But the Grenadan army attacked the house and pinned down the SEALs. During this fight, two marine Cobra helicopters were shot down, and the SEALs found their radios couldn't communicate with the C-130 gunships circling the area.

It took another couple of days before all the resistance collapsed. By the time the operation was over, we had suffered nineteen killed and more than one hundred wounded. It was not a sterling performance: troops not trained to work together in this kind of mission, missed assignments, inadequate intelligence, communications equipment unable to link different units from different services. Vessey's organizational innovations had gone some way toward bringing the chiefs to appreciate their joint roles, but the lessons in jointness and interoperability hadn't filtered down to the forces on the ground. Vessey wasn't happy with the mission; there had been too many hiccups. "We're going down there," he said. "Make it happen." When we landed in Grenada, we went to look at some of the units. The first thing we saw was a number of helicopter crews out of uniform and sort of lollygagging around. We also saw on the runway tarmac a large number of Cuban wounded waiting for treatment by the Cuban doctor, who was set up in a little trailer off to the side. The temperature was well over 100 degrees, the sun beating down on the tarmac; the men lying there were covered with sweat, suffering badly from the heat in addition to their wounds. The Cuban doctor came out of his trailer, his white coat covered with blood. "I need your help," he told Vessey. "You can't leave these people here."

I talked with one of the army officers in charge: "Why do you have them lying here like this?"

"Well," he said, "we have to interrogate them; it's part of our intelligence gathering."

"Get them off the tarmac," I said. "Get them into the shade. Do whatever you want, but not here in the sun."

I don't think the division commander enjoyed the talk Vessey had with him after we had made our rounds of the troops.

We visited Scoon at his residence. He was euphoric over the fact that he and his wife had been saved by the SEALs, who had roped down and then held off the bad guys attacking the house. "I must report to the queen," he said, and we set him up with a satellite phone so he could do that.

Vessey and I toured the island. We saw warehouses filled top to bottom with ammunition and weapons, far in excess of anything the Grenadan army would ever need. There was no question they were for transshipment elsewhere.

The Grenada operation didn't go smoothly, but it did accomplish all its objectives. The students were protected, the Cubans ejected, the Soviet and North Korean ties severed. The country emerged as a functioning democracy, which it has been ever since.

President Reagan made the decision to go ahead with the operation at a moment of crisis. In Beirut, not only did we not achieve objectives, but the marines there met with disaster. The first reports were that 100 had been killed in the truck-bomb explosion. By the time the last body was

Grandpa Michael.

Jimmy and George, age four in 1943. I'm the one on the left.

Front row from left: sisters Jacqueline and Helen; mom Alice; sisters Mary Ann and Loretta. *Back row*: me, Dad, and Jimmy. Jimmy and I are sixteen.

Army football. Number 54, I was a center and linebacker.

I had the most tackles in senior year.

Graduation, June 1961. General Westmoreland hands me my diploma.

At the end of our wedding on February 19, 1966, Karen and I exit the church under crossed swords.

I kept the fused part of the mortar shell that
shredded our operations tent and knocked
me into the back of the bunker at the start of
the Battle of Ap Gu in Vietnam.

In the Oval Office, 1974, where Nixon promoted me to lieutenant
colonel. Nixon wasn't known for dandling children, but when my
daughter Jessica reached out to him, he picked her up.

In the Oval Office with President Gerald Ford in 1974. I'm still deputy White House chief of staff, shortly to be replaced by Dick Cheney.

As commander of the Third Armored Division, I conducted a live-fire exercise.

As commander of the Third Armored Division, I explained the "Nip the Nipple" strategy to SACEUR/CINCEUR John Galvin and Fifth Corps commander John Woodmansee.

Welcoming Russian and Warsaw Pact observers to the last REFORGER exercise, 1988.

REFORGER after-action review, 1988.

Colonel Mark Hamilton, head of the US military group in El Salvador, and FMLN *comandante* Raul Hercules, 1991. Photograph courtesy of Mark Hamilton.

A ceremony for the Fuertes Caminos (Strong Roads) program in Central and
South America, 1992. Tens of thousands of American citizen soldiers engaged
with host nations to construct schools, clinics, and roads.

President George H. W. and Barbara Bush, Karen, and I step down from Air Force One at Howard Air Force Base in Panama, 1992.

SOUTHCOM's motto: "One Team, One Fight."

Reviewing troops with President Bill Clinton at the Normandy American Cemetery on the fiftieth anniversary of D-Day, 1994. Clinton was moved; it was his first visit.

Henry Kissinger was initially opposed to Partnership for Peace. Then he saw its potential.

Richard Holbrooke asked for my blessing during the Dayton negotiations for peace in Bosnia in 1995. A rare humorous moment in a time of high anxiety.

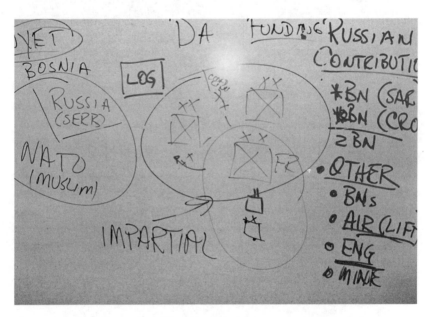

Chart showing Russian requests regarding command responsibilities in NATO's Bosnian force. I called it my "Da/Nyet Chart." I mostly said, "Nyet."

Defense Secretary Bill Perry and I reenlisting Sergeant First Class Kidwell on the Sava River bridge, December 1996.

In Bosnia with my Russian deputy, Colonel General Leontiy Shevtsov, 1996.

Pope John Paul II said the saddest day for him in 1995 was when he had to cancel his visit to Sarajevo. I promised he would be able to go in 1997, which he did.

I presented Colonel General Shevtsov with the Legion of Merit. He asked for a glass of vodka, put the medal in it, and drank the vodka. A Russian military tradition, so I'm told.

Karen and me at my retirement ceremony with the Old Guard behind us, July 11, 1997.

Our daughters Chris, Jennifer, and Jessica with Karen and me.

pulled out of the rubble, we counted 241 dead marines and sailors. The US operation in Lebanon was one that never should have happened.

For a number of years, Lebanon had been a place of sectarian violence, with Shi'a, Sunni, and Christian militias, Druze tribesmen, and the Lebanese army fighting each other in a shifting struggle for territorial and political control. The civil war had been initiated largely by the Palestine Liberation Organization, which had established itself there among Palestinian refugees from Israel. In 1982, Israel had invaded Lebanon to eject the PLO, which had been bombarding northern Israel. It had succeeded in doing that, but afterward the conflict among Lebanese groups had escalated.

A task force of American marines had been inserted initially as part of a multinational effort to oversee the PLO withdrawal. When that was completed, the marines had left, but then in September 1983 the Lebanese government asked the multinational force—Americans, French, British, and Italians—to return.

Vessey had come on as chairman only shortly before this request was made. He was very opposed to stationing American forces there. He wrote a short, pointed memo to Weinberger about it, which I hand carried to Weinberger's assistant, Colin Powell. Vessey's memo told the secretary that the chiefs were not in favor of sending marines to Lebanon. "I urge you," he said, "not to send troops to Lebanon. We are not prepared for such a mission; we are not trained for such a mission." He said it would be like "pouring gasoline on a fire."

Weinberger took Vessey's side and argued against the deployment, but he lost the debate. Our allies were putting enormous pressure on Reagan for America to join the international force, and so, despite Vessey and Weinberger's advice, the president approved the operation.

In these kinds of situations, you give your advice knowing that you might either win or lose. If you lose, but it's important enough to you, you have the option to say, "Okay, thank you, I resign." Otherwise, you soldier on. The troops continue to need strong leadership. In retrospect, I wish I had advised Vessey better. If you say something like, "It will be like pouring gasoline onto a fire," and then the political decision goes against you, you then have to articulate the risk. "We're not trained for this; we're training for what might happen with the Soviets. We're forward deployed in two theaters. You can overrule me, but you need to know that we may lose a lot of soldiers."

After we were told to send in our marines as part of the multinational force, we had to figure out where to position the force. In discussions between the chairman and his counterparts from the other nations involved, it was decided to station the marines around the Beirut airfield. Looking at the map, I wondered who controlled the high ground over-looking the airport. The answer was that the warring factions did. That was part of our undoing. The airport was flat. By not holding the high ground, the marines were in effect sitting in the middle of a bull's-eye.

The multinational force mission was fuzzy. Basically the force was placed there in support of the Lebanese government and army in their attempt to shore up central control and stabilize the country. But that hardly recognized the convoluted nature of the fighting. The marines were in Lebanon as peacekeepers, but there was precious little peace to keep. The American and Western presence inevitably antagonized some of the factions, especially those connected with fundamentalist Shi'a groups. As a result, the marines came under mortar and artillery fire. They dug deeper, and they emplaced special radar that could detect the source of incoming rounds and direct counterfire. But the shelling forced the marines to put even the radar equipment underground.

The people who were doing the shelling were also probing to find weaknesses. Eventually they did. In the after study of the bombing directed by retired admiral Robert Long, it became evident that vehicles had been driving down the road leading to the marine barracks in the period before the blast, reconnoitering. They had determined that a truck carrying a massive explosive device could break through the concertina wire and chain-link fencing around the barracks and crash into the build-ing or at least get near the building before the Americans could stop it. They packed a twenty-ton-stake truck with twelve thousand pounds of TNT, which ensured that even if the truck were stopped some way off, the blast would still destroy the building. The FBI forensic lab later said that it was the largest conventional-bomb blast they had ever studied. The terrorists most likely didn't know that the rules of engagement for the marines required that loaded weapons be kept on safe with no round in the chamber, which made instant action impossible. As a result, the marine sentries had been unable to shoot at the truck as it barreled into the building.

Vessey asked me to participate in Admiral Long's study, which I did, and two months after the event Vessey and I made a trip to Lebanon to survey where we stood now. We landed at the airport, then helicoptered into Beirut for a meeting with Lebanon's president, Amin Gemayel. Gemayel had been elected after the previous president, his brother Bashir, had been blown up by a Syrian bomb. We had gotten intelligence that bad elements in Beirut possessed Soviet antiaircraft SA7 missiles, so we went in very low and fast across the city to the presidential residence.

After Vessey's meeting with Gemayel, we went to visit the marines at the airport. The unit there now had relieved the marines who had suffered all the casualties. "I'll tell you what we're going to do," Vessey said. "They're going to take me up to somewhere to show me the layout of where we are and where the threats are. They'll give me the big, sweeping view. While they're doing that, I want you to get with the battalion commander and the company commanders. Walk the line with them. Get into the foxholes and bunkers. Talk to the troops. I need you to give me the unvarnished truth."

When I met up with the commanders, they weren't too happy about showing me the emplacements. They tried to distract me. "Why don't we sit down and have a cup of coffee?"

"I was told I need to walk your line," I said, "to see where you are." Where they were was not good. When I asked the battalion commander if he had walked the line, he didn't say no, but he didn't say yes either. It was more like a quick, "Well, we've just been here a very short time, and we're just setting up." Walking the line, I did the usual: "Who's on your right? Who's on your left? Let me see your range card. Do you have any artillery targets out in front of you? What's the most likely avenue of approach to your position?" I did not get good answers.

When Vessey came back from his briefing, he said, "What did you find out?"

I gave him the news. "Just what I expected," he said. "I could tell from the leadership, the way they were briefing me, that these guys aren't ready." So Vessey had a "Come to Jesus" with the battalion commander and the commander ashore. "You get this squared away," he told them. "Range cards, interlocking fire. Likely approaches." He was not gentle.

We found other serious problems. The line of communication went from the commander ashore to a ship command post somewhere in the Mediterranean, to the naval command in Naples, to the European Command in Stuttgart, to the SACEUR/CINCEUR in Mons, then back to the command center in Washington. Far, far too much clicking and clicking to get an important decision. That's how to get people hurt. There was no clear chain of command on the multinational side either. It's not often remembered now, at least in the United States, that a few minutes after the marine barracks blew up, a similar truck bomb hit the French barracks in downtown Beirut, killing fifty-eight French paratroopers. It was the worst French military loss since the Algerian War, decades earlier. For the Americans, the bombing had caused the worst single-day death toll since the Tet Offensive in 1968.

A commander's first responsibility is to accomplish his mission; to do that you have to keep your men alive. And how do you do that? You follow fundamental procedures from day one—as I learned the first day I commanded a platoon in Germany. Senior officers as well as young officers need to understand that: follow procedures and get prepared from day one, not "we'll take a week to get the tents set up and get the routine established." Seeing what Vessey and I saw in Beirut made our visit badly disheartening. We had lost many soldiers. We needed to understand how to keep from losing more.

Grenada revealed problems with our own ability to carry out joint operations. In Lebanon, we saw lack of mission clarity, deficiencies in training, inadequacies in tailoring multinational efforts. All these issues made their mark on me; I thought of it as "scar tissue." They educated me about how to effectively run large-scale, joint, multinational operations of the kind that was necessary when I led NATO into Bosnia ten years later.

I absorbed those hard lessons as Chairman Vessey's executive officer. But from my perch there at his right hand, I also saw how the significant buildup of US military forces under President Reagan was based on an emerging geopolitical strategy. We badly needed modernization. We needed the new weapons that could successfully confront the Soviets— the M-1, the Bradley, the Apache, the advanced field missiles and artillery that could strike deep. At the same time, the navy received Aegis cruisers and better submarines, and the air force developed the capability for long-range strikes with precision munitions.

This buildup was not haphazard. We needed to take the advantage away from the Soviets, with their great superiority in numbers and their multiechelon attack plan. The Joint Chiefs were instrumental in the modernization. Their presentations to our political leaders were focused on providing clear military advice. Their testimony to Congress was important because a buildup of this size needed bipartisan support. Vessey was particularly influential here. He had a low-key but precise way of rendering advice. He didn't offend adversaries and critics. Congressional committee chairmen called him, and he gave advice that reinforced the advice he was giving to President Reagan and Secretary Weinberger.

But the Reagan buildup had a purpose that went beyond the purely military: the overall intention was to put pressure on the Soviets and show them that they could not win, that they could not match what the free world was willing to do.

All this modernization was in terms of conventional forces. Nuclear forces were another matter. For years we had tried to match the Soviets' nuclear capability. We had developed the MIRV system, which consisted of multiple independently targeted warheads on one missile. To counter that development, the Soviets had gone to increased throw-weight in order to be able to launch larger missiles at our missile fields and take out more of our MIRVed missiles. So then, of course, we built more MIRVs to get more of their bigger missiles. This race had no foreseeable end, the two sides facing off in what came to be called a policy of mutually assured destruction, or MAD, the idea being that if each side were able to destroy the other, both would be deterred. That meant that if one side couldn't get a completely obliterating first strike in, then it had to have enough second-strike capability as well to make sure of the enemy's destruction.

When Vessey wanted to discuss issues privately with the Joint Chiefs, he would meet with them in his office around a round table he asked me to get for him. No one else would be in the room with them, no assistants or XOs, just the chiefs. In one of these closed-door meetings, he asked me to take notes, so I was there in the back, the only strap hanger. The discussion was about Soviet throw-weight. The Russians were developing a missile with a large enough warhead to take out our entire Montana nuclear field. This kind of huge nuclear weapon would set off a new round in the atomic stand-off.

In the course of the chiefs' discussion, Admiral James Watkins, the chief of naval operations, said, "Wouldn't it be better to save lives than avenge them?" He then presented the idea of having a space-based strategic defense that would give us the ability to shoot down whatever the Soviets might launch against us, no matter how big it was. The theory was that with our advanced technological ability, we could create a space-based system that could intercept the Soviets' intercontinental ballistic missiles very shortly after they were launched. Could we not, Watkins said, put up a protective shield that would save lives instead of answering nuclear strikes with more nuclear strikes?

That was a conceptual breakthrough that had the potential to scrap and replace the MAD deterrent psychology. When the chiefs took the concept to President Reagan, he bought into it instantly; it seemed to him a path toward something saner than mutual extinction.

Of course, no one knew if such a thing were feasible. Just exploring the futuristic technologies involved would be hugely expensive and time consuming. But the president was gripped by the idea that making nuclear missiles obsolete would lead to a far safer world, and his very public advocacy gave the idea a certain credibility. It was, he said in a televised speech to the nation on March 23, 1983, "a vision of the future that offers hope." We were, he announced, "launching a massive research effort."

The idea of eliminating the ballistic missile threat and maybe moving toward eventual denuclearization was dear to the president's heart. But regardless of whether some kind of Star Wars defense would work, the concept linked with what we were doing on the ground. Our buildup there was already challenging the Soviet ability to respond. If we could convince the Soviets that more throw-weight was not going to work either, then they would have to spend untold billions in order to answer us and retool. They were already devoting an inordinate percentage of their resources to defense compared to what we were, all from a budget that was severely stressed. So here was a way for the United States to say, "Is this what you really want to do? Or would it be better for both of us to move toward meaningful treaties and arms control?"

Once the president made his announcement, the Strategic Defense Initiative (SDI) became a political football. But in all that churn, the Soviets were hearing that SDI was a strong possibility. It spooked them and set the stage for the later arms-reduction talks between Reagan and Mikhail Gorbachev and eventually for the collapse of the Soviet Union. Before I left the chairman's office, I saw that process just beginning to take shape. The Soviets were scrambling, and that was exactly the position we wanted them in.

When Vessey and I were sitting up in his sunroom at Fort McNair talking about whether I would take the XO job, he told me it would be for only two years. His wife, Avis, was eager to go back to their home in Minnesota. I told him then that I would take the job for two years, and we shook hands on it. I know that Vessey had told Reagan he would be staying for only that long. But when the two years were up, Reagan asked Vessey to stay for another two, and Vessey agreed.

By this time, I had been promoted to brigadier general, qualified to command a forward-deployed division. I knew that the First Infantry Division (Forward) command slot was coming open, and I had been told I would get the assignment. I was hoping that would happen. The division was based in Göppingen, Germany. I knew the division well from my battalion command with the Blue Spaders. I thought it was the best brigadier's job in the army. So it was a painful moment when Vessey called me in to say that the president had asked him to stay on and he had agreed. He wanted me to stay on with him, to finish the work we had started. Would I do that?

I had a great deal of inner conflict about it. I had been in this joint position for two years. It was time for me to get back to the army, and I really wanted to go to a command. Karen and the kids were excited about getting back to Germany as well. But in the end the idea that you serve your country where you're asked to serve wasn't something I could turn my back on. I told Vessey I would stay.

Vessey finished out his term as chairman of the Joint Chiefs in 1985. (At his retirement, the band played "The Gambler"—"Know when to hold 'em, know when to fold 'em"—the perfect comment on his tenure.) I had been with him for the entire three and a half years of his time in office. Over that period, I had made many decisions and had participated in others that went counter to army positions. I hadn't lost my army identification and perspective, but in a joint position you have to understand that decisions are made for the greater good of the armed forces, not just for your own service. Of course, understanding that way of thinking is one thing, implementing it is another. I learned to do that from Jack Vessey. From the moment he accepted the appointment, he considered himself head of the *Joint* Chiefs. He acted that way, and he put the service chiefs on notice that he expected them to follow suit, no matter how much it might go against their instincts.

As the chairman's XO, I sometimes caught the backlash from this approach. Early on I got a phone call from a very senior army general telling me that a particular issue was going to come up in the "tank" (the Joint Chiefs' meeting room). "This is how we want that issue to go," he said.

I told him, "Wait a minute. That's not how I see my position." I knew Vessey would protect me if the need ever arose, though at another point a different senior officer growled at me after I had told him the same thing, "You will *never* command a division!"

By the time I left the chairman's office in November 1985, I had witnessed an extraordinary transformation not just of the army, so battered from its Vietnam experience, but also of the entire US military. In the army, we had new warfighting doctrine, originating with DePuy and introduced under his successor at TRADOC, Donn Starry. In all the services, we were fielding a new panoply of weapons designed in large part to deal with the Russians and the Warsaw Pact. Under Reagan, the administration was developing a policy toward the Soviets that gave a geopolitical underpinning to our new capabilities.

We were bringing together doctrine and modernization and the training that was enabling us to put the new weapons to good use, all with an emphasis on integrating the fighting capabilities of the different services—that is, on jointness. We had a long way to go on this front. The Grenada and Lebanon operations highlighted serious shortcomings in our warfighting capabilities, but there was no question we were headed in the right direction.

Vessey recognized many of the glaring weaknesses in the command structure. Early on he put together a briefing paper for Weinberger called "A Better Way of Doing Business." He talked there about the role of the chairman, the service chiefs, the Joint Chiefs of Staff, and the Office of the Secretary of Defense. He put great emphasis on the role of the CINCs, the forward-deployed commanders, who had elements of all the services under their command. He opened his office to them—that was one of his first instructions to me. He established direct phone lines between himself and the CINCs that enabled him to talk securely with them. He brought them into the procurement process. To straighten out the problems with interoperability, he put all the vice chiefs together in a group to resolve the problem of different services developing and buying their own systems so that they had ended up with systems—like the communications equipment in Grenada—that didn't work together and were indefensible, unnecessary expenditures. He put Max Thurman, the army vice chief, in charge, and Thurman was a vastly knowledgeable, detail-oriented program manager who could bite your head off. The services began to iron out their differences.

At every Joint Chiefs meeting, Vessey hammered on jointness. He was also very concerned about the quality of the officers coming in as staff for the Joint Chiefs. He had me look at the navy captains and army colonels appointed to the staff. How many had afterward been promoted to star or flag rank? None had! The story was similar for the air force and marines. None of the services wanted to send their best people to joint appointments, even though it was mandated by Title 10 of the US Code. They wanted to keep the brightest for themselves rather than waste them on what they regarded as tasks of lesser importance. "How can we be living up to the law if we don't have the best people coming here?" Vessey asked the chiefs, which gave them all kinds of angst. They didn't like it when Vessey had the J-1 military personnel people come in to brief them about promotion statistics. "Look," Vessey said, "we're not serving the National Command Authority very well if the people being sent here aren't the best we have." That started the impetus toward getting top-quality officers and NCOs onto the staff.

The final big piece of modernizing and reorganizing the military was the reform of the command structure that eventually took place under Vessey's successor, Admiral William Crowe. But Vessey precipitated or institutionalized many of the reforms that became law under the Goldwater-Nichols Defense Reorganization Act of 1986, which streamlined the chain of command, strengthened the chairman's role, and addressed the problems of interservice rivalry. As a battalion and brigade commander, I had witnessed close up the new energy and spirit that flowed into the army in the late 1970s and early 1980s. As chairman, Vessey worked the new realities into the national command structure.

When Vessey retired, I wanted badly to get back to a command position in Europe. It was 1985. No one had an inkling then that four years later the Berlin Wall would come down and six years later we would see the formal dissolution of the Soviet Union. Viktor Chernenko, the old-guard Soviet general secretary, had just died, and a new man, Mikhail Gorbachev, had been appointed to take his place. Gorbachev's reform policies were in the future, and as far as the US military was concerned in the mid-1980s, the Soviet threat on the inter-German border was still very much alive.

10

The Wall Comes Down

With my term up as the Joint Chiefs chairman's XO in 1985, I was promoted to brigadier general, but the army didn't send me to Europe. Instead, Max Thurman, the army vice chief whom Vessey had put in charge of clearing up interoperability and procurement problems between the services, said, "You're coming with me." That's how Thurman talked. His nickname was "Mad Max." He was a hard man to say no to, not that I wanted to.

With that, I was appointed director for combat support systems, which opened my eyes to how decisions were made on research, development, and procurement. My entire career I had been on the tactical and command side; now I was in the nuts and bolts. I oversaw the Humvee program, theater missile-defense program, and various others and got educated on how the force-requirement process works and how essential it is to get that right if our warfighting capability isn't to be undercut. I also got to accompany Thurman as he worked out duplications and conflicts among the services' procurement programs. We found, for example, that the navy and army had separate drone projects going on instead of looking at the need as a collaborative effort, just one instance of wasting money and creating interoperability problems.

Thurman didn't take prisoners in these matters. As recounted in the biography *General William E. DePuy,* Thurman was "the bag man and the hatchet man." "The post, station, and camp commanders treated me very well," he told an interviewer, "because they knew that if I said, 'You don't get a dollar, you don't get it; and if you do get it, you do get it.'" In the same interview, he described docking Fort Benning's budget $3 million, which the commander objected to strenuously. "Fisticuffs ensued," Thurman reported. I attended a meeting where Thurman was overseeing an army/air force negotiation over twenty-five or thirty procurement items in conflict. It was a knock-down, drag-out fight, and Thurman was firing bullets at both negotiators, which didn't perturb the army negotiator, who was used to Thurman's ways, but upset the air force representative so badly that he passed out. A few minutes after they took him away, I leaned over to Thurman and said, "Sir, maybe you should inquire about how he's doing."

"Oh, yeah, right," said Thurman, turning to another air force officer. "How's that colonel doing?"

Resolving these issues wasn't easy. Sometimes the Defense Department was paying General Dynamics, Northrup Grumman, and Raytheon for the same thing. But Max Thurman was a master of both technical and budgeting detail as well as a bulldog. He had a way of bringing order to a situation.

Six months later I finally did get back to Europe, as deputy chief of staff for operations and plans for the US Army in Europe—in shorthand, DCSOPS, USAEUR. Other than commanding a division, this was the best assignment someone of my rank (I was now a major general) could have. It gave me the widest possible overview of our European theater war planning.

The US Army's focus in Europe, as I knew so well, was on how to stop a Soviet attack through the Fulda Gap. I had commanded units from platoon up through brigade that were part of precisely that mission. Fulda was where the big fight was going to happen; we had been thinking about that and planning how to meet it for decades. But USAEUR had a larger scope than just the fight. In time of war, it became a theater army, whose mission was to oversee logistical and other support functions, including organizing the rear of the theater.

A key task here was bringing in the reinforcements that would be required if war broke out. It was always understood that the job of the two corps stationed in Europe was to hold the Soviets until reinforcements could arrive from the United States. The planners believed that we would need ten American divisions to have a chance of success against a Warsaw Pact onslaught and that those ten divisions had to be in the field within ten days of the start of hostilities. That was the planning requirement: ten divisions in ten days. The two corps stationed in Europe comprised four divisions. That meant we would need to get six divisions from the United States to Germany within the given ten days.

When I began looking at that target, I didn't see how we could make it, and when I talked with the relevant people—"How are we going to do this?"—I did not hear anything convincing. What I did hear was a lot of shilly-shallying.

"Let's be very clear," I said. "What you're telling me is that the troops in the Fulda Gap are going to die there. They are going to hold their ground and fight, but if we don't get more troops there in time, the juggernaut that's coming is going to build and build and roll over them. We can fight well for three, four, or five days, but then we get no reinforcements, and the Soviets are still coming with echelon after echelon. No matter how good we are, that's going to lead to only one conclusion."

The two most significant divisions designated as reinforcements were going to come from Fort Hood in Texas. They included corps artillery, corps engineers, attack headquarters, and other essential elements. I asked the planners, "How do we get them here in ten days?"

"Well, sir, they're coming from Fort Hood, so they have to load up at Galveston or Beaumont. From there they've got to come up through the Gulf."

"What if we sent them to Savannah by train and shipped them out from there instead of from Texas?"

"That would save two days," the planners said, so we incorporated that. "What about fast sealift ships?" I asked.

We had eight of those, the fastest cargo ships in the world, capable of crossing the Atlantic in six days. They had originally been built as civilian container ships, but the navy had acquired and converted them. One or two were still undergoing conversion. We expedited that and provided the impetus for building an additional twelve (which were key four years later, in 1990, during the Gulf War buildup). We also found—to our surprise—that the initial air force airlift that we thought was supposed to bring in reinforcements was in fact first going to bring in all the infrastructure the air force needed to conduct the air fight. The air force had its own priorities. So we sat down with the air force to coordinate its needs with the need to move in army and marine troops and equipment.

Our reinforcements were going to come in through Rotterdam and other Dutch ports, so we knew the Soviets would try to shut them down as fast as they could. To help counter that, I had our people plan out how to use the old World War II Red Ball express route from French ports. Then, when we looked at how exactly the Soviets were planning to close down the ports, we saw that they had developed a mobile theater missile, the SS-21, a so-called shoot and scoot. "Shoot and scoot" meant they could drive the SS-21 transporter-erector to whatever launch site they wanted, set the missile up, fire it within five minutes, then leave the site. The missiles themselves could be armed with gas or chemical warheads as well as with conventional or even nuclear warheads. That was a tremendous capability we didn't know how to handle.

But one of USAEUR's intelligence officers, Judith Daley, reported that she was tracking the SS-21 battalions in East Germany.

"Do we know where they go to train?" I asked.

"Yes, sir, we do. We watch them move from their assembly area to their training sites."

Here was an opportunity. Judith Daley knew how long it took them to get from their assembly area to their training areas. We knew where those sites were. We also knew a battalion of SS-21s had quite a large footprint; there weren't that many places in East Germany that could handle a battalion. When I asked her if she could generate a list of potential launch sites, she quickly identified five or six of the most likely.

We surveilled those sites and worked up a plan to take the missiles out if we saw them moving to those places. That was tricky because they would fire only if a war actually began, which meant I couldn't hit them until that moment. When I asked the Warrior Prep Center in Ramstein to run a simulation for us, they incorporated a Soviet attack on Rotterdam using SS-21s armed with gas warheads. The results weren't good.

"My question is," I asked our planners, "what happens in Rotterdam when the ships come in? Who unloads them?"

That's when it dawned on us that all the dockworkers and managers were civilians. "Do they have gas masks or other protective gear?"

"No, sir, they don't."

It wasn't clear what the dock handlers would do in the event of an attack. The likelihood was that they would simply abandon their posts.

Once we ran the exercises and looked at the problems in detail, it was crystal clear that getting reinforcements in and deployed to the front was our Achilles' heel. We were going to be in desperate straits. The Soviets were going to close our ports. We wouldn't be able to get our troops and equipment off the ships, and meanwhile our people would be dying in the Fulda Gap. Ten years later I was able to sit down with the Russian attack generals, who told me that their war plans were indeed designed to prevent our reinforcements at all costs.

We worked and worked the ports problem and made progress dealing with it. We also found that British, Canadian, and even Norwegian troops were also planning to come through the same ports and use the same routes we were, but there were no plans on how to deconflict the disembarkation and forward deployment of troops. We went to the British Army of the Rhine in northern Germany and coordinated those movements with them.

There simply had not been nearly enough detailed thought given to these essential rear-area problems. The focus had always been instead on combat operations, maneuver, and air–land battle. We hadn't completely neglected the rear-area side; our REFORGER exercises always included bringing a brigade in as reinforcement, but the exercises didn't incorporate anywhere near the full spectrum of actual problems we would encounter. We also had forward-deployed depots in Holland, Belgium, and elsewhere that accommodated a brigade's worth or more of armor, so that heavy equipment would be waiting for reinforcement elements when they arrived. So a degree of planning was in place, but the preparations were neither comprehensive nor thorough. The biggest issue wasn't tanks; it was logistics. It was all those sorts of things that would fill out and sustain an army in the field and make it functional. Not just for a day or a week but for the long fight. The attention to detail had simply not been adequate. It all went back to fundamentals. Toothbrush to the right, bristles up.

Working through these and other equally complex logistical problems was challenging, but it was exciting to look at the total picture rather than just the combat side. It took time to get the staff work up to speed, to put all the pieces together, and do it in the context of a joint, combined, interagency, multinational effort. Getting all those pieces to work together put us much closer to being able to fight the way we needed to.

There is a book entitled *America's First Battles* that describes the initial engagements in each of our wars, from the revolution to Vietnam. We lost many of those battles, but not because we couldn't shoot straight. Staffs were not well organized to deal with the problems the mission confronted them with, and they consequently stumbled badly before they were able to get their act together. In Europe, we couldn't afford to lose the first battle. We had to be ready to fight on day one.

I was DCSOPS for two years, June 1986 to June 1988. The dissolution of the Warsaw Pact and the Soviet Union itself was only a few years off, but we did not foresee that. We had the same incentive to keep our readiness at the highest level, as we always had. At the same time, though, thaw was definitely in the air. President Reagan and General Secretary Gorbachev had developed a good personal relationship and had met for several summits. The Intermediate-Range Nuclear Forces Treaty was signed in 1987, and a variety of confidence-building measures were put in place.

One of them was the Military Liaison Commission agreement, by which each side was allowed to send observers to make sure the other side wasn't preparing for World War III. The military liaisons operated under specific rules spelling out where they could and couldn't go and under what conditions. We had a military liaison mission in East Berlin; the Soviets had one in Frankfurt. The main task of the liaison officers was to drive around and observe. Prior to my tour as DCSOPS, the Russians had shot and killed an American major on the US liaison mission team. My predecessor had to investigate why this had happened and to confront the Soviets about it.

During my tour, we had a similar event. Two of our soldiers driving in a marked liaison car were shot and wounded by Soviet troops. The incident took place in Potsdam, just outside Berlin, in an allowed area. The USAEUR commanding general, Glenn Otis, sent me to talk to the Russian leadership.

My counterpart in this meeting was a two-star Soviet general, equivalent to my rank. I brought photographs with me showing that our unarmed soldiers were ambushed. The Soviets had to have known they were military mission people by the license plates and by the type of car they were driving. The shooting had been no accident. It had been a planned ambush. The car had been destroyed, and the soldiers wounded. They could easily have been killed.

This incident occurred just as Secretary of State George Schultz was meeting in Washington with the Soviet foreign minister in talks to further the reductions in tactical nuclear missiles. The ambush and near loss of two American personnel could have been a huge international incident and most surely would have been had they been killed. It was bad enough as it was.

I was prepared for this meeting. I showed the photographs of the incident to my counterpart. "This is outrageous," I said. "Our mission personnel were unarmed. Your soldiers ambushed to kill. Is that the kind of relationship you want?" I then showed photographs of a situation in Frankfurt where a Soviet liaison car had been caught where it shouldn't have been, right inside an American military convoy. The Soviet mission vehicle was surrounded by US tanks. The picture showed an American officer giving the Russians water and offering the use of a phone.

"Contrast this to what you have done here," I said. "Is this your idea of the way to build confidence?" I showed my counterpart the card issued to every American soldier who might come in contact with Soviet liaison personnel, with instructions on what to do if an encounter did happen.

"These were new troops," the Soviet general said. "They had just been brought into East Germany."

"How do you indoctrinate them?" I asked. "Do they get a card like this? Do they get briefed?"

No, neither did they get printed instructions, nor were they briefed.

The Soviets were typically stone cold and gruff in meetings. Despite the diplomatic warming, we were still in the middle of a Cold War stand-off, which was why I was shocked when my counterpart said, "The American general is right. We're at fault. I'm here to apologize." If I was surprised, the other Soviets in the room were stunned. The Soviets *never* apologized.

"We will do better," the Soviet general said. "We'll indoctrinate everyone coming in, and we'll print up a similar card."

Then he said, "I'd like to invite you for lunch."

"Fine," I said. The ambush was intolerable, but the general had surprised the hell out of me.

Over lunch at the Soviet Officer's Club, the general said, "You know, I'm a Soviet officer, but I'm really Ukrainian." Then he pulled out pictures showing scenes of Ukrainian independence from centuries past. The women servers at the club were Ukrainian, the wine was Ukrainian. It was clear enough that the general was trying to tell me something. This man was proud of his heritage, which, he was saying loud and clear, was *not* Russian.

It was after this incident that I began to view the Soviet military in a different light. Although their army was large, it was very poorly disciplined. I later became even more convinced of that when I went on to command the Third Armored Division and after that the Fifth Corps, one of the two corps stationed permanently in Europe.

Most of my time as USAEUR DCSOPS was devoted to the logistical problems of reinforcing and supporting the combat divisions in the Fulda Gap and elsewhere. My next assignment was as commanding general of the Third Armored Division, the "Spearhead." The Third Armored would be exactly in the middle of the Fulda Gap fight if World War III ever did start, one of the units that would need the reinforcements whose arrival I had been working to ensure.

Because of my work at USAEUR, I was far more conscious of the logistical situation; I had a bigger picture of both our own war planning and the Soviets' planning. I knew their order of battle in detail, the tank armies they would bring, where they intended to make their breakthrough, how they planned to get to the Rhine. I had a more precise knowledge of the Thüringer Wald mountain range east of Fulda, where the Soviets had built up a massive concentration of ammunition and artillery. If we didn't punish them for bringing all this power forward, we would really pay the price.

I knew I needed to identify the Soviet main attack early on so that I could maneuver against it. We needed to be able to plan what it would take for each unit to be ready to fight the moment hostilities opened. I talked to my leaders from the division level down to the company and platoon level. But I really focused on how to move the division's battalions and brigades and how to cross-reinforce them, taking artillery or mechanized units from one element and assigning them to another to achieve the maximum effect. We spent a great deal of time studying the terrain and walking it so that my commanders would know the landscape intimately, just as I had done when I commanded the Second Brigade seven years earlier. We used the new simulated battle trainer, or SIMNET, developed by DARPA, the Defense Department's Advanced Research Projects Agency, which was instrumental in the development of the Internet.

I put a special emphasis on gunnery. The Soviets were going to come at us with massive numbers of tanks, so we had to be able to achieve kills with our first rounds and at long range. We utilized new fire-training simulating technology, and I "shocked" the tank and mechanized units, giving them no-notice gunnery tests. I put box scores in the division newspaper to show how well the units did. The troops loved the challenge; the tank and Bradley units responded with consistently high scores. Then we did the same thing with the mortars and engineers. We worked hard at keeping our readiness at a high pitch.

There was still some thought among the army's planners about moving back out of artillery range to lessen the shock of a Soviet attack. But I wanted to engage well forward, so I moved up instead of back. We needed the technological and intelligence capability to predict the Soviets' main attack so we could strike with air and artillery early to disrupt their buildup. The Soviet sledgehammer approach meant that we needed to be a maneuver force, heavily armed but agile and quick to move. I planned to hit the Thüringer Wald salient and take out the Soviets' artillery—that is, nip the nipple, disrupt their assault as it came in, and attack them deep with Apaches and missiles. The point was to take away the Soviets' momentum and disrupt their timing.

To do that we needed to read the battlefield from the other side. In order to set up their main effort, the Soviets would have to begin by positioning various units for assault or support. There was a series of steps they would need to undertake. Understanding those steps would allow us to anticipate the decision cycle, get inside it, and position our own forces so that when the Soviets moved, we would already be countering it.

Reading the battlefield in that way was an artform I truly enjoyed working at. We practiced doing that in the field and in the new wargame simulations. The Red Team commander would move certain elements in ways that would indicate an attack forming up. When we saw these units lighting up on the simulation board, I would quickly reposition forces to meet and thwart what they were doing.

But to succeed in that, we had to be able to maneuver rapidly, to bring forces to bear where they needed to be. We trained to carry out intricate movements. We developed playbooks so that we had preplanned plays that the troops could rehearse—plays called, for example, "Option Right" or "Option Left." We used sports terminology the troops understood. Just calling out a code, "Blue 92," would start off a whole train of artillery, maneuver, air. We war-gamed all of this, both when I was Third Armored Division commander and then on a larger scale when I was promoted to command of Fifth Corps. We rehearsed, and we practiced. We were challenged by the Red Team in every game, but we never lost.

The proof of our training came in the final great REFORGER exercise in 1988. That was the last time we were able to maneuver across country. In that exercise, we went up against the Seventh Corps acting as the Red Team. I set an armored cavalry unit as the screen against the Soviet assault. The Second Brigade dug in as the stopping force, along with the 197th Infantry Brigade. "You're going to be the cork in the bottle," I told them. "You will be the anvil for the counterattack. If you get dislodged, we lose."

Under great pressure from wave after wave of "Soviet" armor, our stopping force held like a rock. When we launched our counterattack, we found a breach on the Soviet left flank. I ordered a German army Panzer division to attack immediately. Five or ten minutes later, the German division wasn't moving. I called the commander again and told him to get going. Timing here was everything. Still nothing, so I spoke to him in German. He said, "Sir, I have the supreme allied commander here with me." General John Galvin was apparently observing the exercise in the German headquarters. The German general was waiting for Galvin's go-ahead. "I don't care who you have with you," I said. "You have to move now!"

The German commander did move. I watched as his tanks practically flew up the road. He hit the opening, and we were deep in the enemy rear with his tank division and our armored cavalry regiment. It was the culmination of all the things we had worked on.

This REFORGER was especially satisfying because we carried it out in front of Soviet observers. As a confidence-building measure, the Warsaw Pact and NATO agreed that when one side held a major exercise, like REFORGER, the other side could attend to make sure it wasn't a prelude to war. As a result, Warsaw Pact officers came in by helicopter and stationed themselves on the top of the hill where I had my tactical headquarters, so they could observe the entire battlefield and follow on my detailed exercise map. They saw the Seventh Corps forces (playing the Soviet units) barreling down toward us. They saw our stopping force hold them. Then they watched our counterattack penetrate through their flank.

They couldn't believe that I hadn't had days and days to rehearse, that the exercise was put in train and executed so quickly. It was a superb opportunity to demonstrate the depth of our training and the effect of our modernized equipment. The message was, "If I can do it here in this exercise, think what I can do to you. If you're coming down with your tank columns, as you will be, we are going to outmaneuver you; we're going to stop you; and we're going to hit you fast and hard. This is the time to understand that you're not going to be able to do what you think you can do."

I knew this demonstration got their attention. I didn't say, "Make peace, not war," but that was what I meant.

The US side was initially uptight about what these observers could be allowed to see. But I said, "Show them everything (not our secret plans, of course). Open every door. Let them see everything, and let them talk to our soldiers. Our soldiers are the best thing we have, so let them talk." And they did talk with our troops, who talked their ears off. That was fine with me. I wanted to impress the Soviets with our readiness, with the way even our private soldiers understood their missions and were trained to carry them out. I wanted them to see up close the power of our weapons systems and our ability to use them.

That was where the reequipping done under Reagan's expanded defense budget came in. It's easy enough to talk about deterrents. But words don't deter. Training, preparation, and superior arms do, and this was what I wanted to impress on our adversaries, especially as I went up in rank to division and then corps command.

In May 1989, as part of the same mutual-observer agreement, I was selected to watch a Warsaw Pact exercise in East Germany. We knew by then about the breakdown in Soviet army discipline. We had reports of fragging, soldiers killing their officers, as we had ourselves experienced in Vietnam. Some intelligence reports suggested that their officers were more afraid of their own troops than they were of us. Of course, neither I nor the other NATO commanders observing the Warsaw Pact exercise were going to learn anything about that. But we had been studying the Soviet military for decades, and now we were going to see them in action.

The exercise was an eye-opener. It was clear that the Soviets had developed East Germany into one vast training area. As a trainer, I caught myself practically salivating over the breadth of territory at their disposal, especially as our own training sites were being increasingly constricted by the West German government. Through the East German countryside, the Soviets had built tank trails, specialized routes that led from their billeting areas down to the border and partly protected the tanks from observation. They didn't need to move along the autobahns; they could bring streams of tanks through the countryside. For all the intelligence and studies we had done, we hadn't known about these trails.

Their exercise wasn't the kind of free-play, force-on-force maneuver and combat that ours was. It was more like a demonstration of how they would follow through on their plans. The Soviets were highly regimented in the way they went about their attack. The commanders showed little initiative. They would not deviate from the orders they were given. An attacking commander would come down Axis X and stay on Axis X no matter what.

The Soviet commanders had little command-and-control flexibility. They weren't looking for agility and maneuver; they were looking for control of force. In a fight, that's extremely important—especially if your forces are not trained to do otherwise. When you have large masses moving around the battlefield, it's important to know exactly where they are in order to maximize your artillery and air support. That discipline is what the Soviets stressed. To them it was a strength. Their intention was to overwhelm us. If you were on the other side and allowed that to happen, without disrupting it, then they were going to hit you like a steel hammer. And once they got through, this whole juggernaut behind them—the second, the third, the fourth echelon—would just come pouring in. They didn't even need much of a hole. But watching this exercise, I felt confident that adaptability and agility were the key to countering their strength. I felt confident that the best tactic was to hit them deep and on the flanks, just what we had been training to do. Actually seeing how methodical and undeviating the Soviets were vindicated the thinking I and others had developed over the years.

At the REFORGER exercise, we had allowed their observers to talk with our troops. Wanting to get a read on their own soldiers, I asked if I could go running with one of their companies. They let me do that, once. On another occasion, I asked if I could speak to a unit. I had seen one very good tank company maneuvering—the only one I saw that was really any good. It happened to be an East German unit equipped with T-72s. When the Soviets gave me permission, I climbed up on the lead tank to talk to the company commander in German, which helped make it a genial discussion. I found that unlike the Soviet tanks, which were filthy inside, the East German tank was spotless. The commander and gunner told me about the various things they were doing and how they were doing them—how the automatic loader worked, for example. I came away convinced that the best-trained and best-maintained tank forces were East German, not Soviet. I saw enough Soviet maintenance to know they were just relying on volume. If one broke down, five more would pass it by.

It was obvious there was little love lost between East Germans and the Soviets. As I was eating breakfast one morning in my Potsdam hotel, an East German general came over to my table to talk. He wanted me to understand that East Germany was hosting these exercises, not the Soviet Union. Other East Germans stopped by, pointedly ignoring a Soviet general sitting by himself not far away. It brought to mind the Ukrainian general who had shown me old pictures of independent Ukraine. None of this spoke well for the cohesiveness of Soviet and Soviet-led forces.

By the time I observed the Warsaw Pact exercise in May 1989, I had been commanding the Third Armored Division for almost a year and a half. In July of that year, I was promoted to command of the army's Fifth Corps, which along with the Seventh Corps constituted the army's permanent presence in Germany. At Fifth Corps, I heightened training procedures and instituted quarterly training briefings with corps leaders. The first slide I showed at these briefings read, "The Fifth Corps exists to fight."

Six months later the target of that mission changed abruptly. On November 8, I got a call from John Abrams, commander of the Eleventh (Blackhorse) Armored Cavalry Regiment, which was stationed right at the border. "Sir," he said, "something's happening down here." Abrams had a close relationship with the West German border guards. They were seeing unusual activity on the other side of the line. "I think the Soviets are going to open the border," Abrams said.

The next day, November 9, the East German government announced that all East German citizens would be allowed to visit West Germany. The Berlin Wall was coming down. That day the Iron Curtain, which had closed off East Europe for more than four decades, became history. In Berlin, euphoric crowds surged through the checkpoints, celebrating the end of their harsh isolation.

One of the first people I called was my old friend Lieutenant General Gordon Sullivan, who was now the USAEUR DCSOPS. He and I had been together in just about every one of our European assignments. Our families had practically grown up in Europe together. Now the outcome of our service and that of millions of GIs who had served in Europe before us was unfolding in massive celebrations of joy in Germany and elsewhere.

Two days later, on November 11—US Veterans Day, no less—two crossing points were opened in my area of the heavily fortified and mined border that ran the length of Germany and beyond—the physical Iron Curtain that had absorbed our attention and planning for so long. That day I flew up to the Fulda Gap in my Blackhawk command-and-control helicopter. It was a crisp, sunshine-filled day; we could see forever. We went right up to the border, close to Fulda. At the two crossing points, long lines of Trabant cars—the legendarily bad East German–produced "Trabbies"—were lined up waiting to cross over. John Abrams's cavalry regiment had three squadrons, which ordinarily rotated at the border every few weeks. But now he sped up the rotation so that all his men could witness this historic event. We also decided to have all the troops keep their weapons inside their vehicles so that heavily armed Americans would not be the first thing the flood of East Germans would see.

I stayed there, near the crossing points, watching. Day and night we saw Germans with flowers hugging and crying tears of joy. I felt overwhelmed, so privileged that I was the commander overseeing this. Twenty-eight years earlier I had watched the wall going up. I had seen people shot down trying desperately to get across. I remembered the flowers and crosses all along the wall, marking the sites where they had been killed. And now East and West Germans were greeting each other with flowers and laughter.

In the middle of all this, two young American soldiers came up to me, two privates. They couldn't have been more than eighteen or nineteen. They were excited and wanted to tell me what had happened to them. "General," one said, "we were caught in a traffic jam in our Humvee with all those East German cars. The whole thing was at a total standstill. Nobody could move. We didn't know what to do. Then the East Germans just started getting out of their cars to come over to our vehicle. They hugged us. They thanked us for their freedom."

"Sir," the other one said quietly, "now I know why I'm here."

His words triggered a distant memory. I had said precisely those same words to myself as a new second lieutenant commanding a platoon in the Fulda Gap. I had seen the crosses and flowers for the dead laid at the base of the Berlin Wall, and I was acutely aware of the Soviet tank armies massed on the other side of the border. I knew why I was there.

And now in late 1989, all the troops felt they were in the middle of something historic. You could feel it in them; you could see it in their eyes and in their faces. Flying low along the border, I had my pilot put down next to one of John Abrams's ground patrols. I pulled a private out and promoted him on the spot. "I hope you'll never forget this day," I told him. "This is the day we achieved victory in the Cold War." I wanted him to remember it through his life, whether he stayed in the military or not. As I write this, we are thirty years out from that day. I'm sure that private does remember, as I and Gordon Sullivan do, as John Abrams did until his recent death, as all those who served with us at that place and time remember.

One other incident from those days stands out for me. I was at an Eleventh Cavalry observation post at the border when two East German boys walked up to the gate. They told us they lived in the East German village that was just a few hundred meters on the other side of the border. There was an East German–Soviet tower on the edge of their village, separated from our post by a "no-man's land" of mines and barbed wire. These two boys had made their way from their village to the crossing point at Eisenach, crossed there, then walked back to our post. They said that every day they and others had looked up at the American flag flying over our post. They said it had been a symbol of hope for them that someday they would get their freedom.

That day felt to me like a vindication of the immense effort that we as a nation and an alliance and an army had devoted ourselves to for so many years. Our commitment to Europe, our role in NATO, what we had done year after year, the risks we took as a nation had brought about a victory—without firing a single shot. We had deterred war by using all the elements of our national power. We did it through arming ourselves with the weapons we needed, by training ourselves in tough, realistic circumstances so that if necessary we were ready to fight, and by working with and standing by our partners in the hard, epic struggle this had been.

11

SOUTHCOM 1

El Salvador

The Berlin Wall came down on November 8, 1989. In the months that followed, I had time to savor what had happened and begin preparing for what was coming next. With the Soviet retreat and the Cold War for all intents and purposes over, the strategic landscape had transformed, though it was impossible to say yet what the new landscape might look like. Whatever the shape of things to come, the US Army was going to have to develop a new definition of its mission and a new approach to strategy and requirements. That was going to be a major undertaking. But meanwhile the two Germanies were moving quickly toward unification. I was working with the Bundeswehr (West German military) about how to engage with what was still East Germany and looking forward to the political, economic, and military integration in the works.

I was enjoying this process immensely when I got a call from Max Thurman, who was now commander in chief of the US Southern Command (SOUTHCOM), which included all of Central and South America. "You're going to get a telephone call," Thurman said, in his abrupt manner. "Just say 'yes.'"

The next day I did get a call, from Secretary of Defense Dick Cheney. Sixteen years earlier Cheney had taken my place as White House deputy chief of staff. "Max Thurman is ill," he said. "We want you to replace him at SOUTHCOM. It's a dangerous area. You're needed there."

Thurman had been the leading advocate for removing Panamanian dictator Emmanuel Noriega, and he had overseen Operation Just Cause in late 1989 to do just that. Noriega was in prison in Miami awaiting trial. But now, less than a year later, Thurman had been diagnosed with advanced leukemia. "We want you to get down there immediately," Cheney said.

This came as a bit of a shock. German reunification was happening, but far more significant as far as the military was concerned was the fact that on August 2, 1990, Saddam Hussein's forces had invaded and occupied Kuwait. President George H. W. Bush had gathered together a coalition of nations determined to eject the Iraqis from the oil-rich emirate and was moving American forces into Saudi Arabia to prevent the Iraqis from advancing any further. The Seventh Corps under Lieutenant General Fred Franks had been ordered to deploy to Saudi Arabia along with many elements from my Fifth Corps, including the Third Armored Division.

When the Soviets under Gorbachev stood down from the long Cold War confrontation, we knew the strategic landscape would shift, but I don't think anyone expected it to shift so quickly or dramatically. We and our international partners were about to go to war with Iraq. The first unit I shipped to Saudi Arabia was a combat aviation brigade equipped with Apache helicopters. I managed to get it there with all its equipment and munitions, sending some elements by train to Livorno, Italy, and loading them on ships there, which cut two days off the travel time. The Apache brigade was the only unit that arrived in the Persian Gulf fully equipped and ready to fight. As soon as they landed, they were deployed to screen the 101st Airborne on the Saudi border. And now, just as all this was happening, I was being posted to a region that had always been regarded as a military backwater, one I didn't know that much about.

On November 20, I turned Fifth Corps over to my old friend David Maddox and flew directly to SOUTHCOM's headquarters in Panama City to check in with my new command. After two days in Panama, I left for Washington for the confirmation process and to start getting myself oriented about what to expect and what was expected of me. My first stop was the Johns Hopkins Hospital, where Thurman was being treated. He was quite ill then but perfectly clear. He told me he enthusiastically supported my new assignment. I thought that he had likely pushed for the appointment.

Thurman's Operation Just Cause, which removed Noriega, had taken place less than a year earlier. Panama was still unstable, he told me, of great concern because of the canal. There were serious insurgencies going on elsewhere in the region—in El Salvador, Peru, Honduras, and Colombia. Narcotics production and smuggling were exploding. I could expect little support or attention from Washington, he said, especially now that General Norman Schwarzkopf's Desert Storm buildup was soaking up every available resource from other commands, including SOUTHCOM. SOUTHCOM needed someone who would be able to operate effectively with few assets in hand.

While in Washington, I spoke with Cheney and Chairman of the Joint Chiefs Colin Powell about the issues they believed were paramount. I met with members of the Senate Armed Services Committee about their concerns, in particular the civil war in El Salvador and the murders of six

Jesuit priests, their housekeeper, and the housekeeper's daughter a year earlier, apparently by a unit of the Salvadoran military.

These and other atrocities thought to have been carried out by the Salvadoran army raised serious questions about US policy in support of the El Salvador government's war against the Communist insurrection led by the Farabundo Martí National Liberation Front (FMLN). In Congress, opposition to aiding the Salvadoran government was growing. There were also residual questions about the Iran–Contra scandal of the mid-1980s. Although those events had taken place a few years earlier, the affair had cast a shadow over Ronald Reagan's last year in office and had undercut the US government's credibility in Latin America.

Daniel Ortega, the Nicaraguan Sandinista revolutionary, had, along with the Castro regime, been funneling arms to the Salvadoran rebels. Ortega had just now been defeated in his bid to keep the presidency, but he was a formidable figure in an unpredictable situation. So Nicaragua, too, was still a concern.

I had visited Panama and El Salvador while I was working for General Vessey. I had read the cable traffic from SOUTHCOM to the chairman. I wasn't naive about the region, but I didn't have a full grasp of the range of problems or their complexity. I knew above everything else that if I were going to succeed, I would need to develop a clear mission rather than just try to deal with problems in a scattershot manner, with no overriding objective.

Four months earlier President George H. W. Bush had given a speech at the Aspen Institute in which he had articulated an American "peace time" engagement strategy—that is, one that fit the post–Cold War environment. Our global strategy now, he said, must be every bit as constant and committed as it was during the Cold War. The strategy had to reflect our interests and our ideals. Our interests were very clear to most, especially now that our access to the Persian Gulf's oil was being threatened. But he also talked about ideals that are part of who we are as a nation: peace, freedom, human rights, democratic government. Our interests and ideals were often intertwined—at least that's how I saw it in Latin America. The president's speech had a profound impact on me, most importantly as a guide for defining goals and objectives. When it came to articulating my primary objectives, the first on my list was "to strengthen democratic institutions."

The Southern Command comprised nineteen countries. My intention was to spend the first thirty to sixty days of my command understanding and prioritizing the problems in these places. I planned to do a theater-wide assessment, to meet with the American ambassadors and military advisers, heads of state, and other national political leaders. I intended to be proactive, to understand where we could be of help, set goals, and develop strategies to meet them. That was my intention.

It didn't work out the way I hoped. My command headquarters and residence were in Quarry Heights, adjacent to Panama City. In my first ten days, from late November to early December, there were three coups, an insurrection, and a war. One crisis flared after another—or, rather, these crises flared simultaneously. Instead of taking the time to visit and assess my area of operation, I needed to deal with overlapping emergencies. I felt as if I had landed in the middle of a CINC stress test.

The day I arrived, the FMLN shot down a Salvadoran helicopter using a Soviet SA-14 surface-to-air missile, equivalent to our Stinger. Over the next few days, they shot down two more government aircraft. The SA-14s were a bad surprise. We hadn't seen them in El Salvador before now. The FMLN had almost certainly gotten them from Nicaragua, which got them from the Soviets. We didn't know how many the FMLN had, but the SA-14s were weapons that had the potential to alter the balance. A few years earlier the CIA's decision to give Stingers to the mujahideen in Afghanistan had led to the defeat of the Soviets there, an ominous precedent.

The Salvadoran air force was the government's most effective tool against the insurgents, who were now about to negate that tool. The morale of the government forces plummeted. We had been supporting the Salvadorans against the FMLN insurgency for more than a decade. The previous year a new president had been democratically elected. It seemed possible that now the battlefield would start unraveling and the country's government might fall victim.

I called Washington to inform the Joint Chiefs that a new, more dangerous FMLN offensive was gaining momentum. But the US national command structure, the chiefs and the secretary of defense, had bigger things on their plate. President Bush and Secretary Cheney had called up National Guard troops and reservists for deployment in the Persian Gulf. The period of enlistment had been extended by 180 days. Our buildup of forces in the Saudi desert was accelerating. The United Nations Security Council had issued an ultimatum to Saddam Hussein to leave Kuwait or face the use of force. Washington had little attention to spare for El Salvador. Most of SOUTHCOM's assets had already been shifted to support Desert Storm.

As I was making plans to fly to El Salvador, Karen called from our living quarters, not far from my headquarters. "There are men out here in combat gear," she said. "They're digging a machine-gun position in our front yard."

I said, "What?"

We were just then monitoring a developing insurrection. Colonel Eduardo Herrera Hassan, one of Noriega's chief henchmen, had staged an escape by helicopter from the prison island where he was incarcerated. He had first stirred up trouble in a police precinct in one of Panama City's suburbs. The next thing we knew, he and a band of armed adherents had taken over the main National Police barracks near the Panama Canal Authority offices. My own command headquarters were nearby, and my living quarters only a couple of hundred yards away, which explained the machine-gun emplacement.

My big concern was that all 10,500 members of the National Police were former soldiers. Herrera was a bad guy and charismatic. He was broadcasting on the police net urging National Police commands in other provinces to revolt. We had no idea how many might decide to throw in with him. If six or seven provinces rallied to him, we'd have a wide crisis on our hands. If any sizeable number of police joined him, it wasn't impossible that he might bring the government down and that we would be faced with the need for another Just Cause. I was in contact with the Joint Chiefs to determine how we could muster whatever combat power might be necessary here. What forces were available? The Eighteenth Airborne Corps was normally assigned to SOUTHCOM, but they were in Saudi Arabia. The Second Marine Division was also on call, but they were either on their way to Saudi Arabia or there already. The Joint Chiefs finally alerted First Corps, based in Washington State, which was normally focused on Korea. The only troops on hand were some special forces and a battalion headed by Bill Hartzog, who was the army commander for SOUTHCOM. (Bill had called me about the gun in our front yard: "I'm not going to let anything happen to your family," he said.)

The police barracks were in a big compound. Herrera was occupying the first floor and basement, where the communications center was. I then learned we had our own people in the compound, too, a ten-man military support group assigned to retrain the police. One of them, Jim Steel, was a friend who had served with me in Europe at various times. We had now mobilized a military police company and an infantry company in case we had to face a hostage situation. But I was able to communicate directly with Steel and his people. "Get out of there now," I told him. "But, sir," he said. He thought he might be able to do some good inside.

"Get out," I ordered. "I want you and your advisers out of there."

Steel was able to get his people out. I had to make a quick decision here. I wasn't going to let this insurrection succeed. The question was: What was the best way to stop it?

There were three options. The best was that the Panama National Police would do it by themselves. The second best would be for us to do it together with the police. The third option was that US forces would handle it alone. I preferred the first option but would carry out the second if we had to. But we clearly didn't want to stop this with US forces alone. The Panamanians had the beginnings of a civilian government. The president, Guillermo Endara, had been in power since Noriega's fall. This was a new, fragile democracy. It needed to be strengthened, which meant Endara had to take this situation in hand. Gringos—us—were an element in Herrera's propaganda. But if the Panamanian government responded, that would be a different story.

I hadn't even had time to meet President Endara personally yet. I reached him on the phone, then I went to see him. My intention was to get him to act. "You are the president of Panama," I said. "You have jurisdiction, not me. It's your business to go in and end this riot that's going on."

Endara seemed frightened by the idea. "I can't do that," he said. But I was insistent. "You need to get a representative in there, a negotiator." He urged me to throw a cordon of US troops around the barracks. I told him he had to commit Panamanian forces, loyal police.

The stand-off at the barracks lasted through the night. But early the next morning the US chargé d'affaires called me (the ambassador was away), saying, "Endara's government really wants this stopped, and they want you to support them."

"If they want our help," I told him, "I need a formal request in writing. I don't want this to look as if we're taking unilateral action."

Significantly, Endara then called a break-of-dawn cabinet and Security Council meeting to get their permission to issue a formal request for help. This was a new, untested government, but you could see the wheels of democracy beginning to turn.

When I received the request, I faxed it to the Joint Chiefs, and Admiral David Jeremiah, the vice chairman, took it to Secretary Cheney. I got back a paragraph giving me permission to render assistance.

Meanwhile, Endara's negotiator was now inside the barracks—which showed great courage. The negotiator told the police inside that anyone who wanted to stay with Colonel Herrera could do that. "Everyone else," he said, "can come out, and nothing will be held against you.

You will be supporting your country and your country's government." Many followed his lead and did come out.

By this time, the government had assembled more than a hundred police at the front gate of the barracks. Bill Hartzog and his troops were in backup, watching, but the Panamanians were taking charge of ending this thing.

Tension was building as we waited to see what Herrera would do. Before the government had mustered loyal police in front of the barracks, Herrera might have thought he held the upper hand. If some of the provinces rallied to him, he would be seen as a national leader confronting the imperialist gringos who had taken over the country. But now, with Panama's own forces facing him and none of the provincial police responding to his appeals, Herrera's options were closing down. The chances were growing that he might just surrender.

Instead, suddenly Herrera and a large group of his bodyguards burst out the back of the barracks, broke through the perimeter fencing, and headed toward the Presidential Palace, only half a mile away. It looked as if there were seventy or eighty of them, men with flak vests and automatic rifles, their faces blackened. Herrera intended to rally people to him along the way and create a confrontation with Endara and the government. But a short way off they ran into a three-man American outpost. The GIs there backed up but then were reinforced by their squad and soon by their platoon. With his men in position, Hartzog called me. "If you can settle this without shooting everybody up," I told him, "do that. I want this thing to end peacefully."

The last thing I wanted was casualties, not ours and not Panamanians. We had already been accused of murdering four hundred Panamanians— people supposedly killed by American troops during Just Cause—and burying them in a mass grave. "Do you think this is true?" I told the press. "I have a platoon of forty soldiers with shovels. You show me where these so-called burial sites are. I will dig them up, and if we find four hundred bodies in there, I will be the first to apologize for my country and for the military. Show me where," I said.

There weren't any burial sites, not for four hundred, not for any number. The accusation was pure propaganda. And I wasn't going to start killing Panamanians outside the police barracks either if it wasn't absolutely necessary, adding to whatever distorted perceptions might be out there. But Bill Hartzog was up to the job, and he had good, disciplined troops. In a tense confrontation, Herrera couldn't decide what to do, and in a matter of minutes Hartzog's soldiers had captured him and the others with him. "No shots fired," Hartzog reported.

"Turn them over to the locals," I told him. "You've done your job."

We had done what we needed to: support the government, not act in place of the government. The Panamanians had also responded well. It was their decision to get forces down to the barracks, their decision to tell the police contingent inside with Herrera to come out, which most of them did, which meant those who didn't were acting against their own country. "This was the first test for Endara," I told Hartzog when it was all over. "We fought Just Cause. Now we're in the government-rebuilding stage. Your troops were magnificent. You stopped them from going to the presidential palace. And you did it without a single casualty."

Meanwhile, in El Salvador the SA-14 shootdowns were ongoing. The first had occurred on November 23, two days after I formally assumed command. The downed aircraft was an A-37 ground-support jet. The second, a Huey helicopter, was hit three days later. The third was an AC-47 gunship, shot down the day before the Herrera insurrection, with the loss of all seven crew members.

The presence of these missiles forced the Salvadoran helicopters out of the sky—the attack helicopters, the medevac helicopters, the supply helicopters. Also the ground-support A-37s. The Salvadoran air force had only two AC-47 gunships, the famous "Spookies" of the Vietnam War, and one of them was now gone. The loss of these planes was especially damaging to El Salvador's warfighting capacity. The Salvadoran army had a limited number of relatively short-range artillery pieces and consequently relied on the air force for firepower. With the logistical and resupply provided by the air force, the army's ground units had wide possibilities for maneuver and could stay out in the field for extended periods. With the air supply and fire support out of action, El Salvadoran forces were forced to reorient the way they fought—not easy at any time, especially not in the midst of the major offensive the FMLN launched just as I took command.

On December 10, seven days after the latest shootdown, I flew from Panama to El Salvador's Ilopango Air Force Base. Karen came with me. I got some flak for that because it was not a safe journey. Because of the threat of FMLN antiaircraft fire, we couldn't make a nice, gentle approach to the airfield. Instead it was a combat descent, where the pilot gets right above the field and then makes a nose dive straight down into it, an extremely steep approach. Karen was steady as a rock, but I couldn't help noticing that her knuckles turned white grasping onto the seat as the pilot started his dive. In many respects, the American Military Group and the American community were at least as happy to see her as to see me. She met with many of the spouses, including the ambassador's wife and the wives of embassy personnel, who were living there under harsh, wartime circumstances. It meant a great deal that the new CINC's wife would take risks to meet and get to know them. That wasn't taken lightly. In Latin America, establishing personal relationships can go a long way. Karen's presence indicated that we had a real investment here, so that was confidence building by itself.

My intention was to assess the situation and decide what was in the best US interest to do. El Salvador had been fighting a bloody civil war against the FMLN Communist insurgency for ten-plus years. More than seventy thousand Salvadorans had lost their lives. The United States had made a very large monetary investment in supporting El Salvador's government. At the same time, there was widespread conviction that the government was deeply corrupt and that its forces had engaged in atrocities and human rights violations, including the murder of four missionary nuns in 1980 and the assassination of six Jesuit priests only a year before I arrived. The memory of the nuns was still very much alive, but the murder of the priests was probably the most significant event of the long war in terms of international coverage and in stoking opposition to American involvement in the US Congress. Political pressure there had resulted in limiting the number of military advisers to fifty-five and had at least temporarily cut off the military aid pipeline.

Once on the ground in El Salvador, I met with President Alfredo Cristiani, who had been elected just a year earlier, and with Emilio Ponce, the minister of defense, whom I had met earlier when I was in El Salvador as General Vessey's XO. At that time, Ponce was commanding a brigade that was well trained and would fight. I was impressed with him then and was happy to see that he was now the defense chief.

I saw some of our Military Group people, including Colonel Mark Hamilton, the group's commander, as well as other advisers and people from the Salvadoran army. The question was: Given the terrible human rights history and the aggressive opposition in Congress, was it worth continuing our involvement in El Salvador? How did that equation work out? In the end, the issue came down to America's national interest: Did we want to preserve this government and work toward building its democratic institutions? And if we did, what steps were called for, especially now that we were in the middle of an FMLN offensive? The Salvadoran army's morale had hit rock bottom. The funding supply had been cut off—$40 million that was in the pipeline but that an angry US Congress had put on hold. For the military, that was like cutting off blood flow to the heart.

Even given all the problems, the answer to the question of whether we should try to build on what was there or allow the FMLN to dominate the battlefield and potentially take power in El Salvador was, to my mind, self-evident. Yes, we needed to work with this government and do everything we could to move it in the right direction. My overriding mission at SOUTHCOM, as I saw it, was to strengthen democratic institutions. El Salvador was not Panama, but the similarities were evident enough: weak, problematic governments that, however, offered the potential for growth as democracies. In Panama, we had just a few days earlier dealt with a threat to that potential. Here in El Salvador, buffeted by an insurgent offensive, we were facing a graver threat.

To assess the situation, I met with Cristiani, Ponce, and Hamilton. I visited a forward brigade to get the smell and feel of exactly what was going on the ground and what was needed.

When I had done my rounds, I came to two conclusions. The first was that we needed to take action quickly to raise the confidence level of the government and the military. The fighting was not going well, especially now that the Salvadoran air force was grounded. The FMLN was a formidable force. It had torn up two of El Salvador's elite reinforced battalions and was making headway in many parts of the country.

What I saw was that we needed to demonstrate that the United States was committed to the fight and would not abandon the government. That meant providing means for the Salvadoran army to fight more effectively. To do that we needed to bring in a surge of weapons as well as aircraft and air force instructors to teach better tactical and evasive techniques to El Salvador's pilots. My second conclusion was that we needed to define a clear mission. What was our objective in El Salvador?

Every military person wants to win the fight against enemy forces, and the SOUTHCOM staff was no different. "The mission in El Salvador is victory," they said. "Really?" I said. This was a highly complex battlefield. It wasn't just military; it was political, psychological, economic, social. The conditions that gave rise to the insurgency were deeply rooted and of long standing. My judgment was that there was no such thing as a military victory here. Winning a military victory over the FMLN was not a feasible mission. When I consulted with Assistant Secretary of State for

Inter-American Affairs Bernie Aronson, his opinion confirmed my own. "The mission there is a negotiated settlement," he said. "I want you," I told our Military Group commander, Hamilton, "to make peace in El Salvador!" And by "peace" I meant peace through a negotiated settlement.

The prerequisite to negotiation was a weapons surge—to bring the Salvadoran army's morale back up and to signal the FMLN that it could not win this war because the United States was not going to abandon our ally. To argue for a surge, right after my visit to El Salvador I flew to Washington. I spoke with Cheney, Powell, National Security Adviser Brent Scowcroft, and everyone else I could get hold of. I told them I had planned to provide an overall assessment after I had visited the entire Southern Command area of operations, but the situation in El Salvador was a crisis that couldn't wait. "I'm trying to bring calm to the chaos that's going on there. We need to infuse new aircraft and other weapons quickly, by the end of January, if we want to avoid a possible disaster there."

The answer was, "Impossible! It will take a year to get security clearance for what you want." "Besides, Powell told me, "Norm Schwarzkopf wants everything you have to go over to the Gulf." Even if it was feasible to give me what I wanted, Congress by law needed a fifteen-day notification. Christmas was coming up, then New Year's. It was not a hopeful scenario.

What my reception in Washington meant was that I had to figure a way to "move without the ball"—a basketball term meaning that someone else is getting the ball, and you have to move independently to help make plays. So that's what I started doing. I needed somehow to scrounge up the arms that would demonstrate our ongoing commitment, and I needed to use these arms to kick-start the Salvadoran army.

Hanging over all my efforts to generate support was the impact the Jesuit priest murders had on Congress and on public opinion generally. The reaction in Congress had been explosive, leading to calls for immediate justice and an end to military aid. The State Department and General Thurman, my predecessor, had been appalled by the murders, and Thurman was ordered to deliver a message to El Salvador's top military leaders: "There is only one way out," he told them. "If some of your people were involved, you need to cough them up." But as of the time I began lobbying for support of a surge in December 1990, there had been no arrests and no trial. The impact those killings had was not going away.

On January 2 of the new year, another atrocity took place, this time perpetrated by the FMLN. On that day an American helicopter flying from San Salvador back to its base in Honduras was shot down.

Ironically, it was taking an alternative route since the more direct flight path would have made it a likely target for the FMLN's SA-14s. But in flying the alternative route, it was hit and brought down by conventional ground fire. The pilot was killed on impact, but two soldiers on board, Lieutenant Colonel David Pickett and Private Earnest Dawson, survived the crash.

FMLN fighters found them, forced them to their knees, and, after waiting an hour or so, shot both in the head.

This cold-blooded execution of wounded and unarmed prisoners of war received sparse news coverage, but it was known. The bodies were recovered, and autopsies revealed what had happened. The FMLN had, of course, committed atrocities before, but these killings happened at a crucial moment in my effort to surge arms to the Salvadoran army. In a sense, they gave my appeals more force. They didn't, however, diminish the sympathy some members of Congress felt for the FMLN.

Representative Joe Moakley of Massachusetts was a leading congressional voice in cutting off our military aid to El Salvador, the head of the so-called Moakley Commission, established to investigate the murder of the priests. In mid-January, I was in the United States on one of my frequent trips to testify to and advise Congress and the Joint Chiefs. Lieutenant Colonel Pickett's funeral was going to take place in Arlington Cemetery while I was there, which would give me an opportunity to pay my respects and speak with his family. I also wanted to meet with Moakley to let him know directly what my assessment was of the war in El Salvador. We did meet, and while we were talking, an aide came in with a message. Moakley turned to me and said that there was an FMLN representative waiting for him, and he needed to excuse himself for fifteen minutes so they could talk.

"Congressman," I said, "I'm about to go to Arlington for the funeral of one of the Americans the FMLN executed. Their plane was shot down; they were unarmed but were captured and then murdered. And you are now going to go meet with representatives of that organization?" My neck was swelling with anger. Moakley left without responding. I left, too, for the funeral.

That was the kind of orientation I was contending with as I looked for how to generate the weapons surge we needed. I managed to find six older-model Huey helicopter gunships that various National Guard units agreed to give me. In the face of Desert Storm's need for all available transport, we were able to fly them down in early January. I also found money for two thousand M-16 rifles. In Panama, we had three A-37 jets that were scheduled to be retired from service; I sent them instead to El Salvador; SOUTHCOM's air wing commander, Brigadier General David Oaks, went with them to teach the Salvadoran pilots how to fly smarter. The Salvadorans named the planes after the three Americans the FMLN had killed: Pickett, Dawson, and Scott. By the end of the month, I had made a good start on demonstrating American commitment and resolve. In the following months, I found ways to bring in hundreds of tons of critically needed ammunition and other supplies and equipment.

The surge didn't happen in a vacuum. In Washington, I was meeting with key senators and representatives and testifying in front of committees. I emphasized in these meetings that my goal was to bring about change. I had no interest in sweeping anything under the rug. I felt that by getting the congressional appropriations we needed, I could assist in the democratization and professionalization of El Salvador's military. The issue was how to balance achieving justice for what had happened to the Jesuits and the four nuns with supporting our strategic interests.

That was the Gordian knot I was trying to cut through, which meant doing a lot of meeting and talking, which became an essential part of the overall campaign I was conducting. This was by no means just a military operation.

The surge in weapons was a demonstration to both the Salvadorans and the FMLN, but it was not a free demonstration. There had to be a quid for our quo. I told Defense Minister Ponce, "We're giving you this, and we're giving you intelligence, but you have got to act. You have got to find them, attack them, capture them, whatever you need to do." And the strategy began to work. With the new equipment and new confidence, the Salvadoran army began utilizing their battalions more effectively, patrolling better, setting ambushes, using artillery and mortar more capably, locating and hitting FMLN headquarters. For all soldiers, success pumps up morale. What looked earlier as if it might become a disaster now began to look like triumph.

At this point, I started going to El Salvador every other week or so to get briefed on what was happening in the field and to further my relationship with Ponce and Cristiani. I also laid it on the line with them about the human rights side. "You need to demonstrate to people in the United Nations and especially in the American Congress that you are doing something about human rights abuses," I told them. "I recommend that you appoint a senior individual to be on the defense minister's personal staff and make him the human rights person. You should make sure you publicize arrests and trials of people who are accused of violations."

They did that. I said the same thing to the Salvadoran army. "Appoint a staff officer, give him a formal designation. Have him oversee this area, and track what's happening. I want to be briefed on what you're doing and what actions you're taking against human rights violators." The army started to do that. It was able to demonstrate that it was arresting officers and trying them. I visited the US Special Forces trainers who were working with the Salvadoran army units. I discussed with them the need to integrate human rights training into combat training. I had told Moakley and other congressional leaders that I was not interested in sweeping anything under the rug, and I meant it. I didn't regard our support as simply offering up all this equipment and intelligence for free. I wanted trade-offs.

The surge created an interesting dynamic in the Salvadoran government and army. With success on the warfighting front and with the confidence US commitment instilled, the civilian government gained an increasing sense of purpose and control. Cristiani was emerging as a strong, democratically inclined leader, which had not been at all obvious when he came to power in 1989 in an election the FMLN boycotted. At the same time, the army became far more accepting of civilian control. Its human rights record improved dramatically. It was as if the military was no longer so afraid that it was going to lose the country that it had to engage in violent suppression and massacres, which had in fact marked its history. The army subordinated itself to the judicial branch and to the political leadership. All of the security assistance I sent went through the president's office. The military had to come to him with their budget and their requests.

I had decided from the beginning that my primary objective in Latin America would be to strengthen democratic institutions. That objective included, very much so, a collateral goal, which was to professionalize the armies of the nations we were dealing with. By "professionalism," I didn't mean just technical or tactical professionalism; I meant institutional professionalism—apolitical posture, civilian control, respect for human rights. In other words, how does a military operate in a democratic political system? We needed to instill in our partners what it means to be a military in a democracy. That was a tall order in a theater where army officers had a history of promulgating coups. But as 1991 wore on, we were definitely seeing the professionalization of the Salvadoran army, part of the growing legitimization of the democratic process there.

We also obviously were making a point the FMLN understood. They saw that we were not going to let them beat the Salvadoran army in the field. Their fighting units were being hit hard. Their hopes of raising a popular revolt and arming the masses were going nowhere. We began picking up signals they were ready to talk.

In the summer of 1991, the State Department indicated to the US ambassador to El Salvador, William Walker, that it might be fruitful to initiate a discussion. Walker did that. He arranged to meet with FMLN representatives, mainly as a sign of American openness. Walker very courageously agreed to do this in Santa Marta, an FMLN-controlled village in the interior. He took with him Dick McCall, a staff member on the Senate Foreign Relations Committee, and Lionel Gomez, a Salvadoran expatriate working for Congressman Moakley. Walker also told me he wanted to take our Military Group commander, Mark Hamilton, because it was felt that without our military involved, a diplomatic contact wouldn't have any weight with the FMLN. So Hamilton went as well.

That evening in Santa Marta, one hundred or so FMLN fighters filtered into the town. The discussions went into the night and over to the next morning. When the Americans got back to San Salvador, the capital, Hamilton reported that he thought they had made progress. They had managed to have frank talks with several FMLN leaders. Hamilton himself had struck up a relationship with Raul Hercules, *comandante* of one of the FMLN's constituent organizations. He thought they had made a promising start. He also told me the meeting looked like a scene from a bad B movie. The whole time they were talking an FMLN fighter wearing a black eye patch and bandana had held an AK-47 on him. Many of the guerrillas had bandoliers crossed over their chests, macho looking but a bad idea for many reasons. They had also passed around a plastic jug of *chicha*, moonshine. The guerrillas were taking liberal swigs, but Ambassador Walker was wary, Hamilton said, so Hamilton had been forced to uphold American honor.

B movie or not, the Santa Marta meeting was a catalyst that opened the way to further meetings. Comandante Hercules even arranged to meet Hamilton at his home in the capital. Hamilton dismissed his security detail. His wife greeted Hercules at the door and served dinner. Hercules had been wounded multiple times. In the ten-plus years of war, his first wife had been killed, then two subsequent wives were also. Hamilton thought Hercules's desire for peace was genuine. "We can make peace with this man," he told me.

Hercules was tired of the fighting and killing. That may have been true for other FMLN leaders, too, especially now that it was clear the military option wasn't going well and that the United States was in El

Salvador for the long run. They weren't by any means giving up, but they were open to serious talks. And what they were getting from us was that although we were committed to supporting the Salvadoran army, we were open to talks as well.

The military side was turning against the insurgents; the political side was, too. In March 1991, legislative elections were held. The army conducted itself well, and observers certified the voting was conducted fairly. The FMLN didn't allow participation in the areas they controlled, but they didn't attack voting elsewhere, either.

We had also been making progress toward addressing the Jesuit case. After the Salvadoran army staff designated a human rights officer, Ambassador Walker and I had a long talk with Ponce about the case. An investigation had been opened into the killings, but the army was stonewalling. "Why don't you cooperate in the Jesuit case?" I asked Ponce. "You're the leader, you're the one who has to set an example. We're providing you with all this equipment; you've got the momentum back. You're in a position of strength. Now is the time to say that the army and you *personally* will cooperate." After some thought, Ponce decided to do that. He put out a letter signed by the top military leadership affirming that they would testify. Then he called the judge and said, "I'm ready to appear any time you want."

After the Santa Marta meeting, serious peace talks started, and by mid-November 1991 they had reached the point where the FMLN announced a unilateral cease-fire. At the end of December, the government and the guerrillas initialed a preliminary agreement, arbitrated in part by the United Nations and facilitated by Mark Hamilton, who had been called to New York to help resolve a number of crucial roadblocks.

The peace treaty was finalized on January 16, 1992, putting an end to twelve years of vicious war. I had been working with this situation for only a little more than a year.

The agreement, formally called the Chapultepec Peace Accords, was signed in Mexico City by the FMLN and the Salvadoran government. It stipulated a series of implementation steps, including the dissolution of El Salvador's Rapid Deployment Battalions, the core of the country's army, simultaneously with the disarming of FMLN forces. These demobilizations were to take place over a year. The government proceeded with its demobilization according to schedule, but the FMLN dragged its feet, which was a major concern. I encouraged Ponce to meet the deadlines regardless of what the FMLN did. "Sir," I told him, "you are the professional military of the democratic government of El Salvador. You are part of a representative democracy. I strongly urge that you meet every require-ment of the peace agreement, even if the FMLN does not. At the end of this compliance period, you are going to remain; the FMLN is going to go away." Ponce decided to follow this advice, against pressure from right-wing hard-liners. He demobilized before the FMLN did. As a result, the army gained enormous international credibility, which put the FMLN under pressure to follow suit, which in the end it did.

The last act in this drama was especially painful. The UN had estab-lished a Truth Commission to examine the human rights abuses and atrocities that had taken place over the twelve-year course of the war. The commission had no legal standing, but it had moral standing in the inter-national community and in the American Congress. At the conclusion of its inquiry, the Truth Commission issued a judgment that the entire Sal-vadoran General Staff, the Estado Major, should resign.

President Cristiani was reluctant to force that judgment. My sense was that he believed it might stoke a right-wing coup against his govern-ment. Again I met with Ponce. We had long before this established a strong personal relationship. I knew he trusted my advice, but how he might take it in this situation I couldn't say.

"I'm giving you my best judgment," I said. "You have won the war. Now you have to win the peace. Cristiani says there's a snag in the peace agreement. It's not going to happen unless you resign. What that means is that if you love your country, you and your staff need to resign. That's my strong recommendation." This was like telling members of the West Ger-man government after the Berlin Wall came down and they had won a great victory that they would have to resign. It was hard for him to swallow.

I visited with Ponce several times. I went with him to see Cristiani. I met with his staff. It was an excruciating process.

"I am not guilty of any of these things," Ponce said. "The Truth Com-mission has no legal basis. I want to take this to court."

"General Ponce," I said, "you can certainly do that. But my recom-mendation is that you take this last step in solidifying peace in your coun-try. You've done great work as a soldier and great work as minister of defense. You've brought peace to your country, largely on your terms. This is now the sacrifice that you need to make."

There was real risk here. In the wings were the extremist elements in the military. If Ponce resigned, what their reaction might be was anything but predictable. In a way, El Salvador was an experiment in the surviv-ability of democratic government. "You have younger people you've trained," I told Ponce. "They'll step in to take your place. This is a choice you need to make."

In the course of our talks, I could see Ponce putting on the mantle of statesmanship. In the end, he made the decision to resign, for himself and his staff. In total, almost a thousand officers left the military. In Ponce's public statement, he said he had made his decision "as a soldier to satisfy the desire for peace of the entire population."

The end of El Salvador's civil war nightmare gave me tremendous satisfaction. But as the final stages of the peace accord's implementation regime were advancing, I received a saddening note from the son of my former mentor General William DePuy. As I knew, DePuy was ailing badly. He had retired from the army in 1977 at the relatively young age of fifty-eight, but he had been *the* key figure in remaking a military that had emerged from the Vietnam War damaged and demoralized. He had been my first commander, my mentor after I came out of West Point. I had known him from my start as a second lieutenant straight through to this point, when as a four-star general I was drawing toward the last part of my own career. Throughout my entire time as a soldier, I had had strong, forceful, even brilliant commanders, but no one had been more important to me than DePuy. Now he was dying, suffering from what had been identified as Creutzfeldt-Jakob disease, with all its devastating physical and neurodegenerative effects. DePuy was near the end, his son, Bill Jr., told me. He had only occasional moments of lucidity. In one of them, he had mentioned my name and said he wanted to see me. "He may not recognize you," Bill Jr. said, "but please come."

DePuy's family had kept him at home as long as they were able to care for him. But the effects of Creutzfeldt-Jakob were so debilitating that he eventually needed the full-time care of a nursing facility, which is where I went to see him.

I knocked on the door of his room and went in. His son was there with him and told him that I had come to see him. I didn't know if that registered at all. DePuy looked diminished, wasted. He couldn't speak. I couldn't tell if he knew me. This was a man so vibrant, so full of vigor and stamina and intellectual power, always a step ahead of everyone else, and now here he was, like this. I knew that if I spent any time at his bedside, I would be caught up in pity, and that was the last thing DePuy would want. I told his son, "It's very hard for me to see him like this."

"I know," he said, "but he wanted you to come."

I tried to talk to him, although it was impossible to express what he had meant to me. I could get out only a few halting words. "We've been so grateful for your leadership. I'm getting toward the end of my career, and I have a lot to thank you for, for so much of what I've been able to do." Utterly inadequate, and impossible to know if he understood or even heard me.

I tried to get some sort of conversation going, although it was obvious that wasn't going to happen. But then he reached up and traced my face with his hand, as if he were saying, "I know who you are." That was nearly too much for me. I told Bill Jr., "I'll stay as long as you want me to. But this isn't easy for me, and I'm sure it's not easy for him." I stayed another ten minutes or so, then I left him, the toughest, most demanding boss anyone could have and the greatest teacher.

12

SOUTHCOM 2
The Drug Trade

The El Salvador military crisis struck just as I took over at SOUTHCOM, as did the police insurrection in Panama. They were separate crises with their own characteristics and levels of threat. But the overall mission I had set for myself—strengthening our allies' democratic political systems—gave me the conceptual framework I needed to analyze these situations and understand what my role, or SOUTHCOM's role, should be. President George H. W. Bush had stressed in his Aspen speech the moral theme of America's democratic values. As events developed in my area of command, that theme in one way or another underlay every step I took. The challenge was how best to engage the powers I commanded to support that effort in a region where we had few resources and where something other than warfighting was the US goal.

El Salvador and Panama were distinct situations, but the same insidious problem was affecting countries throughout the region: narcotrafficking. For ten years, the US national command structure had recognized drug flow into the United States as a major security concern, almost on the same level as the region's Marxist insurgencies.

I saw the drug trade in exactly that way. Drug trafficking was a threat to the vision of democratic development in the region's nations. In the United States, illegal narcotics were killing ten thousand Americans a year. Every drug plane that landed was like a Scud missile carrying death and destruction. The drug problem was costing tens of billions of dollars in police enforcement, medical treatment, rehabilitation, and incarceration. Most of the drugs were coming up from Peru, Bolivia, and Colombia, through Mexico into the United States. But the entire theater was infected by the narcotraffickers as they spread corruption and broke down civil life. The traffickers frequently paid those helping them move their product with cocaine instead of with pesos or dollars, so in poor little countries like Belize and Guatemala cocaine was being sold openly on the streets. With the growth of gangs and cartels, there was no question in my mind that if effective American assistance weren't provided, we were looking at a phenomenon that could seriously destabilize America's southern flank. Combatting the traffickers was primarily a law enforcement task. The challenge as I saw it was to figure out how SOUTHCOM could support law enforcement agencies both in the United States and in the regional countries that were on the front lines. The US military was not permitted to act as law enforcement by the Posse Comitatus Act, but the army in any event had no interest in breaking down doors and making arrests. In addition, the military was instinctively averse to undertaking activities other than warfighting. Other kinds of missions tended to trigger a reflexive negative response. The army was a warfighting organization. It existed to fight wars. We needed to stick to that mission, not drain resources and distract ourselves doing things that were other people's business. That was the historic orientation, which retained a strong grip on military thinking.

By 1989, though, the narcotics problem had reached such proportions that President Bush issued secret National Security Directive 18 ordering the Department of Defense to assist antidrug operations "with all means available." Department personnel would not be allowed to accompany host-government forces in antidrug field operations, but other support activities were to be a priority.

Max Thurman, my predecessor, had begun implementing that directive, looking at budgeting plans for the creation of country teams. But Thurman's efforts were brought to a halt first by Just Cause, the operation that removed Noriega, then by his illness, which left SOUTHCOM without a commander during the months before my appointment.

What I saw when I came in was that dealing with the trafficking problem on a country-by-country basis was not going to work. The problem was regional. If we went after narcotraffickers in Guatemala, they would bounce into Honduras or Panama or Costa Rica. The traffickers had routes set up through the region, and they had the agility to switch from one to the other. If we were serious, we needed to create a regional strategy.

At SOUTHCOM, I began to define what that strategy would look like and how it would operate in a theater where law enforcement agencies had the lead and many countries experienced internal and external problems that might not be conducive to cooperation. "Since we can't be the lead," I asked myself, "how can we facilitate? Can we provide intelligence to our antidrug agencies, the Drug Enforcement Agency, Customs, and the others? What about radar and communication links? Can we provide training and equipment and actionable intelligence to host nations? Can we facilitate coordination?"

As soon as I began exploring options like this, I found that US law enforcement agencies simply did not talk to each other. The situation was like how the CIA, FBI, and local law enforcement agencies in the United States didn't coordinate or share information prior to the terrorist attacks on September 11, 2001. They all were guarding their turf and their own funding pipelines into Congress. I found my guide here in US Army doctrine promulgated by DePuy's TRADOC and incorporated in *Field Manual* 105, which included a section that stipulated, "The Army will not operate alone." Army forces, the doctrine stated, had to be ready to operate together not just with other services but also with other governmental agencies and allies, even where the army was not in the lead.

In our situation, each of the law enforcement agencies—the DEA, the CIA, Customs, the Coast Guard, and others—had a narrow piece of the counterdrug action, but if you put them all together and coordinated them, their effectiveness could increase exponentially. I saw that SOUTH-COM could provide the glue to bring all these other agencies together. We weren't in command; we were in support. We weren't impinging on anyone's budget. We didn't care who got the credit for successes. SOUTHCOM was the ideal organization and structure to establish unity of effort.

I invited the agency czars to meetings in Panama so everyone could get a clear perspective on the potential for cooperation and joint action. I met with the presidents of Colombia, Venezuela, Peru, and Ecuador. They all harbored instinctive fears of American domination, but I told them, "Let me show you what is happening in your country. It isn't the United States that's violating your sovereignty; it's the narcotraffickers." We began to get critical host-nation support for the fight. The motto I used to promulgate this effort to achieve unity of purpose was "Un Equipo, Una Lucha—One Team, One Fight."

I viewed the counterdrug effort the same way I would view a military campaign. In El Salvador, we looked for ways to cut off the reinforcement of supplies to the FMLN and ways to reinforce government forces. In the drug fight, we looked for ways to take the initiative away from the narcotraffickers and interdict their efforts.

For the traffickers, national borders had no significance. The key growing areas were the Upper Huallaga in Peru and the Chapare region in Bolivia. Farmers there grew the coca leaf and made it into paste or base. Then, a mom-and-pop small plane would fly down from Colombia, land somewhere on a road or field, deliver money to the growers, and load on six hundred kilos of cocaine base. The plane would then fly the cocaine back to Colombia, where it was refined, packaged, and distributed out to the United States and the rest of the world.

I got the Twelfth Air Force to put together a huge map display of Central and South America that showed three months of air tracks of narco planes going back and forth between the key countries involved—Peru, Bolivia, and Colombia. There were many hundreds of flights, each one carrying six hundred kilos of cocaine. Seeing the activity laid out like this was a shock. The magnitude of it astonished us.

The picture was like nothing so much as a beehive, with bees flitting back and forth between the producers and refiners and then north to Central America and Mexico with refined cocaine destined for American cities. In my briefings and presentations, I began using the beehive analogy. I drew maps that illustrated the patterns. "What do we do?" I asked. "Do we swat at the bees, or do we go after the beehive, or both? And how do we do it? Can we interdict the narcos' air bridges between their growing, refining, and distribution operations?" Going after the beehive—the growing and initial processing of the leaf—I thought of as the "deep fight." It meant attacking the hive, the queen bee. The transit area—coming up through Central America to our border—was the "close fight." Then there was the "rear fight," which was the smuggling and distribution along the US border and into US cities. We needed to link all that together in a comprehensive plan.

I thought that if we could help the US agencies and the host countries interdict the narcos' ability to transport, the supply of coca leaf would go up, and the price paid to the farmers would go down. If that happened, the campesinos would be more amenable to switching over to alternative crops. Meanwhile, if we could interdict the air bridge, the mom-and-pop pilots would demand higher prices in return for the higher risk, which would raise the price of coke on American streets and cut down use. That was the theory.

The key was first to interdict the air bridge. To do this, we began coupling together the intelligence from airborne warning-and-control system sources and from Customs Department P-3 surveillance aircraft. We had radar that could sweep the skies over most of the northern part of South America. We developed a four-engine De Havilland plane that packed all the relevant technology on board—surveillance, communication, ground and air targeting—and deployed it. We coordinated with the CIA, which used little Schweizer aircraft that could livestream videos. The air links had been the narcos' key advantage, giving them fast and safe transport of drugs and money. But now for the first time we could see them, we could track them, we knew where they were flying and where they were landing. We turned the narcos' advantage into a vulnerability.

I named the comprehensive plan "Support Justice" to signify that our role was to assist law enforcement. I presented my beehive map to the region's political leaders. My message to them was direct and clear—the drug traffickers were violating their sovereignty and corrupting their judges, their police, and their militaries; the traffickers were poisoning their children. I highlighted the resources we could bring to bear, getting their buy-in for emplacing radars at strategic points and establishing communications links. I worked closely with our ambassadors and military attachés to reinforce their country-specific efforts. Since SOUTH-COM was resource poor, we initiated a "surge" approach. We didn't have the wherewithal to fly constantly, but if we knew a host nation was planning a military or police operation, we focused our assets to assist them, intensifying our surveillance and providing logistical support.

We built our capabilities in stages, setting up radar and communications links, coordinating US and host-nation tracking efforts, and training host-nation pilots. We put a command-and-control center in Panama so that any plane going into Latin America would come up on our screens at SOUTHCOM. We sent Special Forces soldiers to help train national quick-reaction teams that could move in on aircraft landing sites, arrest traffickers, and confiscate drug loads. The payoffs began quickly. In an early action in Bolivia, we identified and seized more than forty planes in a joint DEA/Bolivian government operation.

SOUTHCOM's forces weren't on the ground in this action, but we gave substantial assistance. In Colombia, with our intelligence and logistical support Colombia's army began hitting narco planes as they landed and taking down the lab sites they were delivering to. Before long, we estimated we were sweeping up half the total number of flights coming in. Early on, the Hondurans shot a narco flight down, which scared the hell out of the traffickers, who saw that our threat to them wasn't just in Bolivia and Peru; we were now able to attack them en route to Mexico.

With our help, the Peruvians began shooting down planes, which brought a kind of uproar from the Joint Chiefs' staff, who were not enthusiastic about the fact that SOUTHCOM was engaging in activities other than warfighting. The staff had never warmed to President Bush's National Security Directive 18, which ordered military assistance to the counterdrug programs; they didn't think that was what SOUTHCOM should be doing. I was hearing, "You cannot do this. How do you know it's not a doctor or a dentist flying down from Colombia to Peru? Don't you realize you might accidentally kill civilians?" But in the Upper Huallaga Valley a plane taking off at 2:00 in the morning from a dirt field was not typically going to be a dentist from Bogotá. To my knowledge, we never did shoot down a non-drug-carrying plane.

I had a spectacular video from Peru of a plane that had landed on a gravel road in the remote Huallaga Valley. We had tracked the landing and given the information to the Peruvians, who sent a platoon in. When narco guards kept the platoon at bay, the unit moved down the road and shot the plane down as it was taking off. The video captured the plane exploding in a huge ball of flames. I showed it to Dick Clarke at the NSC, who was a leading supporter of our efforts. "This will send shock waves through the narco regimes," I told him. "If we use it right, it's going to be a shot in the arm for all the countries down there."

As the successes mounted, our agencies became increasingly enthusiastic about collaborating with each other. The remarkable Carol Hallet, who was head of Customs, committed her P-3s to the fight and flew down with them, even piloting one. Jack Devine, the CIA's chief of counternarcotics, incorporated the agency's intelligence gathering into the comprehensive effort. "One Team, One Fight" caught on, not just as a slogan but as a reality. At one point, a representative from the US Treasury Department came to see me and announced he was from FinCen, the Financial Crimes Enforcement Center, which I had never heard of.

"Sit down," I said. "What do you do?"

"Sir," he said, "I track the money. I'm here to brief you on what we're finding."

With Treasury's help, we began to nail down the narcos' money flows as well as the details of their operations.

As we gained support and moved from phase one of Support Justice to successive phases, we were able to bring more and more assets to bear. On the Texas border with Mexico, US Customs controlled a series of tethered, intelligence-gathering aerostats—blimplike balloons equipped with radar and communications. The traffickers moved their drugs through tunnels and vehicles at crossing points, but large flows were coming in via small planes that landed in Texas and New Mexico. With Carol Hallet's help, we fed the aerostat information into our interdiction system, which now stretched all the way from the growing regions to the US border.

As we hoped, our combined operations netted increasing tonnages of cocaine. Unfortunately, at times press reports and announcements in Congress about the drug war were reminiscent of the body counts in Vietnam, equating success or failure with quantities of cocaine seized. But body counts had never told the story in Vietnam, and tonnages seized didn't tell the story here. Seizures were dramatic, and with every major success morale among the agencies soared. But the truth was that cocaine production was so vast that even with all the takedowns, lab destructions, and captures, large quantities of narcotics still made it across the US border and onto American streets.

The answer, as I saw it, was to achieve a "steady-state" antidrug action—that is, continual operations in given areas rather than on-and-off single exercises. I wanted to take the initiative away from the traffickers. I wanted to put them under constant pressure. The more resources we could marshal, the more disruption we could cause. I pushed hard on that in Washington, testifying often and trying to squeeze Congress and the Department of Defense for more funding, coordinating with our ambassadors, and intensifying our efforts to promote trust and confidence among the host governments, always looking to further a unity of effort.

I saw the counterdrug war not only as a dam to stop the drug flow but also as a mechanism for furthering military professionalism, military support for democracy, and regional cooperation. I began using American reservists as an element in that strategy. I brought National Guard units down to host countries as part of their training, many of them engineering detachments. They built roads, clinics, and schools in a program I called Fuertes Caminos: Strong Roads. In my three years at SOUTH-COM, tens of thousands of American citizen soldiers engaged with the military and civilians in host countries. The reservists got great training in deploying, conducting missions, and redeploying. At the same time, they reinforced and demonstrated to the host-country militaries the idea of the military's role in a democratic political system; they were superb examples of what it meant. Their commanders interfaced with the local military and political leadership. The reservists gave me the perfect opportunity to further my own relationships and move the generals and ministers of defense to thinking about the proper roles of their armies.

The ties I established helped me enormously in what I conceived as my own role. El Salvador and Honduras had a history of confrontation going back to the "Soccer War" in 1969. That war had ended quickly, but the confrontation persisted. I was able to get both countries' ministers of defense to negotiate outstanding issues, and during my time the border dispute was finally settled. I had success in bringing together the military leaders of El Salvador, Honduras, and Guatemala to cooperate more closely in the antidrug effort. I helped resolve the border dispute between Peru and Ecuador that at one point came very near triggering a war.

One challenge to my requests for more resources was the deep-rooted criticism in the US Congress over the corruption and human rights abuses in the countries I was working hard to mobilize. My efforts toward "democratizing" the militaries in these places were a piece in the puzzle of how to institutionalize the rule of law and protect human rights in these places. This was always a two-steps-forward, one-step-back process. But there were a couple of signal events. One took place in the spring of 1993, when the president of Guatemala, Jorge Serrano, decided to seize power in what was called an *autogolpe*, a "self-coup." He suspended the Constitution and the Supreme Court and imposed censorship, concentrating power in his own hands. In the middle of Serrano's coup, when it was still touch and go, the Guatemalan minister of defense called me at SOUTHCOM. He said he had been directed to surround the Parliament and arrest its members. What were my thoughts about what he should do?

"If you do that," I told him, "we can no longer have a relationship. I told you my goal is to assist you, but in terms of human rights and in terms of your role in the political system, let the political side handle that, not the military. If you take over the legislature, the focus in our Congress will again be on your military and its abuses. You don't want that. Let the political and juridical process work. Keep the military out of it."

The next day he called back. "You'll be surprised and pleased by my decision. We're staying in the barracks."

I don't know that I was totally surprised, but I was extremely pleased. To me the decision demonstrated a step in the maturation of Guatemalan democracy. In the end, Serrano realized he didn't have sufficient backing and fled the country. The Guatemalan Congress then appointed the national human rights ombudsman, Ramiro de León, to the presidency, which he held until 1996, when he was replaced by a rival in a free election.

We had a similar success with an attempted coup in Venezuela, where again the troops stayed in their barracks instead of abetting the coup. (A Venezuelan air force lieutenant colonel named Hugo Chávez led this attempted coup—he was arrested and jailed. Ten years later he became Venezuela's president.) I had serious discussions with each of the region's defense ministers about the role of their militaries and about human rights.

The human element—the relationships I was able to forge—was important, as personal relationships always are in Latin America. The regional antidrug effort was a mechanism that moved Latin governments to cooperate with each other and with us, which allowed for exposure to democratic values in ways that didn't include attempting to shove them down their throats.

My primary goal from the start had been to help strengthen democratic institutions. To this end I used the levers I had available, some of which were significant. But I never lost sight of the fact that I was operating on someone else's turf. My role was to help build; it wasn't to lead. Despite the urgency of the drug fight, I had to hold back the desire to assert American power in ways that undermined our allies' sovereignty. The line was a fine one, which we very nearly crossed in Colombia in the war against Pablo Escobar and the Medellín Cartel.

By the mid-1980s, Escobar and the Medellín Cartel dominated the narcotics trade. It was estimated that he was responsible for 80 percent of the cocaine coming into American markets. *Forbes* magazine considered him one of the world's wealthiest individuals, worth tens of billions of dollars. Escobar's cartel had established sophisticated air and sea smuggling routes through Mexico and the Caribbean. His gunmen were ruthless killers. By the time I arrived at SOUTHCOM, Medellín, Colombia, was considered "the murder capital of the world." In 1991, Medellín and the rest of the country experienced more than twenty-five thousand violent deaths, including the murders of numerous judges, congressional representatives, top law enforcement officials, and leading politicians.

That year Escobar made a deal with the government in which he would be put under house arrest in a luxurious prison that he designed and built for himself. The government promised a lenient sentence and protection against extradition to the United States in return for a cessation of violence and criminal activity. But when Escobar continued drug trafficking, the Colombian president, César Gaviria, decided to transfer him to a more conventional prison. Warned in advance, Escobar walked away from his palatial house arrest and went underground.

Gavrilia's government undertook a massive search operation. At first, the bloody encounters between the government's special Search Bloc force and Escobar's gunmen did not go well for the government. To help with the Colombian effort, the US Joint Special Forces Command dispatched the US Army's Delta Force, which showed up in my office in 1992. The team was headed by Delta Force chief Colonel William Boykin, who went on to become a three-star general. "We have a Presidential Finding," Boykin told me. "We're going to get this guy."

"No," I told him, "*you* are not going to get him. *You* are going to help the Colombians get him. If you get this guy, another narco will just take his place. We'll be down here for another fifty or seventy years doing this. You train the Colombians, you fly the Colombians, you arm the Colombians, but *they* will do the takedown. *They* will kill or capture Escobar, not you!"

Boykin didn't like to hear that. He and his people were raring to go. They were going to find and kill Escobar. "Sir," he said, "we're operating under a Presidential Finding."

"Should I go over this again?" I said. "You have got to understand what we're trying to do down here, what's in the Colombians' best interest as well as ours. You're in my area of operations. I'm the CINC. This is the picture I have for how we've been developing down here and what we're doing. It doesn't include you killing this guy.

"It's one thing for you to go out and get Escobar, and it's another thing to help the Colombians carry out *their* president's order. It's the latter that we're going to do, that *you're* going to do. If you want, you can go back to Washington to get clarification. But this is my area of operations, and this is my intention."

Boykin didn't call my bluff. I got no further directives from Colin Powell. So, at first reluctantly, Boykin and his team devoted themselves to working with the Colombians, whom they did train to a very high standard. They armed them, gave them equipment and intelligence, flew them. With Delta Force's help, on December 2, 1993, the Search Bloc traced Escobar to a middle-class house in Medellín. In the firefight that ensued, Escobar and a bodyguard tried to escape across the rooftops, which was where his pursuers shot and killed him.

In the fall of 1993, we were making substantial progress toward integrating the elements of a hemisphere-wide counterdrug campaign. In three years, we had helped create an effective collaboration among almost twenty US agencies. We had built strong relationships with the region's military and political leaderships. We had alleviated some of the most dangerous conflicts among them and had advanced the cause of civilian control and human rights. We had mobilized these countries' governments to face an insidious common enemy and given meaning to the idea of "One Team, One Fight."

I didn't think this job was close to being finished. Other drug lords would inevitably step up to fill the vacancy left by Escobar's death. (At the time he was killed, the Medellín Cartel was already being challenged by the Cali Cartel. It would take another ten years to get rid of them.) Serious insurgencies were still threatening some of the region's regimes:

the Revolutionary Armed Forces in Colombia, the Shining Path in Peru. Latin America was not a stable theater. The social unrest, the insurgencies, the political fragility were affecting the United States, above all through the flow of narcotics. We were watching illicit drugs tear at the social fabric of our society. That was only going to get worse.

At SOUTHCOM, I had put together an interagency and international framework to counter this assault on our security. But we needed a comprehensive, strategic approach that recognized the seriousness of the situation, and we did not have anything like that.

I had been deeply involved in generating a Presidential Directive (PDD) that defined narcotics as a national security threat and directed the secretaries of defense, Treasury, and other federal departments to undertake a greatly enhanced effort to coordinate our own antinarcotics efforts and assist those of our allies. "Because drug trafficking is a worldwide criminal enterprise that dwarfs the counternarcotics capabilities and resources of any single nation," PDD 14 directed that "the United States will lead in an effort to mobilize international cooperation and action."

PDD 14 was a watershed directive, begun under President Bush and completed under President Bill Clinton. But it was a national directive. What I had in mind was something more far reaching, a treaty organization that would formally bring together all the region's nations, including the United States, and bind them in a unified effort that would carry out planning and implementation and commitment of resources. If we were really going to get control of narcotics trafficking, we needed to institutionalize the groundwork that had been laid. I conceived this organization as mirroring NATO—a *South* Atlantic Treaty Organization. That was where I was headed. But this wasn't a short-term proposition. I needed more time.

In the fall of 1993, John Shalikashvili, who was soon going to take over as chairman of the Joint Chiefs of Staff, called me. I knew my time as SOUTHCOM's CINC was coming to an end, but for three years the narcotics situation had absorbed all my attention and energy. I was caught up by the gravity of it and the terrible damage it was doing to us.

"The president intends to appoint you SACEUR," Shalikashvili said. "Would you have any objection if he did this?"

"I'll serve wherever the president wants me," I told him. "But I have to tell you, I'm really engrossed in what I'm doing here. I think this is a battlefield we need to win. This isn't a business of tanks and rockets and bullets. It's 'how do we come up with a comprehensive approach?' We need a strategy that connects the deep fight, the close fight, and the rear fight. How do we link all that together? That's what I'm doing. We've made a start, but it's just a start. There's a lot more that needs to be done."

But the fact is that once you get asked, you can't really say, "No, thank you. I've got other things to do." I had that experience with Haig (twice) and with Vessey. So before I heard from President Clinton, I wanted him to know that I was very much involved in SOUTHCOM's work and to be sure that he knew the importance of it.

A short time later I got a call to meet with the president in Washington. I understood that he had already decided to do what he wanted to do, despite my talk with Shalikashvili. But I made an effort to dissuade him.

"We have a lot of unfinished business in Latin America," I told him. "We're making headway, but we need to build on that. I really think I could do the best for the country and for you by staying here." Clinton said he understood, but he believed it was more important for me to go to Europe. Given what was happening in Bosnia and other areas of the European command, he was probably right. But at the time I wasn't at all sure.

13

Bosnia 1

Balkan War, Rwandan Genocide

In my interview with President Clinton, we talked about some of the issues I would be facing in Europe, including the rapid drawdown of American forces there. The Berlin Wall had come down four years earlier, the Cold War confrontation had disappeared as the main driver of US foreign policy and military planning. We had thrown Saddam Hussain's army out of Kuwait, so that region at least was stabilized. But Saddam's move had been sudden and unexpected. It underscored how crises could materialize with little or no warning. In the face of unpredictable international developments, Clinton believed, as I did, that NATO would play a key role in the future security of Europe and the United States and that America's leadership of NATO was crucial. President Clinton said he was looking forward to going to Belgium for the NATO heads-of-state summit in January. By then, I would have a few months on the ground in Europe. That would be a good time for us to talk. "You can give me your assessment then," he said.

With that, I left to take over my two new commands: SACEUR, supreme allied commander for Europe (that is, for NATO), and CINCEUR, commander in chief of American forces in Europe.

In the wake of the Warsaw Pact's demise and the Soviet Union's own dismemberment, eastern European nations were trying to figure out what place they might have in this new environment. After almost half a century of Soviet dominance and occupation, they were looking at an unsettled political and social landscape with little to guide their future development. At the same time, the Western alliance was facing its own uncertainty and frustration as it attempted to deal with the carnage going on in the Balkans. The failure of leadership and lack of focus there were glaringly obvious. The different constituencies that had made up Josip Tito's Yugoslavia were locked in the most severe ethnic violence since World War II. Tens of thousands of Bosnian Muslims especially were being murdered and raped and "cleansed," and the UN Protection Force—UNPROFOR—seemed incapable of doing anything about it. When I saw what was happening on the ground, I was amazed at how receptive UN leaders and military commanders were to the idea of using the least force possible, which was allowing the carnage to continue and swell. This was not how I envisaged the UN acting as a force for good in the world.

NATO was involved on the fringes of the crisis. The UN had asked for air support for its troops on the ground and a maritime embargo, and NATO forces were in charge of these operations in support of UNPRO-FOR. But NATO had no ground forces of its own in the Balkans, and the air protection was almost completely ineffectual since missions had to be approved by both NATO's North Atlantic Council in Brussels and the UN in New York City. This "dual-key" approval process meant that almost always by the time a go-ahead was granted, the situation that required air intervention no longer existed.

NATO's role in the Balkans crisis was muddy. Even though the UN was in charge, many in Europe were holding NATO responsible for not dealing with the situation. A large number of UNPROFOR troops were drawn from NATO countries, even while NATO itself was mainly limited to watching Europe's failure from the sidelines.

NATO's role in Europe more generally wasn't clear either. The North Atlantic Treaty Organization had been founded as a mutual-protection alliance that could counter Soviet aggression. The mission of the US Army in Europe had always been to support NATO. That was still valid, but with the uncertainty and instability in eastern Europe, what exactly did that mean now? With the Soviet Union gone, what was NATO's ongoing purpose? The organization's mission needed to be redefined.

I was sure that given Europe's unpredictable and dangerous geopolitical currents, a strong Western alliance would continue to be indispensable. NATO, with its integrated political and military command structure and forty years of experience, was the primary agent here, and NATO required American leadership. No one questioned that. American leadership meant, among other things, an American army that could sustain any future NATO deployment of forces. The problem here was that America's army in Europe was in free fall. When I commanded the Fifth Corps, our total troop strength in Europe had been about 300,000. But with the Soviets gone from Germany, the politicians in Washington were avid to collect the "peace dividend." They couldn't get the troops out of Europe fast enough. We went from 300,000 to 200,000 to 150,000, with no bottom in sight. I thought that was precipitous, especially without a strategy in place for how we were going to preserve the peace we had fought so hard for in World War II and had devoted our treasure and many millions of troops to over forty-five years.

When I made my initial visits as SACEUR to the NATO heads of state, in one country after another I heard profound concern about the United States pulling out. Queen Beatrix of Holland took me aside for a one-on-one talk. "I'm hearing rumors that the United States is truly going to leave Europe," she said. "That would be a disaster. My country was occupied for six years by the Germans. I can't tell you what an impact that had on us and on my family. Most Americans don't understand what it is to be occupied. But we were occupied." All the NATO countries had lived for decades with a current of apprehension that a similar catastrophe was waiting in the wings and that only the US presence had prevented it. "The United States must stay in Europe," the queen said. "You, as SACEUR, represent the American commitment to Europe. This means so much to our stability, to our safety, to our peace."

The Soviet menace had dissipated a few years earlier, but the psychology of apprehension hadn't left. The international scene was still full of danger. The Balkan War, already nightmarish, was getting deadlier. There was trouble between Greece and Turkey and ongoing conflict in the Middle East. Russia was in turmoil. Just before I assumed my new command, a constitutional crisis had erupted there that led to street fighting in Moscow and an armed assault on the Russian Parliament building, with many dead. Boris Yeltsin's grip on power was tenuous; Communist and ultra-nationalist factions were in the wings, and Russia still had twenty thousand nuclear warheads in its arsenal. We might not be facing massed Soviet tank armies in Germany any longer, but we were still in perilous times.

My priority was to stop the free fall of America's European army. It was already obvious to me that if Bosnia weren't to plunge into full-fledged genocide, NATO would have to get involved, and this involvement would have to be in fairly short order. Manfred Woerner, NATO's secretary-general, was equally clear on what the alliance's responsibility was inevitably going to be. I had known Woerner since I was a battalion commander in Göppingen and he was a Bundestag representative from there. He had complained back then about the noise our APCs were making, disturbing the citizens, and I had explained that we needed to maintain the vehicles to be combat ready; I hoped the citizens would grin and bear it. He understood, and we had become friends. Now I was SACEUR, and he was NATO secretary-general. "George," he told me, "NATO is going to have to take action on the ground in Bosnia. I want you to give me your best advice on how we should do that. Don't water it down. My job will be to get political approval for it."

The history of communal and ideological violence in the Balkans was a terrible presage to what was developing there: Muslim/Christian warfare and antagonism going back centuries, the conflict between Serb and Croatian nationalisms, fascist Ustashe terrorists, Serbian extremists, Communist partisans, a culture of heavily armed peasant enclaves. All of that and more were part of the region's identity. Tito had kept the many fault lines from fracturing, but his death in 1980 and the collapse of the regional economy let loose nationalistic ambitions that split the country in pieces and resulted in a series of wars, including the latest and most horror-filled one unfolding now.

All this was happening in a landscape of jagged mountains, stony plateaus, and bleak flatlands that made it some of the most difficult terrain in Europe. I had been told pointedly that no American troops were ever going to set foot in Bosnia. Representatives, senators, and senior leaders in the Pentagon had repeatedly poked me in the chest, telling me I was to understand that "no American troops are going to go into Bosnia!" But once I was on the ground there and had a close-up view, I came to a different opinion. The Balkans had strategic importance. The adversaries there were descending into genocidal conflict right in front of us. Were we capable of just sitting back and watching this happen? Bosnia was testing the West's credibility, politically and morally. In my opinion, Bosnia was a challenge we were absolutely going to have to face.

Almost immediately I began soliciting input from my army, navy, air force, and marine component commanders about the troop levels they thought made sense for us to keep in Europe. I also met with my major NATO subordinate commanders. In the end, it seemed to me that the minimum acceptable force level would be about one hundred thousand US troops. I would have liked more, but the main objective was to get the US side settled down so I could start laying the groundwork for a new NATO strategy. So I decided I'd plant a flag at one hundred thousand and make the strongest argument I could for that number when I met Clinton.

In early January, President Clinton, as he had planned, attended the NATO heads-of-state summit in Brussels. We met afterward for a formal briefing in NATO headquarters. Secretary of State Warren Christopher was with him, along with Defense Secretary Les Aspin, National Security Adviser Tony Lake, and John Shalikashvili, who had been my predecessor as SACEUR and was now chairman of the Joint Chiefs. I brought along all my US four-star component commanders so they could make their own contributions to the discussion.

Standing in front of Clinton and the others at the conference room's big oblong table, I gave my assessment of the situation in Europe, including the conflict in Bosnia and the instability in eastern Europe and Russia. I talked about the challenges we were facing but also about the opportunities. "We need to keep a strong footprint here," I said. "There's still instability; there's still great concern about what Russia is going to end up doing and about what's going to be the future in Europe. My judgment is that we've been drawing down our troop level much too fast. Our responsibilities require a meaningful presence. To do this we need to draw the line on our withdrawal. We need a floor of one hundred thousand troops."

The briefing took about forty-five minutes. In that entire time, Clinton never took his eyes off me. I was used to giving briefings to high-ranking military and political figures; no matter how important the subject might be, there are always at least a few momentary distractions. But Clinton never glanced at his watch, never looked around at his team or at anything else. His gaze never wavered. He was completely engaged.

When I was finished, he said, "George, is one hundred thousand enough?"

You could hear pens and pencils drop around the room. "Yes," I said. "That's it."

Clinton's decision gave me the ability to move forward. Despite the complexity of the Bosnian situation and the other problems in my area, I was more than ready to flesh out my plans and put them in gear. In Latin America, I had developed a comprehensive strategy that unfortunately I had not been given the time to follow through on. I went to Europe with the conviction that here, too, was a fragmented and disordered array of nations and problems where our great challenge would be to develop an overall strategy for how to deal with these new, post–Cold War conditions. What was the mission here, and how could we measure success?

SOUTHCOM had allowed me to crystallize many of the lessons I had learned the hard way, what I thought of as my scar tissue. I had always understood the importance of working with allies and coalition partners. I had seen that as far back as my first deployment, when I had been posted as liaison to the German Second Corps in Heppenheim. Right up through my time as a division and corps commander, I had made every effort to get to know our fighting partners—Brits, Germans, French, Dutch, and others—and integrate our efforts with theirs. At SOUTHCOM, my ultimate objective had been to create a comprehensive counternarcotics strategy that would bring together every one of the countries under attack by the drug lords and cartels. I had worked toward that goal with defense ministers, heads of state, and US ambassadors and separate enforcement agencies. I had coordinated with the UN. All that work had gone toward achieving a unity of effort that was, I believed, the prerequisite for effective action.

In some ways, the situation at NATO was similar. Its charter required all decisions be made by consensus among the sixteen member nations. I was glad to have Secretary-General Woerner at my side, but I knew I was going to bear a great deal of the political challenge in getting the coalition to operate as one—especially as Woerner began to weaken from the cancer he had been fighting for several years.

One lesson that had gotten embedded in me as I assumed higher command positions was the necessity of rendering effective advice. A military commander can't be involved politically, but he has to be politically aware. I had seen that when I worked in the White House and in the chairman's office. I had developed my own approach to it. You can't wait for your political masters to tell you that something needs to be done and then give them your advice on how to do it. You need to be proactive. The point is to anticipate developments and give advice that will help shape political decisions. When you see certain indicators taking place, you don't wait for the train wreck to happen. You give your best advice early on to prevent the train wreck.

I began that effort even before I briefed Clinton. I took every opportunity to tell our US leadership that we needed to start considering using US forces in the Balkans. But that recommendation didn't go over well. There was just no stomach for it. In early October, two weeks before I had assumed command, eighteen US Army Rangers were killed in a poorly thought-out attack on a warlord's headquarters in Mogadishu, Somalia, the famous "Blackhawk down" battle. When I testified about Bosnia in front of the Senate Armed Services Committee, John McCain described the Somalia incident and asked, "What would you do if you run into those kinds of circumstances?"

"If I run into those circumstances, "I said, "I'll get in my plane and fly back here and tell you what you have to do to help me." Which is what I would have done, had it been necessary. But I had studied the Mogadishu fight. I knew it was a badly planned operation. There was a lack of command and control. Communications were poor. There hadn't been any rehearsals. The reserve element that eventually rescued the surviving Rangers hadn't been tied in. There was little attention to detail. Because of all of these problems, we got burned and had come out of Somalia with our tail between our legs. Before McCain's committee, I went on at length about the need for clarity of mission, unity of command, clear rules of engagement, and the need for timely political decisions. These were the prerequisites, I told them, for success.

Later I did get support from McCain and from Bob Dole for US involvement in Bosnia, but in my first months as SACEUR Shalikashvili was telling me, "You have no support in the White House, you have no support in Congress, you have no support here in the Pentagon." I knew "Shali" well. He was a friend. "How about you, Shali?" I asked him. "Do I have your support?" When he didn't answer, I understood how truly isolated I was.

Shalikashvili was certainly right about the Pentagon. Bosnia, I was told, was a quagmire. I was reminded that we had stepped into a quagmire before, which had gone badly. The Germans in World War II had been mauled in the Balkans by the very same people who were killing each other there now. Did I believe these people were less capable now than they were then? If we went in, the body bags would be coming back to Dover, Delaware, by the thousands. Many of the generals who were so rigidly opposed changed their minds later, but my lobbying and advice at the beginning of 1994 were winning zero converts.

I was, though, wearing two hats, my CINCEUR hat and my NATO SACEUR hat. Among other business, the January NATO heads-of-state summit launched two new programs, the Combined Joint Task Force, which set procedures to facilitate the use of NATO forces for any kind of military or humanitarian mission that might be called for, and the Partnership for Peace (PfP), which was conceived as a political mechanism for drawing together countries interested in potentially joining NATO. As SACEUR, I had much of the responsibility for implementing these programs.

In January, two weeks after the heads-of-state summit, I told Manfred Woerner that I wanted to use PfP in an operational context. "If we are going to do missions together," I said, "doesn't it make sense that the part-ner nations should train to common standards, procedures, and doctrine? Some of the partners might want to move quickly toward NATO mem-bership; others might go slower. Maybe PfP could even include countries that might want to work with NATO on certain missions but aren't look-ing for membership. But if we're doing missions together, we need to train to common standards. That's what I want to use PfP for." Woerner approved that approach on the spot. "Make it work," he told me.

I started on it immediately. My overtures about US involvement weren't going anywhere in Washington, but as the situation in Bosnia became increasingly appalling, I was more convinced than ever that we would eventually have to commit forces. Meanwhile, I could be training those forces under NATO's PfP auspices. Once the United States did make a political decision, I wouldn't have to start casting around for how to make the intervention happen. I would be prepared to implement it.

The first thing I did was renovate two unused officers' quarters at SHAPE into a center where we could plan, train, and coordinate PfP exercises and operations. We didn't know whether one country or ten or twenty would join in (we ended up with more than twenty). Most importantly, European nations outside of NATO were attracted to the concept of creating a common way to work together. It was especially interesting to me that Sweden, Finland, Austria, and even Switzerland joined. They were not allied countries, and they had no intention of joining NATO, but they were interested in associating themselves with PfP, which added real assets to whatever potential missions we might be doing.

President Clinton and Secretary of State Christopher considered Partnership for Peace primarily as a path to NATO membership, but I thought of it as a stand-alone operation. I believed PfP could be an important teaching mechanism for former Soviet bloc countries that wanted to westernize and democratize. But I was mainly thinking operationally. When I was asked, "What do you do with the countries that don't want to join NATO?," I would answer, "You train them to common standards because you have to think ahead to one day when we may have to be committed to Bosnia."

I set up training sites in Germany at Grafenwöhr and Hohenfels and constructed a mock Bosnian village. We taught our soldiers there in the cold, the mud, and the snow. We didn't teach just weapons handling and shooting; we taught how to manage situations. What do you do, for example, if you're confronted by a civilian mob that won't let you go down a road? What if someone tries to stop you at a checkpoint? What if you see a woman being raped or someone trying to kill somebody? You can't just sit there; you have to take action. But what kind of action? Do you just shoot them? What do your rules of engagement tell you, and how do you comply with them? We devised exercises and put all the PfP elements through this kind of training in preparation for what I was sure wasn't far over the horizon.

At one point, William Perry, who by that point had replaced Les Aspin as secretary of defense, went up to see the training. "Your colonel showed me around up there," Perry told me. This was Dean Cash, who was running the training. "We were up to our knees in mud and snow. It was freezing. Your colonel said, 'I wish it would get colder. We have to make the scrimmage harder than the game.'"

We held the first big PfP field exercise in Poland later that year, the first of a series. The Poles volunteered to be the initial hosts. They pushed me to make it a large-element, live-fire exercise. What they really wanted was to demonstrate to the Russians that they had big friends. They wanted to poke them in the eye.

"We're not going to do that," I told them. "We're focused on Bosnia and what we're going to encounter there." I didn't tell them that I had no interest in provoking the Russians because I was thinking about how to involve them in the PfP mix.

Over the year, we held eleven more PfP exercises, most in former Soviet bloc countries. Each one focused on how to deal with problems that might confront us in Bosnia, the same situations we were training for at Grafenwöhr and Hohenfels.

In the middle of December 1993, Les Aspin resigned as secretary of defense. In early February 1994, I was meeting with his successor, William Perry, and other NATO ambassadors and ministers of defense when word came in that the main marketplace in Sarajevo had been shelled by Bosnian Serb forces surrounding the city. The marketplace was packed with people hoping to buy or barter for whatever scarce food items they might be able to find. A heavy mortar bomb had exploded in the middle of the crowd: sixty-eight people were dead, nearly two hundred others were injured. It was a massacre.

Sarajevo, the largely Muslim capital of the Bosnia-Herzegovina region, had been under siege by Bosnian Serbs for almost two years. Serb forces had occupied the hills around the city and taken various neighborhoods. Their artillery and mortars shelled the city every day, smashing Sarajevo's infrastructure and leaving much of the city's government, commercial, and residential buildings in ruins. Snipers shot people randomly, keeping the civilian population in a state of constant terror. The seventy thousand or so Bosnian Muslim (Bosniak) troops inside the city were too weakly armed to break the siege. Through 1993, Bosnian Serb shell fire took a constant toll in civilian lives, a daily occurrence punctuated by several large-scale, headline-making incidents. But the February 4 marketplace shelling was by far the worst.

In the wake of this massacre, Perry asked me to brief the ambassadors and ministers on the situation around Sarajevo and its place in the fighting that was creating such misery for all the people in the region, but most of all for the Bosnian Muslims. Afterward Perry and I had a private talk. He had just then come on as secretary, but he had had many years of experience with defense issues and had been an assistant secretary during the Carter administration. I explained to him the outlines of how I saw conditions in Bosnia, the developments we might expect, and what I had started doing with the Partnership for Peace. Perry was a quick read. He understood the complexities very much as I did. It was the start of a close relationship. From then on, I knew I could count on him for support. "You tell me what you need," he said. "I'll try to get it for you.

The marketplace massacre was a shock. UNPROFOR was failing to accomplish even the basic peacekeeping responsibilities. It had no ability to deal with anything like this massacre or to prevent something similar from happening again. In response to the shelling, UN secretary-general Boutros Boutros-Ghali declared a twenty-kilometer exclusion zone around Sarajevo where no heavy weapons would be allowed. For enforcement, the UN turned to NATO.

When Manfred Woerner instructed me to establish the exclusion zone, I went to NATO's North Atlantic Council to set my rules of engagement. "If there is artillery fire from inside the exclusion zone," I asked, "what exactly am I authorized to do?" I explained how quickly an artillery piece can be broken down and moved. "By the time we angle back to where the shot came from, there isn't going to be anything there. What I want is authority to go after the artillery piece itself, wherever it's moved to, as well as the ammunition supplies, the petrol, and the command and control that ordered the shooting. If you want enforcement to be effective, that's what I need." I was presenting to a council composed of civilian ambassador-level representatives, few of whom had much or any military experience. The challenge was not only to convince them of the gravity of the situation but also to get them to understand the military requirements. Fortunately, I had Field Marshal Dick Vincent with me, the British head of NATO's military committee. Dick was an artillery officer. He had been promoted from general to field marshal after the Gulf War and would soon be elevated to Baron Vincent of Coleshill. His use of the English language was far beyond anything I could ever aspire to. He was a persuasive man. The council voted me the rules of engagement I needed.

We then gave the Bosnian Serbs an ultimatum. If they didn't remove all their heavy weapons from the exclusion zone by February 21, we would subject them to air strikes. At first, the Serbs complied, moving their heavy weapons as we told them to. Although the UN had asked us to enforce the exclusion, they had kept the dual-key command structure.

That is, all air strikes needed approval first from the NATO Council, then from the UN in New York, which could take days and often wasn't granted at all. The result was that our ability to effectively hit targets was hamstrung. The Serbs weren't stupid. They came to understand this, and it wasn't long before the artillery and mortars started coming back inside the exclusion zone. Worse, the UNPROFOR commanders on the ground seemed to be doing everything in their power not to call violations or request strikes. I was beyond frustrated. I could see what was happening. With the UN demonstrating its impotence, the Bosnian Serbs under General Ratko Mladić and their political leader Radovan Karadžić were emboldened in their increasingly genocidal assault on Bosnian Muslims. No one was stopping them, certainly not the United Nations. After the war, both Mladić and Karadžić were convicted of genocide and crimes against humanity and sentenced to life imprisonment. But in 1994 as Serbian depredations continued without letup, that outcome seemed unlikely.

On April 6, 1994, two months after the Sarajevo marketplace massacre, an airplane carrying Rwandan president Juvénal Habyarimana and Burundian president Cyprien Ntaryamira was shot down as it approached the Kigali airport. Habyarimana was coming back from signing accords that would have ended the Tutsi/Hutu civil war that had been going on since 1990. No one knew who was responsible for the assassinations (it never has been determined), but hard-line Hutu elements were extremely unhappy with the peace agreement that Habyarimana, a Hutu, had signed. They hated the prospect of sharing power with Tutsis, which the accords required. The day after Habyarimana was killed, Hutu political and military leaders launched a countrywide massacre of Rwanda's Tutsi minority. The attack had obviously been organized long before Habyarimana's death set it off.

Africa was part of my area of responsibility. I was monitoring the civil war in Rwanda, but it wasn't a priority, and the massacres broke out with no forewarning. Once the killing started, though, we were watching closely. The Hutu hard-liners quickly executed all Tutsis and Hutu moderates who were in leadership positions, including Prime Minister Madame Agathe Uwilingiyimana. Within a day or two, every leader in the country who didn't share the Hutu Power agenda was dead.

A catastrophe was unfolding in Rwanda, but I received no guidance from Washington about taking any action. I did get a panicked telephone call from the Belgian defense chief. The Belgians had a battalion in Rwanda as part of the 2,500 member UN force sent to help implement the peace accord, which was now, with Habyarimana's assassination, a dead letter. Ten Belgian troops had been sent to protect Madam Uwilingiyimana, but the prime minister's residence had been surrounded by Hutu soldiers, and the prime minister and her husband had given themselves up in an effort to protect their children, whom they had sent into hiding. The children survived, but she and her husband were shot. The ten Belgian soldiers were disarmed and executed, the defense minister told me. He was distraught, his voice shaking. Could I make some transport available for him? the minister asked.

"Yes, "I said. "Tell me what you need."

He needed to send another battalion down to Rwanda immediately, he said.

"But you've already got a whole battalion there. Can't you use the troops you have there to protect the others? Don't you have the rules of engagement for self-defense?"

"The UN says no," he said. "Our battalion down there is under UN command, and I can't use it the way I need to. I need to get my own force there."

"Okay," I said. "I'll arrange it."

I was shaking my head. A Canadian major general, Romeo Dallaire, was commanding the UN force. He was obviously operating with totally inadequate rules of engagement if he wasn't even allowed to protect his own people. I had never heard of anything like that. Whatever his mandate was, it needed to be changed fast, and more heavily armed reinforcements needed to be sent in with a clear objective. But obviously neither one of those things was happening. I certainly wasn't being instructed to prepare anything militarily. I did get orders, though, to evacuate the American ambassador from the capital, Kigali.

That wasn't going to be easy. I had good intelligence from the Belgians about what was happening on the ground, which was apparently horrific beyond imagining. The Hutu army and genocidal militias were slaughtering the Tutsi population and enlisting or forcing ordinary Hutu civilians to take part in the bloodletting. The road between the embassy and the airfield was about two miles long and was controlled by Hutus who were involved in this killing frenzy. The trip to the airport would be like running the gauntlet. We advised the US ambassador, David Rawson, to drive south instead, toward Burundi. We would meet him at the border.

This extraction had to happen fast, and I had no forces in the region. The US Central Command's area of responsibility was adjacent to mine and much closer to this part of Africa. A good friend, General Binnie Peay, was Central Command's CINC, and he transferred a marine unit to my control, which we quickly airlifted into Burundi. To complicate matters, our communications with the ambassador were cut off, which was hair raising, but I managed to get a C-130 up in the air to serve as a radio relay to the evacuation party.

The convoy started out with the ambassador and other embassy people, but as it made its way toward Burundi, cars and trucks filled with fleeing Tutsis and other refugees joined the procession. From the C-130, we heard that it looked as if several hundred vehicles were snaking along behind the ambassador. The distance from Kigali to the Burundi border was more than a hundred miles. We monitored the convoy's progress and fed the ambassador intelligence, helping the convoy avoid several ambushes. I was sweating bullets until they got to Bujumbura, where the marines had secured the airfield.

A genocide was clearly going on in Rwanda. After we got the ambassador out, I talked with my staff about what was going to happen next, but from Washington I heard only silence. After the fact, the United States came in for severe criticism for not injecting forces to stop the killing. But I doubt the political climate in the United States would have tolerated or supported a military mission. I had been advising everybody I could get hold of that we needed to go into Bosnia, but without any success, and the Balkans were in the heart of Europe, not in an African hinterland few had ever heard of where two equally unknown tribes had been at each other's throats for decades.

The situation in Rwanda was aggravated by the colonial legacy of the French, who considered the country to be in their sphere of influence and had supported and provided weapons to the Hutu-led government in its civil war with the Tutsis. The Tutsis were getting support from Uganda, an English-speaking former British colony, which aggravated latent French Anglophobia. Of course, the UN was also on the ground, with its hopelessly inadequate mandate. Even had there been a desire for it in Washington, direct, unilateral American intervention would not have been welcomed in many quarters. If we had pressed to do it under UN auspices, I would have demanded a different mandate, different rules of engagement, and a different command structure. But it's not likely the French—our allies in Europe, still part of NATO, and a permanent member of the UN Security Council—would have gone along with that. It would have taken a tremendous effort politically, diplomatically, and militarily, and that was simply not in the cards.

President Clinton wrote afterward that the American failure to get involved in Rwanda was one of the greatest regrets of his presidency. Should we have tried to do what was necessary to prevent the atrocities that took place? Yes, we should have. But that is all in hindsight.

The mass slaughter triggered desperate attacks by the Ugandan-based Tutsi relief army led by Paul Kagame. Kagame's forces made steady progress against the Hutu army, but meanwhile the killings accelerated. In three months, *eight hundred thousand* Tutsi civilians and many moderate Hutus were murdered. It took until the beginning of July before Kagame was able to declare victory. The genocide was stopped, but not before more than 70 percent of Rwanda's Tutsi population had been exterminated.

The end of the war was the beginning of another humanitarian disaster. As the Tutsi army advanced, Hutus were fleeing across the border into Zaire (today's Congo). In the final days of the Hutu army's resistance and directly afterward, more than ten thousand Hutus a day crossed over, pitching camp on the hard soil and lava fields in the shadow of Mount Nyiragongo, an active volcano just north of the border city of Goma. By early July, more than a million Hutu refugees were concentrated there, including large numbers of defeated Hutu soldiers and extremist militias.

The flood of refugees overwhelmed the scarce relief services available. There was no potable drinking water—the water of Lake Kivu was polluted, but people had no choice but to drink it. The hard ground made it almost impossible to dig latrines. It didn't take long for cholera and dysentery to reach epidemic proportions.

On Thursday, July 14, I got a call from John Shalikashvili telling me that President Clinton was going to send me an execute order the next day to go to the Rwandan/Congo border and take measures to stop the cholera epidemic. "How much time do I have?" I asked. "I need to put a joint task force together. It may take a week."

"The president wants you to deploy tomorrow," he said.

That night I sent a six-man team headed by a marine reserve colonel down to Goma to assess the situation. The colonel called back that night, his voice cracking with emotion. "The bodies are so stacked up on the road between the airport and Goma that we couldn't get through. We need to do something now!" The next day he gave me a fuller assessment. The facts were very much as we had heard. Cholera was responsible for most of the deaths, definitely from the polluted waters of the lake. The hygiene situation in the camps was indescribable. A reporter for the *New York Daily News* reported on July 27, "The raging cholera epidemic near the border backwater town of Goma, Zaire (Congo), continued to claim lives faster than mass graves could be dynamited out of the volcanic rock blanketing the area. . . . [A]id workers fear that 20,000 may have died since 1.2 million Rwandans fled to Zaire a week ago."

We got the planning going immediately and began looking to bring together whatever water-purification units we had available. As this was gearing up, I was in touch with Secretary of Defense Perry, who was in the Middle East but coming back to the United States. I asked him to stop in Brussels so we could talk. I met with him in his plane, sitting on the tarmac. "I have my execute order," I said, "but I want to make sure we're on exactly the same page. Do you regard this as a humanitarian mission or a military mission?" The genocide perpetrators were larded in among the refugees, along with weapons they had brought with them out of Rwanda. Was I expected to go after war criminals in addition to dealing with the cholera epidemic? Going after them would be a nasty affair. If I had to clean the camps out, I would have to structure my intervention force in a completely different way.

"No," Perry said, "it's not military. It's humanitarian. You are to do everything you can to stop the dying."

When Perry left, I put up a big sheet of butcher paper at the European Command Operations Center. "YOUR MISSION IS TO STOP THE DYING."

Our first step was to get an air-traffic-control team down there. The French were running the Goma airport, but they were only keeping it open ten or twelve hours a day. Goats and cows were roaming around the runway, people were pulling carts across it. We needed the airfield to be open and operating around the clock. With the UN Office of the High Commissioner for Refugees mobilizing its own relief effort and trying to bring some order to the many nongovernment organizations that were also responding to the crisis, I flew to Geneva to meet with Madame Sadako Ogata, the high commissioner for refugees. In a situation like this, everyone wants to get into the crisis area as quickly as possible. What with the limited air access and the primitive roads and paths in the region, when the flow of relief material and aid workers got started, it was going to threaten immense blockages and confusion. "I can give you US Air Force air planners and traffic controllers," I told Madame Ogata. "They'll be in mufti. They'll be able to help you prioritize everything that's coming in. We'll move the water-purification units up front. If somebody wants to deliver something else, they'll have to get in line." Madame Ogata was as focused on the soaring cholera death rate as we were. "You'll do that?" she said. She was appreciative beyond words. It was during that operation that we became close friends, which was extremely helpful with refugee situations we were involved in together down the road.

Our priority was to get water-purification equipment in place. I had an airborne battalion ready to go from Aviano, Italy, to provide protection, but when we understood there was no fighting going on, I held them back to give the water units a chance to fly in and set up. That was a risk. I knew the Hutu army and militia people in the camps had brought weapons with them—even heavy weapons. But I took the chance. Many thousands of refugees had died already, and thousands more bodies were piling up almost on a daily basis.

But there were hurdles to getting the water units in. We sent the first purification unit from Ramstein, Germany, on a heavy airlift C-5, but the French at Goma airport wouldn't give the C-5 permission to land. The pilot, though, evaded the prohibition, flying patterns until nightfall, then declaring an emergency and coming in. We had another C-5 flying from San Francisco with two firetrucks and other equipment aboard, along with a team headed by a civilian former San Francisco Fire Department officer who claimed he knew how to use the trucks to purify water. I talked to the French chief of defense about the Goma airport, and the French did open it up for us.

By then, I had sent Dan Schroeder, my army deputy commander, to oversee the developing operation, and within seventy-two hours of when I received the order we were pumping clean water. We were also mustering water-purification units from the Germans and British and flying them to Goma. The deployments weren't simple, but Schroeder was doing a superb job of keeping things running smoothly.

But both of us were shaken when we got a report that Mount Nyiragongo was showing signs of seismic activity. The volcano loomed over the camps. It had a history of recent eruptions, and its lava flows had the potential to cause huge casualties. (Eight years later an eruption forced the evacuation of Goma: superheated lava flowed through streets and buildings to the shores of Lake Kivu and destroyed a big part of the city. Lake Kivu itself was a natural catastrophe waiting to happen. The lake is a repository of hundreds of cubic kilometers of carbon dioxide and methane, whose release would asphyxiate everyone in the entire lake basin. Exactly that happened at the much smaller Lake Nyos in Cameroon in 1986. A volcano eruption had the potential to trigger a gigantic lake gas explosion. I wasn't aware—thankfully, perhaps—of that potential disaster at the time.) When I was told the volcano might blow, I said, "Please, I'll say whatever prayers you want me to say to whatever god you want me to say them, but, please, I don't need a volcano going off in the middle of this."

The volcano did not erupt, and the purification operation continued unobstructed. From the start of the operation, the cholera deaths began to diminish, from many thousands a day when we first arrived to five hundred and then within a month to one hundred. That was still a high number, but I felt as if we were saving the lives of a significant percentage of the refugee population.

In the middle of this crisis, I got a call from one of my senior on-site commanders, who said he had a State Department representative with him who was telling him that we now had to go in and clean out all the Hutu murderers in the camp.

I said, "Please tell him that I understand he is the president's representative, but he needs to send that request back through the National Command Authority and have it task European Command. If I get the mission, I'll certainly be glad to give input and advice, but please go back to Washington with the request." He apparently never did. I heard nothing further about going after the killers.

As the water-purification effort built, I flew to Goma with Bill Perry to get an up-close look at the operation and conditions in the vast camp. Walking down the line of trucks and machinery, I met the San Francisco fireman who had flown in with his fire engines. He was in his late sixties or early seventies, wearing blue coveralls. He and the US Army major running our equipment had lashed the trucks together with our units, and the big red fire engines were pumping pure water.

Other hoses from British, French, and German operations were hooked into the army and fire engine system. I put my arm around the fireman's shoulders. "I want to thank you," I said. "But how did you do all this?"

"General," he said, "me and the major worked it out. We're Americans. We know how to get things done."

We did know how to get things done, at least in Goma. In Bosnia, that wasn't nearly so clear.

14

Bosnia 2

Srebrenica and the Dayton Accords

At the moment President Habyarimana's plane was shot down in Rwanda, the Bosnian Serbs were conducting a vicious artillery assault on Goražde, a Muslim town of eighteen thousand in southeastern Bosnia, now swollen with many thousands of refugees. A year earlier Goražde was one of six Muslim areas the UN Security Council had designated as "safe havens" under the protection of UN forces. But UN Security Council Resolution 824 had made little or no difference. Bosnian Serbs were rampaging through eastern Bosnia, overpowering Muslim defense forces, killing and raping their way, "cleansing" large regions of their Muslim inhabitants. The European countries weren't calling this "genocide," nor was the United States, nor was the UN, for the same reasons they weren't declaring the Rwanda genocide a genocide. A declaration of that sort would have created overwhelming pressure for a decisive military intervention, which no one had any intention of undertaking.

The safe havens were meant to be areas where the flood of panicked Muslim refugees could gather and receive humanitarian aid. The UN "peacekeeping force," UNPROFOR, was supposed to protect these areas, but with its weak mandate, inadequate armaments, and reluctant commanders, UNPROFOR was incapable of doing any actual protecting. At the same time, NATO air power, which could have shut down much of the Bosnian Serb aggression, was handcuffed by the "dual-key" approval necessary to launch strikes. Meanwhile, in besieged Goražde hundreds of civilians, including many children, were dying under a rain of Bosnian Serb high explosives.

The Goražde situation was critical. As the Serbian attack was going on, I flew to visit NATO secretary-general Manfred Woerner, who was being treated at a hospital in Aachen, Germany. Woerner's cancer was advancing quickly, but even as he grew weaker, his engagement with the Bosnian crisis didn't slacken. I landed on the hospital helipad in my Blackhawk, carrying my briefing books with me. I wanted Manfred to understand how precarious Goražde was, how I needed immediate approval to bring an air attack in because even after receiving NATO approval, I would have to get a go-ahead from the UN. While he was lying in bed, I took him through my charts. I explained what was happening on the ground and what our readiness was. While we were talking, his room television was on, showing by some bizarre chance the Serb bombardment of the hospital in Goražde. It was a surreal moment. We saw the blasts and the smoke billowing up. "I'm in the hospital here," Woerner said, "and those people are shelling the hospital there!" Woerner was sick as hell, but what we were watching set him off. "I will come back and hold a meeting with the other council members," he said. He was wearing one of those flimsy hospital gowns, an intravenous tube in his arm. He got up out of bed, holding on to the stand with the intravenous bag.

"I will walk you to the elevator," he said.

"Manfred," I said, "please don't. Please get back in bed."

"No," he said, "I will walk SACEUR to the elevator."

We trudged down the hall together. I was nearly in tears.

In May, I visited Croatia and Bosnia with NATO's deputy secretary-general Sergio Balanzino to meet with the UNPROFOR commanders. The Security Council resolution establishing the safe areas had not mentioned how the safety of these places could be assured. It demanded only that the different parties should respect UNPROFOR. The resolution authorized an additional fifty UN military "observers" and declared that if the warring parties failed to comply, the UN was ready to "consider the adoption of additional measures."

From a security perspective, this resolution was worse than meaningless; issuing demands without enforcement measures only highlighted the UN's impotence and emboldened the Serbs. The UNPROFOR commanders were beset by indecision and futility. When I asked one UNPROFOR commander, British lieutenant general Michael Rose, what he thought his mission was, he told me it was to protect his troops, not the civilians in the safe areas. I told him that if that was what he thought, he was not doing the job he was supposed to be doing. "Listen," he said, "I've been to war. I'm not going to war with white tanks" (the UN tanks and other vehicles were painted white). "I'm going to protect my troops!"

"You don't understand the mission," I said. "The mandate is to protect civilians in the safe areas. If you don't protect them, what do you think is going to happen to them?" I was so angry I banged my fist down on the table, which startled him and probably everyone else in the room. "How in the world could you *not* protect the safe areas?"

He reiterated that he was going to protect his troops. I couldn't believe what I was hearing. It was just shocking. Balanzino and his two civilian aides were as amazed as I was. The fact was that I held Rose responsible for much of what was happening in the safe zones. I sensed he thought little of the Muslims—he called the Bosniaks a "peasant army," with emphasis on "peasant." I heard the denigration in that description. I restrained myself from saying what I thought: that he had blood on his hands for not enforcing what he needed to enforce and for not pressing the issue with the UN.

As far as I was concerned, the whole UN effort was bankrupt. Bosnia's president Alija Izetbegović had said the safe havens would become refugee death traps, and exactly that was now happening in front of our eyes.

My feelings about all of this came to a head when Rose visited NATO headquarters to brief the North Atlantic Council. As the briefing proceeded, I was making clear my conviction that the UN needed to go to a full-fledged Chapter 7 "peace-enforcement" regime, with all the robust rules of engagement necessary for that mission, rather than clinging to the meaningless Chapter 6 "peacekeeping" mission. "There is no peace to keep," I said, "and UNPROFOR isn't doing even the minimum to safeguard civilians."

Rose said, "How about a 6.5?" He saw me glaring at him from across the table. But the council ambassadors were nodding their heads in agreement. A 6.5 sounded pretty good to them because it wouldn't require the use of force, and none of them wanted to take responsibility for committing ground forces to combat. In their hearts and minds, they were still hoping or maybe praying for a diplomatic solution, even at this stage, when the situation was crying out for a military effort that could put a stop to this rolling genocide.

"Do you have the rules of engagement for that?" I asked Rose. "Do you have the troops trained for it? Because you're talking about crossing the line to robust enforcement. Do you have what you need to do that?"

Of course, he didn't.

Chapter 6.5 was a cute way to get politicians to step a little bit closer but not all the way to what was necessary. I thought it was a recipe for disaster. The safe-haven resolution itself had stepped over the line with its implicit promise of protection. Yet the Serbs were violating the safe havens with impunity, challenging the UN to its face, and UNPROFOR simply did not want to act. Sarajevo was a designated safe haven, as were Goražde, Tuzla, Bihać, Žepa, and Srebrenica—all Muslim towns. Sarajevo was under siege and constant bombardment; Goražde was already critical. Srebrenica's turn was going to come soon.

The Goražde assault hit in early April. The following months saw continual Bosnian Serb depredations: UN food and medicine convoys hijacked, UN troops ambushed, UN troops taken prisoner and held hostage, sieges, bombardments, starvation, civilian deaths in the tens of thousands, terrorized refugees crowding into safe zones that were anything but safe, people fleeing Bosnia any way they possibly could.

Bihać, one of the UN's safe areas, was a city in northwestern Bosnia. Like Sarajevo, it was cut off and besieged. In Bihać, there was almost no food, no electricity, no medicine for the region's one hospital. With an influx of more than 60,000 refugees, the city's population had ballooned to more than 170,000. On November 18, Bihać was bombed by Bosnian Serb jets flying out of the Krajina region using napalm and cluster bombs. I told the NATO Council that this attack violated Deny Flight, the no-fly zone and air operation NATO ran in support of UNPROFOR. This wasn't the Serbs' first violation of Deny Flight. The previous February six Serb jets were bombing a Bosnian factory when they were intercepted by NATO aircraft. In the first air combat in NATO history, F-16s from the air force base in Ramstein shot down five of the Serb planes. The sixth managed to escape back to its base. We hadn't followed that incident with any further action, and the Serbs seemed to have learned the lesson—until the November assault on Bihać.

"Bombing Bihać was a direct violation of Deny Flight," I told the council. "I'm asking authority to hit these planes at their base. We know where they came from. We know where they are. We have pictures."

I did have pictures. We had identified the base they came out of and even the jets that did the bombing, sitting alongside the runway in revetted bunkers. But they were CIA photos, and the agency did not want me to show them. "Those are top secret," the agency told me. "You can't show them!"

"I've got to," I said. "I need the council members to trust that I'm not going outside my authority. They need to know I'm not bullshitting them to get permission to go bomb something just because I think it needs bombing." I did show the pictures to the council; you could see the planes in their bunkers. The council pondered and pondered over whether to allow an air strike. The Serbs had cleverly, or so they thought, used planes that were based at an airfield in the Krajina—territory they had cut out of southeastern Croatia and proclaimed an autonomous Serb region. Of course, no one recognized that proclamation, so the airfield was inside

Croatia, which was off-limits to us. Finally, all sixteen council members agreed. "Okay," they said, "but you can only bomb the runway." We could hit the airfield and render it inoperable, but we wouldn't be allowed to destroy any of the aircraft.

This wasn't exactly a punishment for having violated our no-fly zone and bombing Bihać. It wouldn't take even a third-rate country more than a day or two to repair a bombed runway. But I was willing to take half a loaf, though this was more like a single slice of bread. I wanted at least to do something to demonstrate to the Serbs and the other warring parties that we would find and go after anyone who violated Deny Flight. I also wanted to be able to show the NATO Council that I would comply with its political guidance, which I knew would be important when it came to more difficult decisions later. I was sending a message.

Admiral Leighton Smith, the NATO commander for southern Europe, was in operational command of Deny Flight. Through him, I conveyed instructions to Mike Ryan, the US Air Force leader, on what we had to do (Ryan later became air force chief of staff). "These are our political instructions," I told them. "Bomb right down the middle of the runway."

"There are SAM [surface-to-air missile] sites close by," Ryan said. "Can I get those?"

"Yes," I told him. "You can do that." The Bosnian Serbs had no advanced antiaircraft weaponry; the surface-to-air missiles came straight from Serbia, whose president, Slobodan Milošević, was providing the Bosnian Serbs with weapons, logistics, funding, and even troops.

The air strike was the biggest NATO had ever launched, thirty-nine planes, most of them American, a few French, Dutch, and British. They took out the SAM sites and bombed right down the middle of the runway. It would have been simple to make a small mistake and hit at least one or two of the parked jets, but we didn't do it. I took the photos to the council afterward.

"See," I told them. "Those are the planes that did the bombing. Not one of them was hit. But we bombed the hell out of the runway. I expect they'll have it up and running again in twenty-four hours." Which they did. Poor Mike Ryan told me, "Don't ever give me a mission like that again."

Bihać was barely holding out against the besieging Bosnian Serbs, who at one point penetrated almost to the middle of the city. But on December 20, just before Christmas, Bosnian Serbs and Muslims agreed to a cease-fire brokered by former US president Jimmy Carter. The cease-fire held at first, but by March it was crumbling, and in May another of the war's headline atrocities took place in the city of Tuzla, Bosnia's third largest. Tuzla was another of the UN safe areas. On May 25, 1995, the Bosnian Serbs launched an artillery attack on the city. At 9:00 that evening, a shell exploded in the middle of a café crowded with young people. The Serbs had targeted directly on the site. Seventy-one were killed, and another 240 wounded, a massacre similar to the one in the Sarajevo marketplace fifteen months earlier. Afterward Tuzla's mayor spoke out directly to the UN: "You declared Tuzla and other besieged cities in Bosnia and Herzegovina safe areas. You have worn out all diplomatic means. Innocent children and people are being killed continuously. For the sake of God and humanity, use force finally!"

At the same time, outside of Sarajevo Bosnian Serb forces broke into an UNPROFOR guarded depot, seized heavy weapons, and renewed their shelling of the city. In response, we received permission to bomb an ammunition supply depot near Pale, the Bosnian Serb capital. But when we did that, the Bosnian Serbs raised the stakes by capturing almost four hundred UNPROFOR troops in various areas of the country. They chained some of their hostages to bridges and telephone poles near potential air targets, which was shown on Serbian TV.

Ratko Mladić, the Bosnian Serb military chief, announced his intentions for the UNPROFOR hostages. "The UN has hired a murderer," he declared. "It is called the NATO alliance. It is a hired killer. If NATO wishes to continue with its air strikes, then it will have to kill UN troops because we have placed UN troops and observers around potential targets that NATO might decide to go for. The international community will therefore have to pay a heavy price. And it will not stop at that!"

Throughout the war zone, UNPROFOR was being bullied, and when it did not respond, the next time worse happened. The UN peacekeeping mission was in a death spiral.

In early July, the full bankruptcy of the UN strategy exploded onto the world's consciousness. It happened in Srebrenica, a Bosnian Muslim town in an area that had been the scene of mutual atrocities since 1992. Bosnian villages and hamlets had been subjected to Serb attacks and their inhabitants expelled and killed. Bosnian army forces and militias had done the same to the region's Serb villages. By 1993, Serb units had overrun the Bosniak areas around Srebrenica, and the town itself was besieged. Jammed with refugees from the countryside, with no water or electricity and almost no food or medicine, Srebrenica was a place where terrorized people were dying of starvation and being killed daily by artillery attacks and sniper fire. The conditions there were similar to those in Goražde, Bihać, and Sarajevo, except worse.

The UN had declared Srebrenica a safe haven, but that had little effect on the fighting. Nor were the promised humanitarian relief convoys getting through the lines. An UNPROFOR battalion of Dutch soldiers was in Srebrenica, but they had only light weapons, and they, too, were short on food, medicine, and fuel. They stood no real chance of holding off any kind of determined Serbian assault.

In March and April 1995, Mladić began building up his forces around the besieged town, tightening the noose. On July 6, the assault began. The Dutch battalion knew the town would be overrun and called for NATO airstrikes to try to disrupt the Serb attack. But the UN refused the request, afraid, as it almost always was, of escalating the level of violence. We watched the Serbs advance.

Three days out, two days out, one day out. Approval for the air strikes finally came when the Serbs were right on top of the Dutch battalion, and by then it impossible to carry out without incurring many civilian casualties. Watching this disaster unfold, I was barely controlling my rage. "This is not," I told the alliance, "what we stand for!" I was pushing as hard as I could. "This is going to be a stain on all of us."

By chance, just as the Serbs launched their final assault, the Dutch chief of defense was visiting me at my residence in Mons. At midnight, as the reports from Srebrenica grew increasingly desperate, he tried to call the UNPROFOR commander but was told the commander couldn't be disturbed. When he couldn't get through, he phoned his defense minister, then left abruptly early in the morning.

In a terrible irony, a Dutch air force squadron was waiting at the Villafranca airbase in Italy. It was their turn in the air-support rotation, and they had been sitting on the runway for days waiting for the approval that was too late in coming. On a couple of occasions, they had already taken off, expecting a go-ahead while they were in the air. Later we heard the tape of the Dutch pilots talking directly with the Srebrenica battalion, listening as their comrades on the ground described Mladić's forces closing in on them.

As Serbian forces entered Srebrenica, everyone who could fled toward Potočari, a village just northwest of Srebrenica where the Dutch battalion had its headquarters, a flood of twenty or twenty-five thousand people desperate for protection. The refugees clustered around the UNPROFOR compound. Some were able to crowd inside, but most of them spread out through the neighboring fields. They were pursued there by Mladić's soldiers, including the notorious Scorpion unit that had committed atrocities elsewhere.

On July 12, the killings began. Mladić's tanks surrounded the Dutch compound and ordered the battalion commander to turn over the people who had managed to take refuge there. The commander complied. The Muslims were paraded out, and the men were loaded onto buses, driven off, and executed in a wood a short distance away. Outside the compound, men and boys were pulled out of the crowds of refugees and summarily shot. The rapes started then, too, some of them right in front of Dutch soldiers, who could do nothing but stand and watch. In short order, Mladić's forces began separating the Bosnian men and women. By the next day, mass executions and mass rapes were under way. Corpses littered the ground throughout the area. Bulldozers pushed bodies into open pits, then covered them up. By the time it was over, nearly eight thousand men and boys had been murdered in cold blood. It was the biggest mass killing in Europe since World War II.

I saw part of this on television. Serbian TV triumphantly livestreamed Mladić toasting the Dutch handover of Muslims from the compound and loading the men onto buses. CNN and other broadcast outlets ran the same footage. I had had good intelligence on Mladić's movements as he closed in on Srebrenica. Later I had photographs and made slides of what had happened.

It was a grief-filled day for the Netherlands and a tragic day for the United Nations. In the aftermath, Kofi Annan, who succeeded Boutros-Ghali as UN secretary-general, wrote: "Through error, misjudgment and an inability to recognize the scope of the evil confronting us, we failed to do our part to help save the people of Srebrenica from the Serb campaign of mass murder."

Srebrenica was finally just too much. The massacre of thousands of innocent men and boys and atrocities against women, children, and the elderly galvanized the European community and NATO. British prime minister John Major called a conference in London, inviting the sixteen NATO nations as well as observers from non-NATO countries and nongovernmental organizations.

Major and NATO had gotten out ahead of the American political process, though. After the conference was announced, I got a call from Shalikashvili telling me there was substantial opposition in Congress and even in the administration to sending troops into combat in such a slippery situation.

I was stunned to hear this. The Vietnam syndrome was still coming back to bite us. "Candidly," Shali said, "there's very little support back here."

"That can't be," I said. "NATO's going to give its approval. We're the leader of NATO."

"That's right, but I'm telling you right now there is no agreement that the United States will support a NATO involvement. If you want that," he said, "you'll have to come back and get the president to approve the plan for any deployment."

"I'll be there tomorrow," I said.

I gathered my aide, Ben Hodges, a few charts, and a colonel to flip them, got us all into my plane, and took off.

The next day I was in the Oval Office standing in front of the president's desk with my charts on an easel, looking at President Clinton and his entire national security team: Deputy National Security Adviser Sandy Berger, UN ambassador Madeleine Albright, Secretary of State Warren Christopher, Vice President Al Gore, White House Chief of Staff Leon Panetta, Chairman of the Joint Chiefs John Shalikashvili, Secretary of Defense Bill Perry, and a variety of staffers. The president was sitting exactly opposite me. I had been in this room for briefings back when I was deputy chief of staff to Alexander Haig. Those were fraught times. But I did not think any of those briefings had more significance than this one. I had the deep conviction that the future of NATO and America's leadership role in Europe was squarely on the line.

I was going to be asking the president to commit thousands of US troops to a war zone at a time when the presidential election campaign of 1996 was already under way. Congressional leaders, cabinet members, senior military people, and experts on the area were telling him that if he did that, the body bags would start coming back to Dover, Delaware, with all the dire political consequences that would have. Despite the moral necessity (as I saw it, anyway), Clinton had not yet made the final decision. I didn't have a sense for where he was going to come down. I didn't think anyone else did either.

I started by reviewing the situation. I talked about the violations of UN declarations and how UN troops were under attack. I described the slaughters and ethnic cleansing. I talked about the Nazi extermination of Europe's Jews. "We're now seeing the worst atrocities in Europe since World War II," I said. "The issue is, do we stand by and let it happen? Or do we take action? In all my years with the alliance, the United States has been the leader. The United States *has* to lead!" I then gave an overview of the kind of requirements I would need before we could go in with force: the clear mission statement, the robust rules of engagement, the unity of command, the timely political decision that the United States would have to make, along with the NATO Council.

Clinton waited for me to finish, then asked for questions. There were some, but the only question people were truly interested in was the one Al Gore asked: "How many casualties are you expecting?"

"Any time you commit troops in combat," I said, "or in a wartime situation, there's always the risk of casualties. But if I have the conditions and rules of engagement I've described, I will minimize that." A pat answer, but true.

I knew Shalikashvili and Perry understood what I was saying. I wasn't sure about the others. Everyone there represented constituencies that were telling them in one way or another, "We don't think the United States should be going in there."

Yet Clinton and I had good rapport. We had had a friendly, candid discussion when he first appointed me SACEUR/CINCEUR. He had trusted my judgment when I told him we needed a floor of one hundred thousand US troops in Europe. We had met each other again in Normandy on the fiftieth anniversary of the Normandy invasion, when he had spoken to our soldiers at Omaha Beach, including the aging Ranger veterans who had climbed the cliffs. As he was shaking hands with them, an old vet in a wheelchair saluted and made an effort to raise himself up, which was when we saw that he had no legs. I had stood next to Clinton at those ceremonies. I knew he understood what putting troops in harm's way meant and what kind of cause was worth that kind of sacrifice. I knew, too, that whatever the thinking in the room, I was really addressing an audience of one. Now he stood up and asked if there were any more questions. There weren't. "George," he said, "I approve."

That was an immensely reassuring moment. The president was expressing his judgment in a situation that was going to have profound political, moral, and geopolitical consequences as well as personal consequences for him. I felt strongly that he was also expressing his confidence in me, in our troops, and in the NATO alliance. I didn't think there were many times in our recent history when a president had spoken directly to a field commander and personally given his approval for an operation. I couldn't help thinking back to my master's studies at Loyola on Article 2, section 2, of the Constitution. Here was the "commander in chief clause" in operation.

The London conference called by John Major was held on July 21. Along with NATO secretary-general Willy Claes (Manfred Woerner had died the previous year), I had a chance to speak. The use of real force was finally on the table, and I outlined what I felt needed to be done. I described Ratko Mladić's tactics, how he typically kept a fixing force around whatever safe area he was planning to attack, then quickly brought up armor and artillery from elsewhere. He had been a two-star general in Milošević's Yugoslavian army before becoming the Bosnian Serb military leader. He knew how to maneuver; under his command, the Bosnian Serb forces were mobile and deadly. The Bosniak infantry could rarely stand up against him.

I showed my Srebrenica slides to the conference delegates. I told them, "If you want to prevent Goražde or some other town from becoming the next Srebrenica, you need to allow NATO air forces to respond quickly when we see a massing of forces or shelling. You cannot wait until after the fact and then say, 'Do something!' If you want to prevent more Srebrenicas, I can't go through the whole process of briefing the council and waiting until everyone gets approval from their leaderships. If you want to take effective action, you need to let me, as SACEUR, decide the triggers. If I screw up, I'll take the heat, but I need to have the triggers." Interestingly, the Russian defense minister, General Pavel Grachev, was observing. He agreed with my analysis and, like me, believed that Goražde would quickly fall unless we took early action.

Srebrenica wasn't the end. A week and a half later Mladić's forces took Žepa, a town downriver from Srebrenica. Žepa was another so-called safe area, guarded by a small Ukrainian UNPROFOR unit that was as impotent as the Dutch in Srebrenica. Killings and rapes took place in Žepa, though there was no mass slaughter as there had been in Srebrenica. The Serbs instead simply expelled its Muslim inhabitants to further swell the concentration of refugees in Sarajevo, which was still cut off and suffering under Serb bombardment. As the expulsions and atrocities were going on, our pictures showed a white UN military vehicle sitting there amid the chaos, doing nothing.

Then on August 28 a salvo of mortar shells smashed into Sarajevo's Markale—the same central market that had suffered such a devastating attack the previous year. This time thirty-seven people were killed, and almost a hundred were wounded.

The London conference was a turning point. For me, it had been a chance to give my assessment and advice to the assembled NATO foreign and defense ministers. The end result was a UN-NATO political decision to allow NATO forces to take military action to protect the safe areas on its own volition, without additional UN "dual-key" approval. When the mortar rounds fell on Sarajevo's marketplace on August 28, I had a pre-approved mandate.

For a year and a half, I had been working to prepare both NATO and US forces for eventual involvement. Now it seemed we had finally come to that point, after the deaths of many tens of thousands of innocents and atrocities against whole populations. In my discussions with the NATO Council, I was able to get its members to designate two zones of action, one in southern Bosnia, the other in the north.

Admiral Smith initially wanted a narrow interpretation of the zones of action, but I insisted on a much broader definition that would enable us to attack in depth. I was able to get that and to get approval to attack all elements—command and control, petrol infrastructure, ammunition depots, and other components—that might be involved in artillery or mortar fire on Sarajevo, Goražde, or other designated safe areas.

The London conference political decision came in late July. Once NATO had the go-ahead, Mike Ryan and his Combined Air Operations staff identified sixty or seventy primary targets and ran rehearsals in those areas. By mid-August, we were ready to launch an air campaign from our bases in Italy and from carriers in the Mediterranean. The previous January British general Rupert Smith had replaced Michael Rose as head of UNPROFOR. Smith was smart and energetic, with a sense of mission his predecessor lacked. He was able to quickly identify the Serb unit that had fired the rounds on Sarajevo. Twenty-four hours after the Sarajevo Markale attack, Operation Deliberate Force was in the air over Bosnia.

The attempt to head off war in the former Yugoslavia and then when it did start to negotiate an end to it went back to 1992. It included efforts and plans authored by Great Britain's Lord Carrington and Portugal's José Cutileiro; US special envoy Cyrus Vance and the European Union's Lord Owen; and Jimmy Carter, who was more or less free-lancing. The events in Srebrenica, Žepa, and now Sarajevo gave the Clinton administration a sense of urgency it had not had before. Nor had it had the political will to bring the use of force to the negotiating table. After London, the United States started playing with different cards.

Three weeks after London, Richard Holbrooke, the assistant secretary of state for European and Canadian affairs, took over as President Clinton's lead Balkan negotiator. Holbrooke was a career diplomat with a strong reputation going back to Vietnam, where we had met once or twice when I was Alexander Haig's assistant. He had been assistant secretary of state for East Asia and ambassador to Germany. He was smart, tough, and knowledgeable, not the easiest person to work with—as I was to find out—but a hard-nosed, effective negotiator.

Holbrooke's first meeting with Slobodan Milošević in Belgrade took place on August 30, just as our air campaign began hitting Bosnian Serb targets. These strikes were massive; they had nothing in common with the kind of hesitant, limited missions we had been restricted to previously. I intended them not only to degrade Mladić's military machine but also to convey an unambiguous message that we were going to put a stop to the Bosnian Serb onslaught against the Muslim civilian population.

As Holbrooke was establishing his positions with Milošević, the bombing was ratcheting up. Our planes were inflicting serious damage and providing an unmistakable demonstration of NATO and American determination. As Holbrooke recounts in his book *To End a War*, when he and Milošević broke after their first day's meeting, Holbrooke said, "We'll be back soon, Mr. President, but remember, NATO planes are in the air over Bosnia as we speak."

That first day our attacks went after the Bosnian Serb's artillery and other components, including inside the twenty-kilometer exclusionary zone around Sarajevo that the UN had declared back in February 1994, which the Serbs had paid little attention to. Over the next two weeks, as Holbrooke pursued shuttle diplomacy with Milošević, Croatia's president Franjo Tudjman, and Bosnia's president Alija Izetbegović, we at times temporarily halted and then resumed the bombing to assist Holbrooke's efforts. He had undertaken an exceptionally complex task, and while he was negotiating, he would call me to urge us to step up the bombing in order to give him greater leverage. I was sensitive to that, but, of course, he wasn't knowledgeable about the details of our capabilities, targeting priorities, or timing requirements. "Dick," I told him, "leave it alone. It's our business. We know what we're doing here."

Though Holbrooke's efforts and NATO's were bound at the hip, our objectives weren't identical. NATO was working to protect the Bosnian civilian population. We were responding to atrocities. We were supporting the diplomatic process, but our primary objective was to stop the killing. Holbrooke's ultimate goal was to maneuver Milošević into a peace deal, and he regarded NATO's military effort primarily as the fist end of his negotiating tactics.

To get his point across unambiguously, he invited me to sit in on sessions in Belgrade with Milošević and in Zagreb and Sarajevo with Tudjman and Izetbegović. There's no question my presence sent a message, especially with Milošević. I was the face of our military power and our will to bring force to bear. Holbrooke was using me to indicate the heavy hitting he had in hand. I was happy enough to play that role; the tactic got Milošević's attention.

Milošević was glib and sophisticated; many people considered him charismatic. He had been a banker before he got into politics. He was now essentially running the Bosnian Serbs, supplying them, financing them, giving them direction. He had a first-rate understanding of the use of force. Holbrooke told me often that the bombing was directly responsible for the progress he was making.

I also insisted on being part of the process in order to make sure that whatever tasks we were given under an eventual agreement (assuming there was one) would be clearly defined and attainable, that our rules of engagement would give us the authority to do what was needed. I was determined to make sure that any agreement wasn't going to be couched in the typical murkiness that often characterizes diplomatic compromises. As far as military elements went, I wanted a document that could be read in clear operational terms.

Political or diplomatic leaders often sacrifice clarity because of their eagerness to make a deal. My concern was that whatever deal was made, it had to be enforceable. Assuming Holbrooke could come to terms with Milošević, NATO troops were going to be on the ground in Bosnia implementing the agreement's requirements. Given the deep hatreds, the vast amount of blood that had already been shed, and Bosnia's history of violence, those requirements were not going to sit well with one or maybe all of the parties. I wanted to make sure that whatever deal he made would be enforceable. If there was a point of contention, I wanted to clear it up early rather than face uncertainty once we had committed troops. We had made that mistake in Somalia by not giving clear military advice while diplomatic arrangements were being made. I was determined the same thing wouldn't happen in Bosnia. Giving clear, proactive advice was a way to preclude that result, so I kept closely engaged in what Holbrooke was doing in order to create the best conditions for success once NATO ground forces were called on. Whatever Holbrooke was saying to Milošević, I didn't want him obscuring what I was going to have to do on the ground.

By the second week in September, the bombing was taking a huge toll not only on the Bosnian Serb military but on the Serbs' emotional resources. We destroyed heavy weapons, ammunition bunkers, command-and-control facilities, and the main communications center. In Pale, the Bosnian Serb administrative capital, we hit the big mountainside fuel tanks. On

September 10, we launched Tomahawk missiles from the USS *Normandy* in the Adriatic and took out key elements of the Serb antiaircraft defenses. The Tomahawks had a devastating impact. The Serbs were suffering badly from our bombing campaign, but their antiaircraft systems posed a danger to our pilots, and the fog and heavy overcast caused delays and aborted missions. The precision-guided Tomahawks, in contrast, were impervious to weather. Long range and all but undetectable, they appeared out of nowhere and destroyed their targets with pinpoint accuracy. Knowing their use would be considered an escalation, I had gone to the NATO Council beforehand for approval. The strikes not only took out the Serb air defenses but also created outrage, fear, and deep apprehension. They were a decisive signal. I could feel that they broke the Serbs' spirit. In one of our Belgrade meetings, Milošević's foreign minister told me, "You have got to stop. You have just got to stop!"

"You get every single heavy weapon out of the Sarajevo exclusion zone," I said. "That's when we'll stop."

I had photos of where all these guns were. We had inserted people on the ground who had counted them. That evening the Serbs started driving or towing more than two hundred heavy weapons out of the exclusion zone. UNPROFOR commanders had been telling me for a year that the weapons in the zone were mostly rusted hulks. I knew that was nonsense, really no more than an attempt by Rose and his subordinates to defend their inaction. These weapons were dangerous and serviceable, and they were registered on targets in the city. Now, for the first time in four years, Sarajevo was free of bombardment and the threat of bombardment. Sarajevo had undergone the longest siege of a major city in modern history, longer than the Nazi sieges of Leningrad or Stalingrad. I told the Serbs, "Don't play games with me. Once you tell me you have everything out, I'm going back to look."

On September 14, Holbrooke and his team in Belgrade were given a document signed by Ratko Mladić, Republika Srpska president Radovan Karadžić, and Slobodan Milošević formally committing the Bosnian Serbs to removing their weapons and opening the main highways to the city. Holbrooke didn't sign; he told them he had no authority to represent NATO or the UN. Holbrooke's assessment after two weeks of hard negotiating was that the Bosnian Serbs "respected only force or an unambiguous and credible threat to use it." I could have told him that before. We were doing peace enforcement here, not peacekeeping.

Operation Deliberate Force lasted from August 30 to September 20, 1995. It included four hundred aircraft, mostly American from bases in

Italy and carriers in the Mediterranean, but also British, French, German, and Dutch. Seventy percent of the bombs dropped were precision guided. The targeting had been extremely careful, and the NATO pilots did a magnificent job, hitting only military, not civilian, targets. They had rehearsed their runs numerous times, which gave them the ability to be exceptionally accurate. When the NATO Council became concerned over possible collateral damage, I was able to present satellite pictures that showed, for example, how we would hit barracks while leaving a directly adjacent Red Cross–marked building unscathed. Even Milošević was amazed by how we had carried out such a massive bombing campaign while causing so extremely few civilian casualties. In one of our meetings, he actually asked me how we had done that.

As Holbrooke shuttled between the Balkan capitals, at NATO's headquarters we were planning how to deploy ground forces. Whether or how this might happen would depend on the outcome of Holbrooke's efforts, but we were going to be prepared for whatever might eventuate. There was zero doubt that NATO was going to be responsible for implementing any agreement that emerged.

The plan for a deployment was crucial. It had to incorporate all the prerequisites I wanted—clarity of mission, unity of command, robust rules of engagement. We were at a historic moment. NATO forces had never been deployed outside alliance countries, and this was going to be a major mission, potentially a combat mission, in an unpredictable, violent environment in the middle of winter in some of Europe's worst terrain.

We started with a plan that had been developed earlier but had serious deficiencies and went to work forging a new one. It was a painstaking process. For me, it was also a nerve-wracking process. Time was absolutely of the essence here, but the plan had to cover every detail we could anticipate. The need for attention to detail had been part of my DNA for a long time, but I also needed to get this thing done and approved so I could start training up for the specifics. I needed to move quickly to get the force up to speed. Holbrooke's timetable depended on how he might be able to herd three hard-headed, angry heads of state—Milošević, Tudjman, and Izetbegović—into an agreement, if he could do that at all. But if he could, I was damned if I wasn't going to be ready to deploy.

The final plan was called OPLAN 10405: "In response to a request by the United Nation's Security Council, it is anticipated that the North Atlantic Council will authorize a NATO operation to implement the military aspects of the peace agreement in the former Yugoslavia with the following objectives." It identified and defined the objectives—this provided the clarity of mission I needed. It gave me the robust rules of engagement I required to go into a rough place and deal with rough people. It spelled out the command structure and called for sixty thousand troops, to be identified as IFOR—the Implementation Force. We named the operation Joint Endeavor.

After a flurry of refinements, we finished the document and typed it up, and I gave it to the chairman of the NATO Military Committee, Dick Vincent, telling him, "Let's get this thing approved so I can start training the force."

The North Atlantic Council was scheduled to convene at a special NATO ministers of defense meeting, scheduled for Williamsburg, Virginia, on October 5. We presented it at that meeting, going over the entire document carefully, paying special attention to clarifying the rules of engagement for the benefit of the nonmilitary ambassadors. Unlike UNPROFOR's "peacekeeping" rules, the new IFOR rules gave me the right to use force against anyone who attempted to interfere with the implementation of whatever might be stipulated in an eventual accord. I had the right to enforce compliance.

Approval of OPLAN 10405 put every one of the NATO nations on board with that. They all did sign on, with the exception of Greece, which had close economic, diplomatic, and cultural ties with Milošević's Serbia. But we found a way around that, allowing Greece to agree in principle but register its objection in a footnote.

On October 7, the North Atlantic Council and the defense ministers formally agreed to a combined force to be deployed in Bosnia-Herzegovina, led by NATO, with SACEUR the overall military authority and Admiral Smith, NATO's southern Europe commander, in operational command. When the vote was taken, there was silence for a moment. Everyone in the room felt the weight of this historic decision. After forty-six years, NATO was entering new territory.

All this time Holbrooke and his team had been busy brokering terms with the belligerents. He was helped along by the shifting fortunes of war. Croat and Bosnian forces were for once making significant progress against the Bosnian Serbs, who had suffered serious losses from our Deliberate Force bombardment and weren't getting the usual plentiful assistance from Slobodan Milošević. The Serbian economy had been devastated by the economic sanctions the UN had imposed in 1992 and continued since then, enforced by NATO's sea blockade. The strain was telling badly on Milošević, who was also tiring of his relationship with Mladić and Karadžić. With the stars aligned the way they were, Holbrooke finally succeeded in getting Tudjman, Izetbegović, and Milošević to sign onto a cease-fire. Mladić and Karadžić agreed also, although Holbrooke left it to Milošević to deliver their signatures. From the start, Holbrooke had refused to deal with them personally.

President Clinton announced the cease-fire on October 5. From that point, all sides began preparing for final peace talks, to be held at Wright Patterson Air Force Base in Dayton, Ohio. In western Ohio, Dayton offered few distractions, and the military setting would be a helpful background reminder of American power.

The Dayton negotiations began on November 1. Now that everyone had decided that more bloodletting would not benefit them, they had to face the hard postwar issues: which territories would go to whom, troop- and equipment-withdrawal requirements, the repatriation of refugees, the political relationships between the various government entities, the organization of postwar elections, the re-creation of civilian life, the treatment of war criminals.

None of these issues was easy, and IFOR was going to be responsible for enforcing compliance with the military elements and securing the environment so that effective civil government could emerge. Carl Bildt, who had been the European Union's chief representative to the Balkans, was appointed high representative for Bosnia-Herzegovina, with the primary task of organizing and holding elections for that entity.

Since a working civilian government was the desired end state for that conflicted region, Holbrooke's team believed that Bildt should have overall control of implementing the accords. My advice was exactly the opposite. "This is a political decision," I told Holbrooke, "but what's necessary is that I go in first and create a secure environment for elections to take place. We still have killings and atrocities going on, even with the cease-fire. I've got a mandate to go in and stop that, to collect the weapons and the ammunition, separate the sides, and enforce the boundaries. Let me do what needs to be done. Once I've done that, it will be time for Bildt to take charge. If Bildt's in charge of the whole thing from the beginning, it could easily turn us into another version of UNPROFOR. No one wants to see that. It's an unacceptable risk."

During Dayton, Holbrooke and I were in touch regularly. After a day's negotiating there, he would call me. Nine or ten o'clock at night in Dayton was two or three in the morning at my residence in Mons, Belgium. The phone would ring, waking Karen and me up.

"Who's that?" she'd say.

"It's Holbrooke from Dayton. It's tough times over there."

Sometimes the calls were about specific military questions, but the larger subject was the civilian/military issue. I had shown Holbrooke my chart with a large *M* (military) and a small *c* (civilian) transitioning to a large *C* and a small *m*. They knew where I stood on this. My NATO forces would have six months to secure the region, then Bildt and his team would take on the civil society operation. "You guys can run it if you want to, but I'm telling you what my recommendation is."

At one point when Holbrooke was having trouble with Milošević at Dayton, he asked Bill Perry and me to come and help. Milošević was a smooth operator; he could be charming, he was smart, he spoke English fairly well. But he was deeply complicit in the atrocities that his partners, the Bosnian Serbs, had perpetrated. I was concerned that Mladić and Karadžić had been so successful for so long at bullying and intimidating UNPROFOR that they might perceive IFOR as just another iteration of the same. They were unstable and rabid enough to make that kind of mistake.

I brought Bill Nash with me to the Dayton meeting. Nash was the major general commanding the First Armored Division, which was going to be the lead NATO force in Bosnia. Nash was an armor officer. Like most armor officers, he had a tough, macho way about him. He smoked big cigars. His demeanor impressed Holbrooke, who wrote that our physical presence sent its own "potent message."

I made it abundantly clear to Milošević in Dayton and in my own one-on-one meetings with him that we were not going to be the new UNPROFOR. "Let me be clear on the difference between UNPROFOR and IFOR," I told him. "I am coming with a NATO force. I am SACEUR, a NATO officer. I am also a United States Army officer. I have a mandate from the sixteen countries of NATO and also from my own country. I am coming with robust rules of engagement, and I am in overall command. What Bosnian Serb forces did in Srebrenica and Sarajevo and other places will not be tolerated. If anyone points a tank or a gun at my forces, we will shoot to kill. All my soldiers know that. If someone points a rifle at them, they don't have to go back to Boutros Boutros-Ghali or to me either for permission on what to do. They know what to do. They will react, not just to hostile acts but also to any hostile intent." I was trying to get inside his head and his gut. I wanted him to know just what was going to happen if anyone wanted a confrontation.

I would sit through Milošević's meetings with Holbrooke, and sometimes my patience would wear thin. Afterward I would say to Holbrooke, "What came out of that? What was your intent? You're exchanging diplomatic talk with a thug. You're dealing with a thug here who has been killing people and condoning killing people. You're talking about conditions and niceties, and you think he's going to come over to our side and help us?"

I knew what Holbrooke was trying to do, and I appreciated the skills he was bringing to the task of dealing with someone as tough and slippery as Milošević. I knew as well as Holbrooke did that the ultimate resolution here was diplomatic, not military. But it was our use of force and the threat of ramping that force up even further that had pushed Milošević to the negotiating table in the first place and was giving Holbrooke the leverage he needed to move the talks the way he wanted them to move.

The negotiations did progress, with more than enough dramatic confrontations and heart-stopping moments. In hindsight, they went relatively quickly, although I'm sure that wasn't the way the participants experienced them. By November 21, three weeks to the day from when the talks kicked off, the final document was signed and announced at Wright Patterson's Hope Conference Center (now the Hope-Holbrooke Conference Center). While others' speeches were going on at the signing ceremony, Holbrooke was thinking, as he wrote in his memoir *To End a War*, "After the behavior we had seen from some of the participants at Dayton, I was more worried than ever about implementing the agreement."

That wasn't my concern. I didn't know what we might encounter, but I had clarity of mission. I had the backing of the alliance and of my president. I trusted my commanders. I had sixty thousand well-trained NATO soldiers poised now to move into the forbidding Balkan landscape with its traumatized, bitter, heavily armed peoples.

15

Bosnia 3
The NATO Army

IFOR's deployment was going to take place in the face of the three armies—Croat, Bosnian Serb, and Bosniak—that had been waging no-holds-barred warfare over Bosnian territory for four years, two hundred thousand soldiers all told, armed with artillery, tanks, and air defense systems. As specified in the Dayton Accords, IFOR had three primary military tasks. The immediate mission was to separate the warring armies and enforce the agreed-on boundaries, more than fourteen hundred miles of difficult terrain. Then we were to oversee land transfers among the three entities; that was to be completed within 45 days of our deployment. Within 180 days, we were to ensure that all the warring factions within Bosnia were demobilized and their heavy weapons placed in cantonment areas. The intention was that we would take six months to secure the region, which would then be ready to conduct elections, the essential piece in the reconstruction of civil life.

To start this process, we were going to have to deploy quickly and impose ourselves decisively, including dealing with any military opposition. Mladić and Karadźić had been dragged kicking and screaming into the agreement, but they weren't signatories, and it wasn't clear how much control Milošević really had over them. Mladić was a competent armor commander, and neither he nor Karadźić was a stable personality. What they might decide to do on the ground as opposed to what they were forced into by Milošević during the Dayton negotiations was an open question.

We divided IFOR into three commands, French, British, and American. Bill Nash, who had sat in with me in Dayton, commanded the American-led element, which we were calling Task Force Eagle. His First Armored Division was the spearhead; his command included a Turkish brigade, a Polish/Nordic brigade (with troops from Poland, Denmark, Estonia, Sweden, Finland, Latvia, and Lithuania), and a Russian brigade.

The NATO deployment as a whole was historic, the first time ever that alliance troops were going into non-NATO territory. Even more historic was Russia's participation. For forty-five years, NATO and Russia had stared angrily at each other across the Iron Curtain, each side planning how to destroy the other. Now, only a few years after the breakup of the Soviet Union, we were partners in trying to implement peace. That was a phenomenon, an unmistakable sign of optimism for the post–Cold War world—dashed all too soon but very much alive then.

Our interaction with the Russians had begun shortly after my appointment as SACEUR. On one of my first visits to the European Union headquarters in Brussels, I was told that Russian defense minister General Pavel Grachev would like to meet me. Grachev was at the Russian embassy. Would I go to see him?

I didn't know Grachev. When I asked about him, I was told he didn't have a sterling reputation. He had commanded an airborne division in the last years of the disastrous Soviet war in Afghanistan; he had been accused of corruption in the Russian pullout from East Germany. But he was a friend of Russian president Boris Yeltsin and had led the faction that opposed the revolt against Gorbachev, which brought Yeltsin to the presidency. Yeltsin had appointed him defense minister. He was apparently one of the Russian president's drinking buddies.

"Yes," I said, "I'll meet him. I don't know what we'll discuss, but I'll meet him."

The next morning at 9:00 a.m. I was at the Russian embassy being introduced to Pavel Grachev. Aides rolled out a cart with an assortment of liquors and whiskies. I asked for coffee. Grachev had vodka. Nothing serious happened; we mainly exchanged pleasantries. But we did break the ice, which turned out to be important later on.

The NATO heads-of-state meeting in January 1994 had launched the Partnership for Peace program. Among the nations that had signed up were many of the former Soviet Republics as well as Warsaw Pact countries. I saw PfP as a teaching mechanism to further democratization and as a training organization to introduce NATO standards. To me, those objectives were part and parcel of a wider vision for a post–Cold War NATO that would include antiterror operations, humanitarian endeavors, and a range of activities meant to resolve conflicts before they became shooting wars. Most former Soviet Union and Soviet bloc states still had Communist-style militaries and leftover Communist governments, but they were changing, and we were figuring out how most effectively to engage with them. I saw PfP as a big part of that process.

But beside the larger vision, I also regarded PfP as a training ground specifically for a potential multinational Bosnian operation. Manfred

Woerner and I had agreed on that shortly after PfP was established, and as the organization grew, I began thinking that we might be able to include Russia itself.

The next time I met with Grachev, I described to him how PfP was training to common standards so that we could, in my opinion, step in to end the slaughter going on in Bosnia. "Can you be part of that?" I asked. "That would be helpful, especially with the Serbs." I was drawing my concept of this for him on a napkin. "If we worked together, we could bring peace and stability there instead of what's going on now, which isn't good for any of us."

Grachev liked the idea. He didn't commit immediately, but he liked it. Yeltsin must have also because in June Russia formally joined the PfP.

Now, a year and a half later, Secretary of Defense Perry began talking with Grachev about the possibility of Russia joining with NATO forces in some way. The Joint Chiefs had suggested attaching a platoon or two of Russian combat engineers to one of our engineer elements. Perry asked me to consider it.

I gave the suggestion a lot of consideration. Attaching a small Russian engineer unit seemed like a weak symbol of cooperation, to say the best for it. If we were going to bring in the Russians, what I wanted was a front-line Russian force integrated with our front-line forces. That would be meaningful operationally—it would give me a step up with the Serbs—and it would serve as a bond between our two countries that could have positive consequences beyond Bosnia. (In fact, it did lead to the NATO-Russia Founding Act of 1997, which we hoped would serve as a roadmap for cooperation "on the principles of democracy and cooperative security." In the age of Vladimir Putin, that concept appears to be an idle fantasy. At the time, it didn't seem like that at all but rather a strong possibility.)

When I opened a discussion with Grachev about this, he was in favor. He wanted to do it, in principle. The sticking point was that the Russians couldn't acquiesce to putting themselves under the command of the United States or a US-led NATO. The very thought gave them heartburn.

After thinking about it for a while, it occurred to me that our army doctrine concerning command relationships could give us a way around the problem. Army doctrine differentiated between operational control and tactical control. Operational control means command over setting objectives, organizing forces, and assigning tasks. Tactical control refers to the direct command of forces that are tasked to accomplish the missions set for them.

Tactical control—the command of forces deployed in the battle-field—needed to be in Bill Nash's hands. But I thought I saw a way of including the Russians in operational control.

"If you send me your military representative," I told Grachev, "I'll make him my deputy for Russian forces in Bosnia. I'll exercise control as overall military authority, but I will give Russian forces their mission through my Russian deputy. He will be the one issuing the orders to Russian troops. That way we can preserve unity of command, which I need to have, but Russian operational orders will come through a Russian. Tactical command will be in my division commander's hands."

Grachev thought the operational side sounded all right—Russian forces getting their orders from a Russian general. But what did I mean Russian troops would be under an American's tactical control? I could feel him digging in his heels. "I cannot give you tactical control over Russian troops," he told me.

"Let me explain," I said. I knew Russian military doctrine didn't break down command and control the same way ours did. "Russian troops would be part of Task Force Eagle—four brigades, American, Turkish, Baltic/Scandinavian, and Russian. That's our Multinational Division North. My two-star, Bill Nash, is in command. The mission for your brigade comes through your guy, the deputy to the supreme commander. But here's what we mean by tactical control." I showed him a map.

"This is the area of operations. Let's say for a moment that you are General Nash. Your area of operations has one road going through it. That's the supply and logistics line for all your elements. Who needs to control who comes down that road? What are the priorities? Who needs to control the food and ammunition supplies? Who needs to control the timing? Who needs to decide which reinforcements come through?"

"If I'm the commander, I do, of course," said Grachev.

"Of course. Who needs to control where the division's artillery gets placed, where the logistical points are, where the communication points are, the POL [petroleum, oil lubricants]?"

"I need to control all that," said Grachev.

Being a military professional, he added two or three other things he would need to control if he were the division commander.

"That's exactly what we mean by tactical control," I said. "That's how we differentiate it from operational control. That's why tactical control has to be in one person's hands, my division commander's.

"But of course you retain ultimate authority over your troops. All the NATO nations have that. If you don't like a mission you're given, you can pull your forces out. That happens very rarely, but you have the right to do it. But I have to retain unity of command. I can share operational control over Russian forces with a Russian deputy, as I explained. But my division commander needs to have tactical control. If you can't accept this, I'm not going to be able to accept your participation. Either you agree with these conditions, or I'll shake your hand, and we'll depart as friends."

Grachev accepted them. When he did, I briefed Secretary of Defense Perry and Javier Solana, who was now NATO secretary-general. With everybody in agreement, Grachev sent Colonel General Leontiy Shevtsov, whom I appointed my deputy. Then Shevtsov and I planned how to work together on key principles: unity of command, coordination of air–ground operations, logistics coordination, intelligence sharing, and rules of engagement. Our agreement then went back to Moscow for approval by the Russian General Staff and Grachev, who authorized the deployment of a Russian brigade under the operational control of myself as SACEUR. That was a great day for NATO. It demonstrated how extremely far we had come in our military-to-military relationship with Russia, with all its potential for the Russian–American political relationship.

Once all the details were settled, we drafted a formal agreement, which I had printed up in both English and Russian, the Russian in Cyrillic script. Shevtsov and I signed, then Perry and Grachev did (for many years the original document was on periodic display at the National Defense University). I had a large chart made up that read, "Russia Plus NATO Equals Success in Bosnia."

This agreement was not well received all over the place. A half century of enmity and confrontation didn't just suddenly lose its grip on minds, and not many thought we could really pull it off. Skepticism ran deep on both sides. All of America's military leaders had been conditioned throughout their careers by confrontation with the Soviets. For the Russians, America had been "the Main Enemy," and NATO was nothing more than America's pawn.

At a dinner Prince Charles hosted for defense chiefs and ministers, I found myself sitting to the right of Russian foreign minister Yevgeny Primakov. After Prince Charles finished his introductory remarks, Primakov turned to me.

"General," he said, "why do you have this NATO expansion? Why do you want to put NATO in Poland and all those countries right on our border? This gives us great concern."

"Foreign Minister," I said, "first off, these are democratic nations. They have a right to do what they want to do. That's their prerogative now that they are free nations." I didn't know if the "free nations now" might have been a little off-putting.

"You know," Primakov said, "if you get into Poland, you're going to threaten our nuclear sites in that part of Russia."

"No," I said, "that's not correct. NATO expansion does not threaten your nuclear sites. We don't have to be in eastern Europe to threaten your nuclear sites. We have submarines and many other means to threaten those sites. What NATO enlargement does"—this took him off balance— "what NATO does is secure your western flank. Your threats are to the south and east, China and the Caucasus. That's where you ought to be concentrating your effort. NATO isn't planning an attack against Russia. We want to try to work together with you."

When Shevtsov had first arrived in my office with his team of five or six other officers, there was a certain awkwardness. This wasn't a one-to-one talk, as with Grachev; we were actually going to be working with these Russians. Were our interactions going to be strained, or could we establish a friendly, working rapport? When they came into my office, they all stood stiffly at attention in front of my desk in their big hats.

"General," I said, "please sit down." They sat down, and I offered coffee. I told them I had to make sure they understood that I was the overall commander. I went over the rules and the formal relationships. "We need to build trust and confidence in each other," I said. Then after we had talked for a bit, I asked Shevtsov, "Where would you like to go? What would you like to see?"

The first thing he wanted to look at was the air operations center. Fine, I thought. We flew in my plane to Villafranca, Italy. I didn't announce to the operations center that I was coming; I just went in and sat down with Shevtsov in a back row to watch what was going on. The air force does things in an extremely organized air force fashion. Charts were going up to show tasking orders. Lights were coming on to show what was happening and where. A group of pilots was sitting in front being briefed for their next mission. Shevtsov was looking intently at everything. I asked the pilots to turn around and introduce themselves; one was a Brit, another French, another Dutch, others from various NATO countries.

"Tell us what you're doing," I said.

"We're enforcing Deny Flight," they said. "We're keeping anybody from dropping bombs. We're protecting lives there."

Shevtsov next wanted to go to the NATO Allied Rapid Reaction Corps in northern Germany, which was going to serve as the headquarters for the land component of IFOR. I sent Shevtsov there by himself. Instead of going with him, I called my British three-star who was in charge and told him to "open every door. Show him everything you can. No secrets—I want him to see what you're doing."

"Where else?" I asked when he got back.

"I'd like to see your EUCOM headquarters in Stuttgart," he said.

I looked at him. EUCOM—central command of the US Army in Europe—was not NATO but of course was in support of NATO. "This guy's done his homework," I thought.

"Okay," I said. "You can go there by yourself."

I called my deputy there and told him the same thing I had told my commander at the Allied Rapid Reaction Corps. "I'm sending this Russian, Shevtsov." I went over who he was and what he was going to be doing. "I want you to open every door for him."

When Shevtsov came back from Stuttgart, he didn't ask to see anything further. He apparently had seen enough. I knew he wasn't just interested in how we handled command and control; he was looking for signs of a NATO or American attack plan against Russia. But he hadn't seen anything to suggest that, and he had seen a lot. The Cold War had conditioned the Western allies with a fear of Soviet aggression. It apparently had conditioned the Russians similarly.

"We don't have a plan to attack Russia," I told Shevtsov. "We know you have a plan to attack NATO, but the only thing we have is a defense plan. We're not going to attack Russia. We're ready to defend the NATO countries, but we have no attack plan." After Shevtsov had seen everything and understood the chain of command I had devised with Grachev, the Russian General Staff sent me a deployment order, with details about the brigade it was sending for me to include in IFOR. That was the official signal that the Russians were in with the rest of the coalition. I assigned my special assistant, Steve Covington, as my liaison with the Russians. "One Team," I thought, "One Fight."

As Shevtsov and I got to know each other better, he told me that he had commanded the First Guard Tank Army directly opposite us in the Fulda Gap when I was Third Armored Division commander and then Fifth Corps commander. His mission then was to punch a hole through our forces there. Grachev had earlier told me that he had commanded the Soviet operational group of airborne and Spetznaz (Special Forces) that was to drop behind the Rhine River to blow the bridges there, which would shut off the allied front from reinforcements.

Shevtsov's tanks were intended to break through our defenses at Fulda and marry up with Grachev's assault group.

We knew the attack plans, but not all the details Shevtsov was telling me. Needless to say, I was fascinated. What an irony this was and how unimaginable only a few years earlier. The two Soviet commanders I would have been head to head with, now working with me. Who could have guessed?

"I knew all about you back then," Shevtsov said. "We knew what you were doing. The thing was, we couldn't match your buildup. We couldn't get the advantage we needed."

They couldn't do that because of the new M-1 tanks, Bradley Fighting Vehicles, and multilaunch rocket systems we had acquired during the Reagan buildup. I had seen it coming as far back as my time as John Vessey's XO. Our buildup had sent a convincing signal. Then we had put Star Wars on top of that to neutralize whatever giant throw-weight missile they might develop—even though Star Wars was no more than a bluff. Despite President Reagan's enthusiasm, we didn't even have the theory necessary to start building it. But the US assertion of force on the ground and the specter of a Star Wars ballistic missile defense created *the* critical turning point in the Cold War, which my new Russian friends now confirmed.

After Dayton was completed, I went to see Milošević in Belgrade. He had signed the Dayton Accords on November 21. Along with their other major stipulations, the accords suspended the economic sanctions that had done such damage to the Serbian economy. Lifting those sanctions was Milošević's primary objective in the negotiations. Now they were suspended, but they wouldn't be lifted until the accords were fully implemented, which meant he was strongly motivated to cooperate with those charged with implementation, namely, IFOR.

The bulk of the First Armored Division would be traveling into Bosnia by train through Hungary, but I wanted to bring a strong lead element in as quickly as possible to establish our presence. The airport in Tuzla, Bosnia, would have been the best entry point, but the weather was so bad that Tuzla was closed down. That meant I needed to bring our advance forces in through Belgrade, Milošević's capital.

"If you really want to be part of the solution," I told Milošević, "you'll let me come in through your airport here."

This was the man who more than any other individual was responsible for starting the Balkan War. The Bosnian Serb forces that had done so much of the killing had earlier been part of Milošević's Serbian—that is, Yugoslavian—army. Ratko Mladić was a general in his army. The

Bosnian Serbs' weapons, munitions, and funds came from Milošević. But with Bosnian Serb forces in retreat and suffering under our air assault and with the economic sanctions biting him, Milošević had gotten religion. He understood which way the wind was blowing, and that had brought him to the negotiating table. Now he was eager to demonstrate his cooperation. Or so it seemed.

On December 16, our planes began landing in Belgrade. The entrance of NATO forces into the city was worldwide news, covered by a crowd of press reporters and photographers, with dozens of TV cameras beaming images back to every country where the Bosnian War was on the front page. I watched the Second Brigade combat team emerge out of the giant C-17s with their APCs and other armored vehicles and form up on the tarmac, the cameras rolling. I knew their colonel, John Baptiste, as a first-rate trainer and leader. His troops looked tough and disciplined. They made the kind of impression I knew they would in the heart of Milošević's country.

I went out onto the tarmac and inspected them. I had been preparing these troops for more than a year. On the one hand, I was filled with pride for these soldiers; on the other, I could hardly believe we were here, after all the fruitless cajoling and frustration, watching from the sidelines as UN forces were assaulted and humiliated time after time.

Our arrival in Belgrade conveyed a definitive message, if one was needed—this was for real. The United States was now involved. The Second Brigade Combat Team was, in army terminology, a "quartering party." Their mission was to reconnoiter for the presence of hostile forces, mines, and other impediments, secure the area, and locate positioning for tanks, artillery, and supplies. They were the advance element for Task Force Eagle, whose nucleus was Nash's heavy-armored division with all its M-1s, Bradleys, and artillery. Nash was heading a truly formidable force, capable and intimidating. I had told Milošević, "Don't futz with me" (using slightly more colorful language). In case he didn't understand well enough, when I got to Belgrade, I told him more explicitly, "Get all your tanks and artillery into a cantonment area, get them into buildings, get them back in the barracks, not out here where they're going to confront my troops."

Milošević put on a gracious air, but I wouldn't hazard a guess at what his inner thoughts might have been. He provided guides and an escort to take us from Belgrade into Bosnia. All the terrain was rough, but the major obstacle was the Sava River, which the brigade needed to cross. Then, once they established security and prepared the ground, the First Armored Division would follow them in.

It was bitter cold, gray, freezing weather. But the weather wasn't the problem; the Sava was. It is one of the longest rivers in Europe, the biggest tributary of the Danube, which it joins at Belgrade. We planned to cross the Sava into Bosnia at the Croatian city of Županja, but the river was at flood stage. A season of heavy rains had swollen the Sava to three times its normal size.

Our combat engineers began building a pontoon bridge on December 20, but the volume and raging flow of water together with the flooded approaches forced us to stop while we brought in large bridging sections on the C-17s. I had some concerns about this; I was determined to move into Bosnia quickly, with no show of hesitation or any weakness. But the engineering commander told me not to worry. "We've been building bridges for the army for two hundred years," he said. "We've always completed them, and we're gonna complete this one."

Inside one of the engineers' tents, some of the officers and men were huddled around a pot-bellied stove right out of World War II, the men and everything else in sight covered with mud. I shook a few hands and said, "Okay, who wants to reenlist?" There was a murmur of laughter. Then one of the soldiers said, "Sir, I'm Sergeant First Class Kidwell, and I want to reenlist. But not right now, sir. I'll reenlist when the bridge is complete. I want to reenlist on the bridge."

Sergeant Kidwell said "when," not "if." I loved those combat engineers.

The prospect of moving a heavy force across this swollen river recalled a visit I had made to France's Meuse River along with my staff and several French and German military historians when I was commander of the Fifth Corps. I had wanted to see the site where German tank commander Heinz Guderian crossed the Meuse in 1940 and put the French to flight at Sedan, the battle that led to defeating the French army and trapping the British Expeditionary Force at Dunkirk.

With all the streams and rivers Guderian had already crossed, by the time he got to the Meuse, he was more or less out of bridging equipment (there's a well-known picture of him in his half-track looking across the river through his binoculars). He needed to cross quickly to hit the French while he had surprise with him, so instead of waiting for additional equipment, he ferried tanks over on rafts. Any force is extremely vulnerable crossing a river, especially on rafts or boats. Guderian took the risk. On the western side of the Meuse, the French had an armored division and a motorized division. If they had launched an attack while Guderian was astride the river, the outcome of Germany's World War II attack on

France could well have been extremely different. Had the French defeated Guderian or even just stopped him at the Meuse, many millions of lives might have been saved. But the French commander didn't move. According to the somewhat embarrassed French historians, he felt he needed another twenty-four hours before he was ready. The crossing was a master stroke by Guderian and a catastrophe for the French and British.

I wasn't at all sure what might be waiting for me on the other side of the Sava. Looking at the swollen river, Guderian was on my mind, but so was Srebrenica, the slaughter of innocents, and the potential for more slaughters. I wanted to get across quickly to begin moving on my objectives.

From where I was, the far side of the river looked okay, but I wasn't taking any chances. Everything isn't usually as good as it might appear. I landed in my helicopter on the other side next to a perimeter manned by a scout platoon that had inserted itself earlier. When I jumped down, I went instantly into DePuy mode. I walked the line with the lieutenant in charge. I didn't like what I saw—no range cards, no artillery concentrations. I called Bill Nash: these were his troops. "Bill," I told him, "you better get down here. These people are flat on their asses."

Meanwhile, the C-17s were flying in the bridging sections we needed. Chinook heavy-lift helicopters delivered them to the crossing site, where they lowered them into the water so that the engineers in small boats could guide them into place. Given the torrent, the skills they were demonstrating seemed extraordinary.

On December 31, the first Abrams tank rumbled across the longest pontoon bridge the army had built since World War II. Perry and Shalikashvili came down and walked across it with me. Halfway across, there was Sergeant First Class Kidwell with the reenlistment NCO. I reenlisted him right there in front of the secretary of defense and the chairman of the Joint Chiefs, no doubt one of the highest-level reenlistments in history. While Shalikashvili was there, I told him I wanted JStars to give me a picture of everything on the ground in Bosnia. JStars was the air force's specialized surveillance and targeting system incorporated into E-8 planes, developed from the Boeing 707. The system was used experimentally in the Gulf War, where it proved very successful. JStars radar was capable of tracking all vehicles stationary or moving in the regions it flew over. It would give me the ultimate eyes and ears on the territory we were about to move into.

"Deploying JStars will cost millions," Shalikashvili told me, blanching a little.

I said, "Shali, I'm telling you, I need it. I don't know what's on the other side of the river. If we're going to be successful, I need to have eyes over there before I start putting people in harm's way."

Shali did give me JStars. As we got ready to bring Task Force Eagle over, I had pictures that showed our big tank column extending back for miles. On the Bosnian side, we saw nothing in the near areas, not a vehicle moving. Toward the west, though, we picked up Bosnian Serb forces. We could see tank units, even individual tanks, but they were far enough off, so I had confidence that we could cross without being disturbed.

Our first objective was to separate the opposing forces. The Dayton Accords specified that this and the other implementation tasks needed to be completed within six months so that elections could take place. As IFOR spread out along the boundary lines, I was concerned that we might face a violent reaction by one or maybe all of the warring factions. That didn't happen. The Serb and Croatian leadership—Milošević and Tudjman—apparently had decided to honor the spirit of the agreement they had signed, in general if not in detail.

Bosnia's president Izetbegović was less inclined. As the Bosnian Serb army withdrew, Bosniak forces began moving forward in clear violation of the agreement. I felt, as did most people in the United States and Europe, that Bosnia's Muslims were by far the greatest victims in this war, but it would have been disastrous to allow the Bosniak forces to attack as we were getting the Bosnian Serbs to return to their barracks. I made it clear that we weren't going to tolerate it and that if they didn't stop, IFOR would take action against them. Fortunately, the warning was enough, and the Bosniaks pulled back. That didn't completely end the problems, though. Serbian special forces made sporadic raids on the Bosniaks, and Muslim mujahideen were slipping across the lines to cut Serb throats and sow panic. Again, I made it clear we wouldn't tolerate aggression from either side. "There's a line here," I said. "Anyone who crosses it is going to suffer the consequences."

"You're going to come down on the Muslims?" Shali asked. "You know, we're on their side here. They've been the good guys in this. They've been the victims."

"My mission from NATO is to implement Dayton on all sides," I told him. "I hope the United States is on board with that. If we're going to have peace here, we have to prove our will to everyone concerned. Whoever violates is going to face the consequences, whether we have to shoot them or just turn them back. They are not going to cross the line."

In the course of our actions, IFOR forces came across an Iranian "camp" that was still training Bosniak terrorists. The camp housed all sorts of terrorist equipment, vests, bombs, bomb-making equipment, rocket launchers. IFOR troops took the camp and captured some of the Iranians, and we told the Bosnians, "Get the rest of them out!" Several hundred Iranians left.

The cross-border incidents, the Iranians, the prohibited-weapons caches, and other problems were part of my concerns early on. But I had anticipated these kinds of things, and I had the mandate to deal with them. I had a clearly articulated mission, the enforcement capability, and the political support I needed. As a result, in the six months Dayton had stipulated for IFOR-enforced implementation we had achieved all our objectives. Admiral Smith and his team had done an outstanding job in directing IFOR in the field. We had separated the warring forces, overseen the return of territory, and made sure all heavy weapons were sequestered in cantonment areas. We had created the secure environment necessary for elections to take place and for the emergence of civil authority and reconstruction. On the chart I had made up for Holbrooke and others, big *M*, Military, little *c*, civilian, were ready to morph to big *C*, Civilian, and little *m*, military.

As we were nearing our implementation goals, I received an invitation to meet with Pope John Paul II in the Vatican. John Paul, of course, was Polish. Poland had hosted our first PfP joint exercise, and a Polish unit was performing well as part of the Polish-Nordic Brigade in Bill Nash's task force. I didn't know if that had anything to do with the invitation, not that it made any difference. I was delighted to go, even if it was only for a grip-and-greet photo op.

Karen came with me, as did my aide Ben Hodges. We flew to Rome, then a car took us to Vatican City, where we drove through a labyrinth of tunnels that ran under the Vatican's buildings. When we stopped, an Italian military assistant said, "General, the Swiss Guard is forming up for you to inspect." About fifteen of the guards were there, dressed in their ceremonial costumes. I said hello, shook some hands, thanked them, and then we were led through four or five huge rooms to the pope's office, where a cardinal came out and said the pontiff would like to meet with me privately first. I wondered what was going on; I had thought this was going to be a brief introduction and photograph.

In his spartan office, John Paul asked me to sit down and began asking detailed questions about the Bosnian operation. He had obviously been thoroughly briefed. "I understand you haven't lost any soldiers there," he said. "How do you do that?"

I took him through some of the story, the training, the political direction, and so on, keeping it brief. He listened carefully.

"The worst day of my papacy last year," he said, "was when I had to cancel a trip to Sarajevo because of the violence."

"Your Holiness," I said, "you can go to Sarajevo next year, one year from now. I will guarantee your safety."

I said it without thinking, but our peace operation was going so well I thought that in fact I could keep him safe.

"I want you to know," he said, "you are not just conducting a military operation. What you are doing has strong religious overtones."

A year later John Paul did visit Sarajevo, appearing before a massive crowd in the Sarajevo stadium, where he made a powerful plea for peace, forgiveness, and reconciliation. In the bombed-out Sarajevo Cathedral, he conducted a service before Catholic worshippers as well as representatives of the Islamic and Jewish communities.

Dayton had given us six months to secure the environment. By the end of June 1996, we had accomplished that. The next, essential step in bringing some kind of stable civil life to Bosnia was elections, scheduled for September 14. The overall authority for the reconstruction of civilian life had been given to Carl Bildt, former prime minister of Sweden. In December 1995, as I was preparing IFOR to move into Bosnia, I had talked to Bildt about his plans. "I have a secretary, a cell phone, and a briefcase," he had told me. "That's all I have. They've given me no staff or anything else." Bildt had been named high representative for Bosnia and Herzegovina, an imposing title but without any resources to go with it. The result was that preparations for civilian control had been delayed and inadequate.

I wasn't happy about this. A stable, civilian-led Bosnia was the end state envisaged by the accords, and we had been working hard to establish conditions for that to happen, starting back in January 1994 with our initial PfP preparations. When the US Senate Foreign Relations Committee asked me about progress, I described what I was seeing. Holbrooke was sitting across from me, and I could sense his agitation when I talked about the slow, inadequate response on the civilian side. Even though I had the military authority and Bildt the civilian, the Dayton Accords were very much Holbrooke's baby, and he nurtured a strong, emotional sense of ownership.

Bildt was the overall civilian authority, but responsibility for carrying out the elections had been assigned to an American, Ambassador Robert Frowick of the Organization for Security and Cooperation in Europe.

Frowick was a very good administrator, but he, like Bildt, had been given few resources. As IFOR was moving toward completing its objectives, Frowick came to ask for my help. When I asked how the election preparations were going, he said, "I've been trying, but the problem is I just don't have what I need to get it done."

"Do you have the polling places?" I asked. "Are you able to print ballots and the other election material?" No, he said. He didn't have the staff to set up polling places; he had never received any material to print.

Holding these elections on time was going to be critical. In order to do that successfully, we needed to build on the momentum of IFOR's peace enforcement. Frowick didn't have the resources, but the fact was that I did, and part of my mandate was to assist in elections. I had anticipated that we would be providing security at polling places and for the voting generally, but with time passing quickly I sent Frowick forty civil affairs personnel to help with preparations.

Those officers and noncommissioned officers came from reserve units, mainly from eastern Pennsylvania. If any people deserved awards for their service in Bosnia, they did. In their normal civilian lives, which we had yanked them out of, they were lawyers, managers, police chiefs, and businesspeople. They developed a detailed plan and a strict schedule. They printed ballots, established polling places, and took care of a hundred other necessary tasks. They helped Frowick through all the steps leading to elections, which were held successfully at the stipulated time. Frowick credited them with the success. He said it couldn't have been done without them, which was satisfying to hear. But I was also thinking that we should have done a better job from the beginning in linking the military and civilian efforts. Better-thought-out cooperation and mutual reinforcement would have given us a more effective grip on the postwar reconstruction of normal life.

Our civil affairs people were also a huge help to Madame Ogata, the UN high commissioner for refugees, in her effort to assist the tens of thousands of refugees and displaced persons to return to their homes. The civil affairs unit put together a staff study that identified the work the various towns and regions needed to do to facilitate the return and reintegration of refugees, and they helped lay out plans to get the towns and regions to agree to these returns, a complicated business considering all the ethnic cleansing and movement of peoples that had taken place. The return of refugees took longer than we had hoped, especially in areas where they were minorities, but eventually the Office of the High Commissioner for Refugees was successful in doing that. I thought it was a great example of how the civilian and military sides could work together in these kinds of situations. We did that as well in the return of Hutu refugees to Rwanda, though that story is beyond the scope of this book.

I had been closely involved in making sure the Dayton Accords clearly identified IFOR's military tasks. But one area where the accords had a great deal of ambiguity concerned war criminals. The framework agreement stipulated that the warring factions had the responsibility for apprehending and turning over war criminals to the International Court of Justice at The Hague. Yet there was a lot of pressure for IFOR to help round up individuals who had been indicted. This was a slippery slope. Mladić and Karadžić had been indicted, but we knew they traveled with large protective forces. Going after them might easily set off a fight. In the entire time of our deployment in Bosnia, we had not had a single combat death. I didn't think a well-planned capture action would turn out badly, but everyone remembered Somalia and the Rangers killed and wounded there. As a result, I went to the North Atlantic Council to get political clarity. "What exactly do you want me to do?" I asked. "What are my orders with regard to war criminals? Do you want me to hunt them down and arrest them?"

The council put that question to their lawyers, who came up with a typical lawyerly solution. No, we were not to hunt them down and arrest them. But if we "came into contact" with an indicted criminal, we could apprehend him. We had to come in contact with that person as opposed to going out and actively looking for him. There were about seventy individuals on the indicted list. We made up wanted posters with their pictures and distributed them throughout the force, but the mission was still vague. I felt strongly that the indicted criminals, particularly after Srebrenica, should be standing in the dock in The Hague, Mladić and Karadžić first, so I was trying to figure out how to be proactive within our guidance.

One of the things I thought we could do was collect intelligence that could lead us to finding ourselves in a place where we might come into contact with someone on the list. If, for example, we knew a criminal was traveling on a certain route, we could set up a roadblock that would result in contact. I cleared this with NATO secretary-general Solana. Then Solana and I met with Judge Richard Goldstone, chief prosecutor of the International Court, to explain how I was planning to proceed. With that, we began an intense intelligence operation to see if we could get any actionable information. It was a difficult process. We would get reports that either Mladić or Karadžić was sipping tea at some café in

Pale or Banja Luka, but both were extremely elusive. Networks of families and sympathizers gave them cover. Our plan was that if we did find them, IFOR troops would set up a ring of security, and a special force with police powers from outside would come in to make the arrests. That entailed its own problems; the IFOR troops would probably be Americans, French, Germans, Italians, and others, which meant it would be a real challenge to keep any operation from being compromised and getting our troops caught in a trap. We had to take all those factors into account, but that was our action plan.

IFOR's mandate was for a year's deployment. In that year, we had implemented all the tasks laid out in the Dayton Accords. By the end of 1996, though, it was clear that in the war's aftermath a continued NATO military presence would help keep any volatility dampened and would facilitate the reconstruction of civilian life. I briefed Secretary-General Solana and the North Atlantic Council on a concept for continued NATO involvement, and we worked out an extended mandate with the UN, diminished the size of the force, and renamed it Stabilization Force (SFOR) in place of Implementation Force. Over the next few months, Leighton Smith relinquished his command to Admiral Joe Lopez, and General Bill Crouch, the army commander in Heidelberg, was designated as head of SFOR, which made for a smooth transition as we entered the new year.

As I passed the three-year mark as SACEUR, I began to think about retirement. I knew I could stay on in that position; the slot didn't carry a time limitation with it. My friend Shali also talked to me about succeeding him as chairman. My old boss, former chairman Jack Vessey, did too. He didn't have to remind me that he had stayed on two years after he had wanted to retire. But at that point I had been on active duty for thirty-six years, moving every few years, putting the burden of keeping the family physically healthy and emotionally whole on Karen, and switching the children from school to school as we moved from place to place. I had great pride in many of the things I had accomplished. But most of all I loved being with troops. I had lived my entire adult life with soldiers. I had never lost my admiration for them or my deep feeling of being one of them. I looked at the soldiers I commanded, and I saw them as the embodiment of America's most precious qualities, young men and women from every one of America's communities of place, color, ethnicity, religion, willing to do the hard training necessary to defend the nation and ready to put themselves in harm's way for that cause, which meant giving their lives if they were called on to do that. Separating myself from the community of soldiers would be a painful, wrenching thing to do. But I was tired. I thought it was time.

My last visit to Bosnia included a stop with my old unit, the First Battalion, Twenty-Sixth Infantry, the Blue Spaders I had fought with in Vietnam and commanded in Germany in the mid-1970s. Seeing them again was a moving moment for me. I reenlisted some troops and shook a lot of hands. It was emotional and difficult; no unit I had ever served with over all the years had meant more to me. As I moved along the line, a big African American sergeant caught my attention. "Sir," he said, "I've been with you for years, ever since Vietnam. I don't understand, sir, . . . how can you leave us?" I looked at him, and we shook hands. Then I had to quickly turn away.

I set my retirement for early July 1997. I had entered West Point in 1957, which would make it an even forty years, a nice round number. It sounded right.

In late June, SFOR's commander Bill Crouch told me we had obtained actionable intelligence on two of the indicted war criminals. He gave me a window when we could mount the action that happened to coincide with the Madrid NATO Summit, which President Clinton would be attending. Crouch told me that one of the targets would be in Prejidor, a Bosnian Serb city near the Croatian border. The second was apparently planning to go fishing at a remote lake. We knew the second one would have bodyguards with him.

In Madrid, I met with President Clinton and Secretary of Defense William Cohen to brief them on what was about to happen; I also met with the British foreign minister Robin Cook and defense minister George Robinson. American Special Forces and British Special Air Services (SAS) teams were designated to do the apprehensions. These teams had been training together for capture or kill missions in England. We knew that at least one of the targets would be dicey, the one with the bodyguards. The SAS group going in there would tell them to put their hands up but wouldn't shoot first, which meant there was a chance the bodyguards might start a fight.

"This action isn't risk free," I told the president. "We'll have the area sealed off and helicopter gunships on hand, if it comes to that. But in a situation like this there's always risk involved." Clinton gave his go-ahead for the US team. Cook did that for the British team. I briefed the NATO Council as well and got its specific approval. In Somalia, when the shit hit the fan, all the diplomats and political figures who had pushed for the capture mission had scattered and ducked for cover, leaving the commanding officers out in the cold. This time we had specific guidance and approval. We trained for the approved mission, and we had political as well as military accountability.

We didn't want the capture to take place during the summit in case something went wrong, so we scheduled it for directly afterward. By chance, my retirement and change-of-command ceremony was going to take place in Stuttgart on the same day. I would be handing over my CINCEUR command to Wesley Clark there, then my SACEUR command a few days later in Mons. At Stuttgart, I was in the middle of the ceremonies on the parade field with Clark and Shalikashvili when someone passed a note to me. "Mission accomplished. One dead, one wounded." It didn't say who was dead and who wounded. I gave the note to Shali, who gave it to Clark. "I tried to clean this up before you got here," I told Clark, "but now you've inherited it."

After we passed the flags, I found out what had happened. Six SAS operators had sprung the trap, but a bodyguard had gotten off a shot, wounding one of them in the leg before they killed him. The war criminal himself and his colleague in Prejidor had been captured.

That's how you have to do it, I was thinking. That was the essence of a fundamental principle I had been teaching for years. That was how you needed to act, with anticipation, training, a clear objective. That's how you keep your troops safe—these troops I was saying good-bye to now, lined up on the parade field in front of me. Not a single one of the sixty thousand men and women I had led into Bosnia had died in combat.

In February 1996 during IFOR's deployment, Defense Minister Grachev came to visit. I flew with him from my headquarters to the Russian brigade's headquarters in one of Bosnia's big hydroelectric power stations. It was the usual winter's day, cold and gray with heavy snow flurries. Visibility wasn't good, and as our helicopter hovered, it seemed as if we were lowering ourselves into the nest of power lines that stretched out from this godforsaken giant dam. But these pilots were the best; in a sense, I was showing them off to Grachev. These are my troops, I was saying. Look at how good they are at what they do. I also wanted to convey that though the Russians in this place were his troops, they, too, were mine. We were in this together.

That was my main message. I meant it to set the stage for what I was going to ask him. Talking in private, with only an interpreter present, I told Grachev that the Russian liaison to Milošević in Belgrade was a problem. He had been giving Milošević distorted information and advice that were hampering IFOR's efforts. "He's trouble," I told Grachev. "He's playing on Serb–Russian brotherhood. We're looking for success here, and he's hurting our chances. What I would like is for you to relieve him and get him out of there."

"That's a problem," Grachev said. "It would be a personal risk for me. He's got high connections, and he's extremely popular."

But Grachev acquiesced, and shortly afterward the liaison was gone. That was an important event, indicative. We needed to make our alliance with the Russians work politically and diplomatically as well as militarily, and this incident told me we were on the right path.

Reflecting on that period from a distance of twenty-plus years now, I am convinced that at the end of the Cold War we, the United States, made a fundamental mistake. We did not reach out to the Russians effectively and with goodwill. Instead we humiliated them. To them, it seemed we didn't respect them as the great nation they still considered themselves and in fact still were, with strategic interests in many parts of the world. We instead bathed in the euphoria of the Western victory. I know that is not how many commentators view what happened, but I saw it firsthand, on the ground.

I did everything I could to counter that. The alliance we put together with Russia for Bosnia gave me a platform, which I regarded not as an end in itself but as a strategic stepping stone. As NATO's military commander, I had substantial credibility. In the various visits I made to Russia, I explored possibilities and advocated for cooperation. During one of those visits, Thomas Pickering, the US ambassador in Moscow, gave a dinner. Grachev and I sat at a round table with Pickering. "In 1945," Pickering said in his opening remarks, "Generals Georgy Zhukov and Dwight Eisenhower sat at this table together." Neither Grachev nor I would have thought of comparing ourselves to those predecessors, but there we were, working together and breaking bread together.

In the interviews I gave in Moscow, I reiterated, "Russia is a great country, and Russians are a great people who have a clear strategic role to play in the world. Your joining us in Bosnia is a groundbreaking effort to cement this relationship that we need to develop for the benefit of both our countries." On May 27, 1997, while I was still SACEUR, the NATO-Russia Founding Act was signed in Paris: "Based on an enduring political commitment undertaken at the highest political level [the parties] will build together a lasting and inclusive peace in the Euro-Atlantic area on the principles of democracy and cooperative security." The Founding Act formally ended the Cold War.

I believed we were at a turning point rich with potential and that the West would be best advised to view Russia as a strategic partner, if not as an ally. We had common interests, which we could pursue together to turn us away from the kind of confrontation that characterized our conflict with the Soviet Union—despite the geopolitical realities that draw Russia and the West toward contention rather than cooperation. After my retirement, I tried to impress on the SACEURs who followed me that their mission was to build up our relationship with the Russians.

That did not happen—unfortunately, in my view. That was one, if only one, of the factors that lined the path to our situation today, where the eastern European nations apprehend ever more clearly the strength of Russia's aggressive advance and the softening and retreat of America's protective presence.

I had turned away from the big sergeant on the parade ground at Stuttgart so he wouldn't see me choking up. I thought for a moment that maybe I really was leaving too soon. Chance had given me those commands at a historic moment. The Soviet Union had collapsed only two brief years before I came on as SACEUR. This was the moment in time when both Russia and NATO needed to reset their geopolitical agendas and were casting around for how to do that. Both were asking, *"Where do we go from here?"*

Neither had the opportunity to contemplate this question in tranquility. Russia was reeling from economic dislocation and political turmoil. NATO was watching the impotence of the European Union and the United Nations to resolve a bloodbath in Europe's historically most volatile region.

When I arrived in Europe to take up my duties as SACEUR, the first item on my agenda was to stop the rapid and unconsidered withdrawal of American forces—whose primary mission was to support NATO. Since I was both SACEUR and CINCEUR, I was right in the middle of the debate about where we should be going from here. President Clinton's approval of my proposal to stabilize US force levels gave me the ability to turn my attention to NATO and its future role, just as NATO's political leadership was addressing exactly that issue.

On January 11, 1994, the NATO summit launched two programs that gave shape to the general thinking about NATO's future direction. One, the Partnership for Peace, provided a mechanism for nations outside NATO to associate themselves with NATO procedures and missions. The Clinton administration regarded PfP membership mainly as a pathway to

NATO membership, which would now be open to eastern European states still fearful of Russian intentions—for good reason, considering their post–World War II experience with the Soviet Union. The second program was the Combined Joint Task Force, which streamlined the Western alliance's ability to field and control NATO forces.

The thrust of these two programs indicated that NATO's future role would be mainly an enlargement of its past role. NATO had been organized to provide western Europe with a common defense against Soviet aggression. PfP and the Combined Joint Task Force envisioned expanding that mission to include eastern European countries.

I looked at the two programs differently. As I told Manfred Woerner, I wanted to use PfP operationally. That is, I saw it as a mechanism for engaging countries in a potential military role in Bosnia. Bosnia—in my opinion—was an intolerable humanitarian catastrophe that was going to have to be addressed with military force. If that did eventuate, it would have little or nothing to do with the Soviet Union. I was looking at NATO not in terms of its anti-Soviet founding mandate but rather as a way for the United States and other nations to ally themselves for what was essentially a humanitarian mission that would need to be accomplished by military means. Because PfP provided mechanisms for non-NATO countries to cooperate with NATO countries, I also saw it as a way to create and nurture collaboration and alliances among nations that might have certain interests in common, nonmilitary as well as military, even if they weren't formal allies. This mandate, of course, wasn't anti-Russian either. In fact, I saw it as a possible way to include Russia in a broad collaboration of western and eastern European nations.

I drew up a chart to visualize what I was thinking, for myself and others. I entitled it "THE NEW NATO." The chart featured a big arrow consisting of four segments: NATO's Article 5 (each NATO nation's fundamental agreement to come to the defense of any other that might be attacked); PfP; the Combined Joint Task Force; and "Counterproliferation" (against the spread of nuclear weapons). The arrow's spearhead read "Crisis Management," representing the broad scope of emergencies NATO might be called on to address.

Underneath the arrow, I listed the elements the new NATO would foster among its members and PfP associates—Mutual Trust, Solidarity, Adaptability, and Clarity of Purpose—all of them linking Europe and North America, with American leadership.

Mutual defense, NATO's original raison d'être as defined in Article 5 of the North Atlantic Treaty, was still the heart of NATO doctrine and was still operative (Article 5 was invoked the first time after the United States was attacked on September 11, 2001). But I saw conflict prevention as NATO's priority. The new post–Cold War NATO, I believed, should promote democratization and stability and should regard its mission as preventing crises from developing into conflicts. In the new geopolitical landscape, I believed strongly that NATO needed to shift from its traditional reactive posture to a proactive posture. It had to be ready to engage with an array of missions, not just warfighting. To do that required an engagement strategy that fostered alliances and allowed for mutual training. Partnership for Peace embodied that engagement strategy.

I fleshed out this concept before the North Atlantic Council and at various NATO-sponsored conferences, the first one a meeting of defense ministers in Norway in the fall of 1994, where I first used the phrase "the new NATO." By then, I had renovated space for PfP headquarters. Liaison officers from Poland, Hungary, Romania, the Czech Republic, and a dozen other PfP countries—many of them former Soviet Socialist Republics—were working next to each other and with each other, coordinating plans and building trust. Russia itself had joined PfP several months earlier.

The new NATO could be, I believed, a driving force in resolving conflicts in the future. It would have the ability to muster and train allies, coordinate with civilian agencies, and mobilize the necessary political decision making that could make intervention successful. It could coordinate with the UN, as NATO did in Bosnia. That was, I knew, a tentative vision. Had I stayed on instead of stepping away when I did, I could have shaped that vision more concretely, even as the winds of change began to blow in adverse directions.

Those adverse winds have become stronger and more threatening in the years since my retirement, and NATO stands again in need of defining its identity and its mission. It needs, I believe, to become something like "the NEW NATO" I envisioned then. But that transformation requires, above all, strong American leadership.

To address the array of severe challenges we currently face—Russian aggression, Chinese economic and military rivalry, terrorism, North Korean and Iranian nuclear dangers, climate change, global refugee crises, pandemics (I am writing this chapter in April 2020 in the midst of the COVID-19 worldwide pandemic)—the United States cannot back away from leadership. In doing so, we court not only a breakdown in the moral universe of liberal and democratic values that are the bulwark of human dignity and the decent interaction of peoples but also the further deterioration of the world's ability to avoid disasters and heal its wounds.

But such profound problems are never amenable to single efforts. Their resolution requires leadership with the wisdom and pragmatic adeptness to muster the resources of friends, allies, and strategic partners who may or may not be friends and allies. Without that kind of leadership— American leadership—we stand in danger of being overwhelmed by the fateful changes unfolding around us.

I was intensely proud of the work we accomplished in Bosnia, and I know the many nations that helped us accomplish it were equally proud of their contributions. Together we stopped the dying and protected the living, which was a signal achievement. But leaving when I did was also a deep regret that I have carried with me ever since.

Epilogue

My retirement ceremony was held on July 11, 1997, at the Fort Myer parade ground adjacent to Arlington National Cemetery. That Friday was the hottest day of the year. Generals Vessey and Haig were there, along with hundreds of friends and colleagues from my forty years of service. I trooped the line of the Old Guard and stopped to speak to a few of them. I listened to the warm words spoken by Secretary of Defense William Cohen, who had succeeded Bill Perry; John Shalikashvili, still chairman of the Joint Chiefs; and army chief of staff Dennis Reimer. A great number of my West Point Class of 1961 were there, as were old friends from Pottsville. Karen and our children, Jessica, Jennifer, and Chris, were in the front row with our two grandchildren at the time, Kaitlyn and Devin. Karen stood at my side as Secretary Cohen presented me with the Distinguished Superior Service Medal.

Finally, my turn came to speak. I thanked everyone for their kind words. Then I spoke to the troops:

I soldiered with you in the rain, the mud, the snow, in war and peace. You did your job without complaint; you walked your post.

You did your duty; you served your country with great distinction.

You won the Cold War and are preserving the peace and preventing conflict. None of the historic events of the past decade would have been possible without your steadfast discipline and professionalism.

Stay ready! You are the watchmen on the gates of freedom.

The future is bright. You are creating a better world for our children and grandchildren.

You are this country's greatest asset.

Take care of each other, look after one another. You will always be in my thoughts.

I will never forget you!

God bless you and good-bye!

Index

A-10 Warthog ground-support
aircraft, 97
A-37 ground-support aircraft, 155,
159–60
Abizaid, John, 75, 76, 123
Abrams, John, 145, 146, 147
Abrams M-1 battle tanks, 114, 223
AC-47 gunship aircraft, 155
Agnew, Spiro, 81
AirLand Battle doctrine, 24, 101, 109,
114
Albright, Madeline, 204
Allied Rapid Reaction Corps, 221–22
allies: Joulwan and inclusion of
Russian forces in NATO's Balkan
Implementation Force, 216–23,
235, 238; Joulwan on the value of
working with, 1–2, 27–28, 113;
Joulwan's forging of relationships
as commander of the First
Battalion, Twenty-Sixth Infantry,
98–99; Joulwan's regional
approach to antidrug operations in
Latin America and, 167–78,
183–84; Joulwan's response to the
Balkan War as SACEUR and,
183–84, 185–87; Partnership for
Peace program and, 185–87,
217–18, 236–37, 238
American Military Group (in El
Salvador), 156, 158, 162
America's First Battles, 138
Annan, Kofi, 203
anthracite coal mining, 3, 5
Anthracite League, 6
antiaircraft defenses, Serbian, 211
antidrug operations: George H. W.
Bush and National Security
Directive 18, 168, 171; Joulwan

as head of SOUTHCOM and
development of regional approach
to, 167–78, 183–84; Presidential
Directive 14 and, 177
antitank weapons, 96, 100–101
antiwar movement: Joulwan's
interactions and dialogue with, 47,
50–57, 58–60, 63–64; riots of
1968, 57–59
Apache helicopters, 149
Ap Gu, Battle of, 40–47
Armor School, 28, 48, 49
Army of the Republic of Vietnam
(ARVN), 70–72, 73
Army of the Rhine (Great Britain),
137
Army War College: Joulwan as an
instructor at, 106–9; Joulwan as a
student at, 102–6; Joulwan's
classmates at, 109
Aronson, Bernie, 158
Arter, Bob, 65, 67, 68–69
ARVN. *See* Army of the Republic of
Vietnam
A Shau Valley, 69–70, 71, 72
Aspen Institute, 150
Aspin, Les, 182–83, 187
Atlantic Command, 121
atrocities: Balkan War and, 187–88,
196–203, 206, 207; El Salvadoran
civil war and, 156, 158–59, 163;
Rwandan genocide, 189–92
Augsburg, 110
Austria, 186
autogolpe, 174

B-52 bombers, 45
Balanzino, Sergio, 197, 198
Balkan War: 1994 shelling of the